THE MAKING OF A LEFT-BEHIND CLASS

Educational Stratification, Meritocracy and Widening Participation

Fred Powell, Margaret Scanlon, Patrick Leahy,
Hilary Jenkinson and Olive Byrne

First published in Great Britain in 2025 by

Policy Press, an imprint of
Bristol University Press
University of Bristol
1-9 Old Park Hill
Bristol
BS2 8BB
UK
t: +44 (0)117 374 6645
e: bup-info@bristol.ac.uk

Details of international sales and distribution partners are available at
policy.bristoluniversitypress.co.uk

© Bristol University Press 2025

British Library Cataloguing in Publication Data
A catalogue record for this book is available from the British Library

ISBN 978-1-4473-6794-9 hardcover
ISBN 978-1-4473-6795-6 paperback
ISBN 978-1-4473-6796-3 ePub
ISBN 978-1-4473-6797-0 ePdf

The right of Fred Powell, Margaret Scanlon, Patrick Leahy, Hilary Jenkinson and Olive Byrne to be identified as authors of this work has been asserted by them in accordance with the Copyright, Designs and Patents Act 1988.

All rights reserved: no part of this publication may be reproduced, stored in a retrieval system, or transmitted in any form or by any means, electronic, mechanical, photocopying, recording, or otherwise without the prior permission of Bristol University Press.

Every reasonable effort has been made to obtain permission to reproduce copyrighted material. If, however, anyone knows of an oversight, please contact the publisher.

The statements and opinions contained within this publication are solely those of the authors and not of the University of Bristol or Bristol University Press. The University of Bristol and Bristol University Press disclaim responsibility for any injury to persons or property resulting from any material published in this publication.

Bristol University Press and Policy Press work to counter discrimination on
grounds of gender, race, disability, age and sexuality.

Front cover image and cover design: Andrew Corbett

Contents

Acknowledgements		iv
Preface		v
1	Introduction: Aristotle's curse	1
2	The cultural politics of educational stratification	35
3	Public education, universities and widening participation	73
4	The psycho-politics of meritocracy: IQ + effort = merit?	105
5	Snakes and ladders: aspirations and barriers	128
6	Social class and parental attitudes to education and career choices	149
7	Structural racism and Traveller education	163
8	Conclusion: Global lessons	178
References		184
Index		196

Acknowledgements

The research team would like to sincerely thank the six DEIS schools that took part in the project, particularly the students, teachers and parents who shared their insights and experiences. Thanks are also due to the youth and community workers and representatives from the Irish Traveller community who were so helpful in interpreting the social context. We are extremely grateful to the UCC students who participated in the research, and to our colleagues in the UCC Access Office for their participation and support. Finally, we would like to gratefully acknowledge the funding from the Irish Research Council that made this project possible.

Preface

The slogan 'Equality of Opportunity' offers a starting point for a discussion of the asymmetrical relationship between education and social equality that has divided society and endangered democracy. It evokes a policy paradox that has created a 'left-behind' class; the members of which, to paraphrase Robert Putnam (2000), have been consigned to 'bowl alone' in the social wilderness of disadvantaged communities. The 'left-behind' live precarious lives located on the periphery of post-industrial society. These largely forgotten people are a universal social phenomenon across the cities of Europe and North America, as deindustrialisation hollows-out the traditional working-class in Western society. The 'left-behind' are problematised in the media as a marginalised group that has failed to engage constructively with economic change in a globalised world. They are in social reality victims of poverty, discrimination and social exclusion.

That is the sociological approach adopted in this book to an important and complex equality issue. It goes to the core of the cultural and economic context of social life in Western civilisation. The French public intellectual and internationally renowned sociologist Pierre Bourdieu (1930–2002) observed: 'Sociologists are in a very rare position. They are unlike other intellectuals, since most of them know in general how to listen and to interpret what is said to them, to transcribe and transmit it' (Bourdieu and Grass, 2002: 68).

The connection between democracy and education is a cornerstone of Western civilisation, as the philosopher and education reformer John Dewey (1859–1952) has pointed out, calling education 'a necessity of life'. Dewey, in his 1916 book *Democracy and Education*, equated education with life itself, which is diminished by its absence. Each generation is challenged to build education anew, as if reinventing the world. It is, as Dewey (1916: 1) put it, 'the renewal of life by transmission'. In the era of the 'knowledge economy', which seeks to instrumentalise higher education, Dewey's humanistic vision is challenged by neoliberalism representing a return to market values, social discredit and individual responsibility in a globalised world.

This book sets out to explore the relationship between the global and the local through the prism of educational disadvantage in territorially stigmatised communities. Professor Peadar Kirby (2008: 2) has commented in relation to the influence of the local sphere on political and social discourse:

> [T]o me all our politics and all our social scientific knowledge is ultimately rooted in the local; that is not to say that it is limited by the local but it is to say that unless our knowledge of a globalised world is ultimately related to the daily life experiences of people as they

work, interrelate and make life for themselves in local communities in whatever part of the world, then it is not useful knowledge and it runs the risk of imprisoning and oppressing human beings rather than liberating and enhancing them.

In the book we seek to reflect the global-local duality by offering a synthesis of: (1) international theoretical and policy debates about educational equality; (2) local studies of educational disadvantage, eliciting the views of students, parents and professionals; and (3) addressing the structural racism that Travellers and Roma experience within society in general and the education system in particular.

The ideal of equality of educational opportunity based on merit (commonly referred to as 'meritocracy'), is explored in the context of a 'political fiction' (Reich, 1971) that defines the dominant public conception of fairness. It is juxtaposed with equality of condition, in terms of broadly equalising life chances between citizens, and 'opportunity pluralism', seeking to create more pluralistic routes to accessing higher education that widens participation. While the book uses Ireland (reputedly the most globalised society in the world) as a locus for analysis of local community studies, the theoretical and policy context is firmly located in the wider sphere of European and planetary politics.

Pierre Bourdieu (1998) regarded globalisation as a counter-revolution or 'restoration' of pre-democratic society in which politicians have lost their moral courage and social vision. He argued that politicians have essentially capitulated to a globalised capitalist order, publicly represented by the International Monetary Fund, the World Bank and the G7. These oligarchies of power and wealth in Bourdieu's view have elevated the economic over the social, copper-fastening inequality as an inevitable part of life. Bourdieu viewed the state as a bulwark against global market dominance and called for a European social state.

The assertion to 'think globally, act locally' encapsulates the contemporary debate about sustainable communities in which community is often presented as an 'imagined village' – an idyllic construct remote from the social reality of a globalised planet (Powell, 2009). The African proverb 'It takes a village to raise a child' captures the essence of the enduring importance of community in social life. Globally, many communities face serious adversities: poverty, insecure housing, unemployment, health problems (physical and mental), addiction, crime, domestic and community violence and underachievement in educational performance. It is the latter issue that provides the sociological backdrop to our study.

The empirical research reported in this book was carried out in local disadvantaged communities (urban and rural) within the European Union (Ireland), purportedly one of the richest regions in the world. Yet, many of its inhabitants are excluded from access to higher education on the basis of merit. Widening participation is promoted as the policy solution to inequality. Irish universities in 2014 made it a core principle of a Charter for Civic and Community Engagement with civil society. Civic and community engagement has been described as the 'third mission' of universities – complementing teaching and research (Hunt Report, 2014). Widening participation is a basic principle of this engagement strategy. We examine the international research evidence and local data and record the voices and views of people from disadvantaged communities in relation to their experience of educational inequality.

The book explores educational stratification as a reflection and agent of deep class and ethnic divisions in contemporary society. We pose several fundamental questions. Is meritocracy fair? Will widening participation achieve an inclusive higher education system, based on the principle of social justice? Or, are barriers to access more deeply and subtly embedded in the cultural codes of the Western hierarchical socio-economic system? Does this make widening participation a policy chimera? We approach these challenging questions in a spirit of enquiry and hope, inspired by Pierre Bourdieu's observation: 'This is why one must speak out: to restore a sense of utopian possibility, which is one of neoliberalism's key victories to have killed off, or made look antiquated' (Bourdieu and Grass, 2002: 66). The constraints of social and economic reality and the 'utopian possibility' of social justice are always in profound tension in democratic society.

This book originated from an empirical research project funded by the Irish Research Council and based at University College Cork (UCC), National University of Ireland, entitled *Widening Participation in Higher Education*. The project raised major questions about educational inequality and social justice, encapsulated in the metaphor of a 'left-behind' class. While the fieldwork was carried out in Ireland, we set the book in an international context because that is our European and global reality. In our view the questions we raise go back to the origins of Western civilisation and the social hierarchies it has created. Educational stratification historically reflects social stratification. Meritocracy, according to its critics, paradoxically constitutes a system that perpetuates social inequality (Littler, 2018; Markovits, 2019; Sandel, 2020). The paradox is evident in widespread support for the principle of merit across the social class spectrum, despite divergent results between social classes at the expense of lower socio-economic groups. The reason for this apparent consensus is, in our view, the public acceptance of a metafiction that merit is a fair and objective basis for allocating university admissions. Widening participation in higher education seeks to redress the resulting imbalances in access to the higher education system.

Meritocracy has been essentially at odds with the social justice values of the welfare state. However, it fits comfortably with the ethos of neoliberalism.

The welfare state has been in decline since the 1970s, as neoliberalism has become more influential in reshaping public policy around market values and individual responsibility, while simultaneously dismantling the institutional architecture of social democracy. The moral principle of redistribution of wealth, that shaped 20th-century social policy, is now openly disavowed in the 21st century, as social inequality returns to normative acceptability on the political agenda. Widening participation in higher education has been viewed as a progressive alternative to 'welfare dependency' by 'Third Way' advocates of post-socialist politics because of its perceived potential for empowering the declining working class and minority ethnic groups. However, in 2023, this consensus was dealt a serious reversal by the US Supreme Court, which outlawed affirmative action. It would appear that the pursuit of equality, which is at the core of democracy, is under siege from conservatives who wish to restore the past as the future. Have we reached an inflection point in the Western narrative of progress?

Equality, as a one-dimensional class construct, is increasingly challenged conceptually by complex equality, shaped by intersectionality, which is – conceptually – primarily based on class, gender and race, and the interconnected forms of discrimination and disadvantage that these social groups experience. An unequal world is being reimagined in our minds as complex and multidimensional. This is changing public perceptions about personal identities (who we are) and future biographical possibilities (what we can become). Education has emerged centre stage as being of critical importance in reshaping the self in this new world order. Those who are left behind in this quest for personal development and financial prosperity are increasingly problematised, marginalised and potentially demonised. Yet, our study shows that many young people from disadvantaged backgrounds aspire to participate in higher education (largely with the support of their parents), indicating a major shift in working-class aspirations towards participation in higher education in post-industrial society. They face barriers, however, both visible (economic) and invisible (cultural) that frustrate the realisation of their aspirations. Tensions between personal identities and individual biographies may also be an ontological challenge in educational progression, which we will investigate. Irish Travellers and Roma in particular face poverty and discrimination in a world of extreme marginalisation, where only 1 per cent of Travellers access higher education and Roma remain a largely hidden population.

Tackling inequality offers the key to unlocking access to the higher education system. Meritocracy currently defines equality of opportunity as 'equal chances to become unequal'. Equality of condition offers an alternative approach based on a radical vision of social justice. But it raises major cultural, social and political questions. How can social justice be democratically achieved in accessing higher education? Is widening participation the answer?

Opportunity pluralism has also been posited as a more flexible approach to accessing third-level education through widening routes to participation. This book explores these complex social and educational issues that are polarising society.

The book is written as part of a wider context of educational experience and practice. The UCC School of Applied Social Studies was founded in 1989. Several of the authors have played key roles in its development and evolution. We sought to make a difference by opening up access to students who were previously largely denied admission to university because they lacked the requisite formal qualifications. Our thinking was significantly shaped by the work of the inspirational Brazilian educator Paulo Freire, who championed adult education as an act of liberation. We sought to pioneer critical pedagogies, curriculum reforms, open-book examinations, student-centred learning methods and vocational degrees for mature students. We wanted the student experience to be empowering both personally and intellectually. Our approach also sought to reach out to disadvantaged communities through widening participation. We aimed to enable everybody who aspires to learn to share in knowledge equally as a founding principle. It turned out to be a very positive experience that created a vibrant learning environment. Many of our graduates found their voice in civil society and went on to make their mark in public life and civic leadership. We dedicate this book to all of our students from whom we have learned much about the world.

1

Introduction: Aristotle's curse

Hierarchy and privilege in education: an old story in new language?

Anya Kamenetz (2022) observed: 'For the majority of human history, most people didn't go to school. Formal education was a privilege for the Alexander the Greats of the world who could hire Aristotles as private tutors.' Aristotle (384–322 BCE) is widely regarded as one of the greatest philosophers in human history. His thinking continues to shape our social and educational world views over two millennia later. In modern society what is called 'the invention of childhood' has made public education at primary and secondary levels compulsory up to the mid-teens (Aries, 1973). But at least half the Western population are left behind when it comes to participation in higher education, creating a new form of stratification in society that reflects the durability of hierarchical classical social and cultural attitudes towards access to the knowledge.

Meritocracy during modernity has replaced aristocracy in the perpetuation of an elite society, creating a conflict with the core republican values of liberty, equality and solidarity, which are the foundation principles of modern democracy. Access programmes help to redress educational inequality, but they do not fundamentally change the social structure and meritocratic culture that characterises higher education in an elitist world. As one former disadvantaged student, who achieved a PhD, has asserted (*The Irish Times*, 18 September 2021):

> I'm what is commonly known as an 'access' student: I come from 'an under-represented group'. I am a charity case, an experiment. I am one of the students that was allowed in because someone fought hard against the elite education system that believes that intelligence is measured by school performance. Someone recognised that people like me also had the potential to be people like you.

Widening participation in higher education is arguably the greatest challenge facing democracy in building a 'knowledge society' during the 21st century. The renowned Brazilian educationist Paulo Freire explains why: 'Education … is the practice of freedom, the means by which men and women deal creatively with reality and discover how to participate in the transformation of their world' (CivicEducation.org, 2021). Professor Linda Doyle (Provost, Trinity College Dublin) has stated, 'I think access and excellence are not opposing things' (Doyle, 2021).

In this opening chapter we chart and explore the social and policy landscape that provides the backdrop to the book, and discuss its intellectual rationale. We start by explaining the emergence of the neoliberal concept of the 'knowledge economy' in the age of globalisation. The chapter then moves on to address the seminal issue of the meaning and definition of a 'left-behind' class as a consequence of this conservative policy shift. It is followed by a discussion of the role and responsibility of higher education in building a 'knowledge society' as part of its historic humanist legacy. The aims, objectives and methodology of the study are then presented, as well as a discussion of the metapolicy questions arising from access inequality. We follow this with an analysis of the origins and contemporary democratic challenges for education that frame the debate about educational equality. The chapter explains what DEIS (Delivering Equality of Opportunity in Schools) schools are about and their role in disadvantaged communities. Finally, we set out the book's structure and content.

The knowledge economy in the age of globalisation

In the 21st century we have entered the fourth industrial revolution, driven by a new digitalised technology based on mobile devices, renewable energy, artificial intelligence and internet connectivity. It is largely shaped by a transformative meta-technology with implications for education and how we understand learning in an era dominated by growing social inequalities (Piketty, 2014). The Irish Taoiseach (prime minister), Leo Varadkar, is reported to have proclaimed on retaking office in 2022 his 'passion in terms of education and opportunity that we continue to drive forward in ensuring no child is left behind' (*The Irish Times*, 17 December 2022). Ireland's modernisation since the 1960s, which has brought about major economic and cultural change, has been primarily due to investment in education. Ireland was ranked in second place in the Progress in International Reading Literacy Study (Pirls), which examined reading skills among hundreds of thousands of pupils across nearly 60 countries during 2021 (*The Irish Times*, 17 May 2023).

While Ireland has among the highest rates of participation in higher education within the European Union, a significant section of the population has been left behind by this transformative change. Ireland is far from unique. There is a global problem of educational stratification that effects many societies in the 21st century, where competitive economic principles substantially inform public policy making. A futurist vision of higher education has emerged in the 21st century, encompassed in the policy goal of building a 'knowledge economy'. Will it be socially just or economically elitist?

The concept of a 'knowledge economy' is based on creating a system of consumption and production powered by elite intellectual capital. Roberto Mangabeira Unger (2022: 7–8) in his book *The Knowledge Economy* frankly acknowledges the inherent elitism of this model of economic development: 'The distinction between an insular albeit multi-sectoral vanguard and the rest of the economy – a collection of rearguards – has become a power engine of inequality of opportunity and capability as well as income and wealth.' In a knowledge economy, educational stratification has promoted what Fritz Stern (1961) called 'cultural despair', leading to nihilism and populist authoritarianism.

In 2001, at the dawn of the new millennium, the US under President George W. Bush enacted the No Child Left Behind (NCLB) Bill. The US intended to position itself at the cutting edge of development, by closing the achievement gap in education through boosting the performance of poor and minority ethnic students, learners with English as a second language and children with special education needs. The initiative was driven by standardised tests in reading and maths at the expense of humanistic subjects such as history, social studies, foreign languages and the arts. It lacked adequate funding and many schools failed to meet their targets in terms of enhanced student achievement. The NCLB, which held schools accountable through the yardstick of Annual Yearly Progress measurement, was deemed a policy failure and was largely replaced under the Obama presidency in 2015 by a less draconian schools regime, reflecting the evolving complex institutional roles of schools as community centres that not only teach students to read and write but also provide childcare for working families, food for hungry children and a sense of community cohesion for neighbourhoods (*New York Times*, 4 September 2022).

Arguably, the lessons to be learned from the NCLB debacle are: school underperformance cannot be resolved by standardised tests; a child's performance is heavily influenced by poverty and discrimination, the alleviation of which requires political will, crisis-level funding and wealth redistribution similar to that spent on the coronavirus pandemic or the energy emergency; the recognition of the right to equality of condition (entitlement to similar life chances) among all children as the basis of education in a free and just society; and the evolving role of publicly funded schools into community centres that seek to enable all children to thrive.

The ideas of sociologist Pierre Bourdieu are fundamental to our analysis. Annette Lareau (2011: 363) comments that Bourdieu's work 'provides a dynamic model of structural inequality, it enables researchers to capture "moments" of cultural and social reproduction'. Bourdieu unlocked the meaning of educational inequality in his theory of cultural capital. It broadly describes the values, skills and ideas that are recognised in society and confer advantage or disadvantage on individuals, who possess or lack these attributes. Bourdieu's contribution to deepening our knowledge and understanding of educational inequality has been seminal in broadening the debate beyond a purely economic analysis to incorporate the more hidden influences of culture. This book sets out to examine the challenges involved in achieving social justice posed by educational inequality, which raises fundamental social and moral questions. How do we explain it? What can we do about it? The answers, according to Bourdieu, are to be found deeply embedded in our culture, where meanings, signs and symbols of success and, ultimately, opportunities in the social structure are generated. We will return to a more extensive analysis of Bourdieu's intellectual contribution in Chapter 2.

In addressing the causes of social inequality and how it shapes educational opportunities, Victor Hugo's famous comment in his 1869 novel *The Man Who Laughs*, that 'the paradise of the rich is made out of the hell of the poor', resonates and illuminates down the centuries. The story about two young disabled people has been made into many films in different languages over the years. Hugo reminds the world of the seminal importance of emotion as the foundation of ethics and the need for a caring rather than a competitive society. That is arguably the moral basis of a free and just society, which, during the 20th century, we called the welfare state.

The emphasis in the debate about the meaning of freedom is on what the political philosopher Isaiah Berlin, in a published inaugural lecture at Oxford University in 1958, famously called *Two Concepts of Liberty*. Berlin's thesis has been broadly interpreted in political discourse as 'positive freedom' (liberty from debilitating social conditions including hunger, want, ignorance, as collective democratic and republican goals), as opposed to 'negative freedom' (liberty to pursue individual interests, goals and choices without coercion). The pursuit of both concepts of liberty should be possible in a pluralist democracy, but inevitably there are tensions. Education is a classic example of a struggle over political values that raises searching questions about the meaning of freedom in modern society. For some citizens positive freedom is highly constrained in 21st-century affluent Western society.

Guy Standing, in a challenging presentation to the World Economic Forum on 21 June 2018 observed:

> A term widely used in 2017 was the 'left behind' implying that a growing number of people had fallen out of the traditional working-class and left insecure and impoverished, while the majority had steamed ahead. The term 'left behind' has been used semantically as a broad brush depiction of discontented people who support populist movements and sentiments, in the US, UK, Germany, France and elsewhere.

Standing added to his depiction of the 'left behind' that they 'are relatively uneducated and mostly come from families and communities that have experienced deindustrialisation or live in communities mostly made up of those who relied on industrial wage labour in the past'. Standing concluded his commentary by stating somewhat unsurprisingly that, in psycho-political terms, the 'left behind' 'tend to be resentful'. The analysis offered by Standing to the World Economic Forum, originally developed in his influential book *The Precariat* (2014), evokes the visual imagery of the Four Horsemen of the Apocalypse at the gates of the citadel of democracy.

Robert Reich (2021), a former US Secretary of Labor and political columnist, also makes the connection between the anger and alienation of the left behind and their lack of access to college degrees, good jobs and a decent place to live. Essentially, Reich is warning that a marginalised segments of the population are unable to find pathways through the education system that will enable them to live economically, socially and culturally fulfilling lives in the era of globalisation. The gulf between the haves and have-nots was exposed during the 2022 French presidential election, won by the centrist candidate Emmanuel Macron. While the voting difference was partly explicable in terms of income differentials and regional voting patterns, educational stratification also significantly influenced the election outcome. In sociological and cultural terms, a left-behind class has been identified in peripheral France, embodied in the angry *gilets jaunes* movement, reflecting 'a profound re-stratification of the entire population according to educational attainment' (*The Guardian*, 30 April 2022). These developments suggest democratic society has reached an inflection point, symbolised by the Washington riot on 6 January 2021. Democracy is being disrupted and social cohesion fragmented.

'We are ghosts': the social construction of a left-behind class

The 'left behind' are part product of our socially constructed (culturally invented) public imaginary of life at the bottom of the social class hierarchy and, as Loïc Wacquant (2022: 2), in reference to the related concept of an 'underclass', asserts, a deflection from social reality (largely out of sight) that is embodied in the precarious lived experience of a very deprived section of the working class. This social group has historically been called 'the poor'. The cumulative evidence in voluminous public reports over the past century is that poverty and discrimination, rather than individual behavioural characteristics, define the social reality of the poor and oppressed and is the fundamental cause of being left behind in society. But society does not necessarily choose to see it that way and act on the evidence. As Henry Giroux (1994: 330) has suggested, poverty is ultimately attributable to a 'poverty of values'. Denied an active voice in the public sphere, the left behind feel like 'ghosts' in a world from which they are largely excluded socially, living in spaces described as 'deprived' or 'disadvantaged' areas.

We have adopted the term 'left-behind' class because it offers a powerful metaphor for a market economy and politically polarised society that is divided by class and ethnicity. Western society describes itself as a 'meritocracy', meaning 'equal chances to become unequal'. The social reality, however, is that educational stratification, which largely determines individuals' biographies, income and well-being, has produced a deeply polarised society. Civic virtue and moral prestige have become reflexively equated in a stratified education system, shaped by the possession of cultural, social and financial capital, as described by Pierre Bourdieu. This moral order arguably constitutes the paradox of our times that is disrupting democracy, undermining social cohesion and threatening individual liberty.

As the welfare state is systematically undermined by austerity policies designed to shrink the size of the state and lower the tax burden on the rich, collective responsibility is being replaced by a new ideology called 'neoliberalism' that evokes the classical liberal laissez-faire economics of the 19th century. Its ideology is embodied in the conservative concept of the small state, involving the devolution of caring responsibilities to voluntary organisations and families – known as 'subsidiarity' in political jargon. Neoliberal ideology opposes state intervention in economic and social affairs, which it views as the defence of negative freedom. The German writer and winner of the 1999 Nobel Prize for literature, Gunter Grass, has observed: 'Irresponsibility is the organising principle of the neoliberal vision' (Bourdieu and Grass, 2022: 71).

Social democracy has adapted to neoliberalism by embracing a new social policy agenda based upon key themes, including opportunity; responsibility and community. It initially promoted this new political strategy as the 'Third Way' –purportedly fit 'for a new era of information-age capitalism' (Geismer, 2023: 18). When Professor Anthony Giddens published *The Third Way* in 1998 the 'new' strategy had a philosophy, enabling it to occupy the political centre ground. However, critics dismissed it as 'Thatcherism with a human face', as evidence of its inability to tackle growing social inequality mounted (Geismer, 2023: 19). Neoliberal ideology was clearly setting the political agenda in the new era of information-age capitalism. Even social democrats were embracing neoliberalism through the adoption of the Third Way. The pursuit of equality through the redistribution of wealth is being fundamentally undermined as a political goal. Social democracy is in decline. Poverty is rising. The labour movement is also in decline and the consequences for the working class were very serious. The precarity of the 'gig economy' replaced trade unions and workers' rights in many areas of the burgeoning neoliberal economy (such as business services). As Gunter Grass notes: 'For years I've tried to tell the unions you can't only attend to workers while they are working; as soon as they lose their jobs they fall into a bottomless pit' (Bourdieu and Grass, 2002: 67). For many 'the bottomless pit' meant a future without hope in a left-behind class (Case and Deaton, 2020).

The re-stratification of society wrought by neoliberalism is a product of this restoration of classical liberal economic values. It has promoted a poor-law mentality in social policy with an emphasis on workfare, welfare conditionality, self-help and charity. The problematisation of a section of the working class as left behind has emerged as a concomitant of this process, invoking Victorian moralism (deservingness) in political, media and academic discourse, while seeking to excuse the social consequences of rising inequality and the residualisation of the welfare state.

The dynamics of class are addressed by Faiza Shaheen in the foreword to a research report produced by two progressive UK think tanks – the Runnymede Trust and CLASS – entitled *We are Ghosts: Race, Class and Institutional Prejudice*. Shaheen asserts: 'It also needs to be noted that the original idea of "working-class jobs" has shifted dramatically, and hence we need a new understanding of what it means to be working class' (Snoussi and Mompelat, 2019: 3). The Gothic imagery of *We are Ghosts* was inspired by one of the participants' comments on the barren landscape of working-class life in deprived communities in contemporary Britain. The report contends: 'The current conception of working class in public debate is often based on a mixture of misinformation and mythology, fails to recognise working-class voices and agency, increases division across racial lines, and is divorced from the lived realities of those experiencing race and class injustice' (Snoussi and Mompelat, 2019: 5).

There are four core elements that negatively impact on 21st-century working-class life: precariousness (financial, food and fuel insecurity; homelessness and lack of a safety net); prejudice (disrespect for class identity and ethnicity); place (territorial stigmatisation and sense of neglect and abandonment) and power (powerlessness and lack of voice), which are highlighted in the Runnymede/CLASS report. These factors deconstruct the complexity of the lived experience of working-class existence in the 21st century. The report offers a pessimistic assessment of working-class life in modern Britain and makes some positive proposals for change in the direction of greater equality.

This social pessimism is also reflected in US research. In 2020 a seminal contribution to the 'left behind' narrative came in the publication of a study – *Deaths of Despair and the Future of Capitalism* – written by two social scientists, Ann Case and Noble Prize winner Angus Deaton. This influential book, based on sophisticated data analysis, illuminates the generational catastrophe of Western deindustrialisation that is turning into a psychosocial apocalypse of 'dying of despair' ravishing the American working class. Case and Deaton

(2020: 3) discovered 'the increase in deaths of despair was almost all among those without a college degree', observing:

> The four-year college degree is increasingly dividing America, and the extraordinarily beneficial effects of the degree are a constant theme running through the book. The widening gap between those with and without a bachelor's degree is not only in death but also in quality of life; those without a degree are seeing increases in the level of their pain, ill health, and serious mental distress, and declines in their ability to work and to socialize. The gap is also widening in earnings, in family stability, and in community. A four-year degree has become *the* key marker of social status, as if there were a requirement for non-graduates to wear a circular scarlet badge bearing the letters *BA* crossed through by a diagonal red line.

In their analysis, referencing Michael Young's 1958 satirical book, *The Rise of Meritocracy*, Case and Deaton (2020: 3–4) conclude:

> The elite can sometimes be smug about their accomplishments, attributing them to their own merit, and dismissive of those without degrees, who had their chance but blew it. The less educated are devalued or even disrespected, are encouraged to think of themselves as losers, and may feel that the system is rigged against them. When the fruits of success are as large as they are today, so are the penalties of failing the tests of meritocracy. Young presciently referred to the left behind group as 'the Populists' and the elite as 'the hypocrisy'.

How far does the circle of equality extend in social reality? Are all people equal in a meritocratic society, or are some excluded because of social class or ethnic identity? Political rhetoric often obscures social reality. Education illustrates this disjunction between political rhetoric and social reality in meritocratic society. Yet, it is hard to recognise divisive social consequences of merit because of the justificatory rhetoric of fairness and objectivity that shrouds the meritocratic education system's deep and often invisible inequalities. Educational stratification is one of those social phenomena that is publicly known and unknowable simultaneously, exposing a profound and disturbing social hypocrisy in our world, rather like the historic child abuse scandals (Powell and Scanlon, 2015). Its moral defence rests on the principle of equality of opportunity. It is assumed the system is fair and just. The poor are deemed to be responsible for their own failures, due to social pathology, such as mental illness, alcohol consumption, drug abuse, family instability and so on. In the new 'Dark Ages' of today, virtue is linked to class positioning in the 'great chain of being' – a hierarchical belief that all matter and life is divinely determined and beyond the human realm to change without interfering with a preordained natural order, most notably traditional family and property rights. Meritocracy provides the ethical reasoning for the re-stratification of society. As Michael Young (1958: 152) put it: 'Castes and classes are universal and the measure of harmony that prevails within a society is everywhere dependent on the degree to which stratification is sanctioned by its code of morality.' Education, shaped by the possession of cultural, financial and social capital, as Pierre Bourdieu has argued, is at the core of meritocracy (see Chapter 2).

Educational stratification is one of the greatest challenges confronting democratic society in a secular age. To understand our cultural institutions, we need to grasp the distinction between social forces, such as class privilege and racial domination, and the source and function of moral authority in our society. Unless these value issues are addressed, it is hard to see how the fabric of democracy can be preserved. Arguably we need to confront the myths that obscure educational inequality from full public scrutiny and start a discussion about the justification for a fundamentally divided education system in the 21st century.

In this book educational stratification will constitute the philosophical and sociological framework in terms of its attempt to reframe class relations by replicating the elitism of the past in the present through replacing hereditary privilege by a merit-based system. Critics argue meritocracy does little for the working class: 'Hence, while the myth of meritocracy lionizes individual success stories and "hard-working families", social mobility has failed to transform whole communities. This has led – at best – to a few successful working-class people, who leave behind otherwise depleted working-class communities' (Snoussi and Mompelat, 2019: 4). It does not 'level-up' communities. Widening participation in higher education has emerged as the answer to the crisis in access, but it does not guarantee equality.

Meritocracy embodies a conservative policy towards social change by appealing to a metafiction of fairness and objectivity at the expense of social equality and human flourishing. It involves, as George Orwell described in his novel *1984* (2000: 37–38):

> the labyrinthine world of double think. To know and not know, to be conscious of complete truthfulness while telling carefully constructed lies, to hold simultaneously two opinions that cancelled out, knowing them to be contradictory and believing in both of them; the use of logic against logic, to repudiate morality while laying claim to it. … Even to understand the world 'doublethink' involved the use of doublethink.

Meritocracy has provided a popular metanarrative for the retention of educational stratification in democratic society, by publicly representing the system as fair and objective.

Critical pedagogical thinkers, including Paulo Freire, Henry Giroux and Peter McLaren, challenge this double thinking. Peter McLaren (1994: 45) has observed:

> In our hyper-fragmented and postmodern culture, democracy is secured through the power to control consciousness and to semioticize and discipline bodies by mapping and manipulating sounds, images and information, and forcing identity to take refuge in forms of subjectivity increasingly experienced as isolated and separate from larger social contexts. The idea of democratic citizenship has now become synonymous with the private, consuming citizen and the increasing subalternization of the other.

Critical pedagogy theorists also explore the possibilities of liberation from hierarchy and oppression. Paulo Freire (1921–1997), one of the most influential educationists of the 20th century, prophetically equated education with the experience of freedom –both in terms of challenging autocracy and democratising democracy. Henry Giroux (1994: 331) argues: 'Cultural democracy encourages a language of critique for understanding and transforming those relations that trap people in networks of hierarchy and exploitation.'

The 'left behind' reputedly experience a lack of purpose, identity and dignity, which democrats around the world ignore at their peril, as the insurrectionary events in Washington on 6 January 2021 powerfully demonstrate. Our findings suggest that educational aspiration is not lacking among the working class and ethnically marginalised in society. They seek agency and empowerment but are constantly constrained by the social structure they mistrust, shaped by class and White privilege.

During the 21st century the social construction of the working class as 'left behind' (the problem), the barriers it confronts within a meritocracy (the cause) and widening participation (the policy solution) constitute the issues we wish to discuss in this book. We view this process through the lens of educational stratification and are reminded that the baleful effects of meritocracy in the form of a widening gap in social equality is an indictment of modern democracy. What can society do about this widening gap? Widening participation in higher education as a strategy to achieve greater social class convergence is currently promoted in public policy as the answer. But is it? Is it working? Or is it just another policy elixir intended to divert attention away from the *real* causes of educational inequality: poverty and social inequality? We seek to find out in this book, which reveals high-achievement aspirations among the working class in our empirical study. We discuss alternatives to the popular ideal of equality of opportunity, such as opportunity pluralism and equality of condition. Our study will evoke bell hooks' (2014) concept 'talking back' in addressing these questions of deep-seated inequalities in accessing higher education, through reflecting the critical voices of the research participants in the UCC study 'Widening Participation in Higher Education'.

Higher education: building a knowledge society

Higher education has traditionally been the preserve of the social and economic elite. This reality belies a paradox. Traditionally, society at large has been required, through taxation, to financially support higher education. In the 21st century the state is increasingly withdrawing from funding universities, creating a massive problem of student debt. Universities have consequently been seen as having public responsibility to promote the common good through the pursuit of cultural, scientific and economic goals that go beyond the narrow interests of the academy. Equally, institutions of higher education are expected, as the distinguished US jurist, Ronald Dworkin (1998: 100) has observed 'to help improve the collective life of the community, not just protecting its science and culture, or improving its medicine, commerce or agriculture, but by helping to make that collective life more just and harmonious', concluding: 'our universities and colleges are surely entitled to think that the continuing and debilitating segregation of the United States by race, class, occupation and status is an enemy of both justice and harmony'.

In Europe, in the early decades of the 21st century, we are also faced with serious challenges in higher education. These include the challenge of social inclusion in an increasingly multicultural society, during an era when widening participation is being promoted as one of the means to 'redistribute the possibilities' (Giddens, 1998: 109) of upward social mobility. Social inclusion, however, cannot simply be reduced to improvements in access quotas. It needs to be backed by significant investment in the educational and social infrastructure that enables individual agency and personal empowerment. Education has emerged in the 21st century as the key to preserving an ethical civil society as the cornerstone of democracy, in which each citizen is empowered to make their individual journey towards the acquisition of knowledge in order to protect the humanistic values of our civilisation – based on personal freedom, human rights and social justice.

Paulo Freire, as a philosopher of praxis and author of the iconic book *The Pedagogy of the Oppressed* (1970), advocated the transformative practice of self-development and cultural empowerment through 'conscientization' (consciousness-raising). His theory of education viewed knowledge as the basis of cognitive justice and human agency, achieved through gaining critical consciousness about the world we inhabit, its power imbalances and the possibilities of democratic change. *The Pedagogy of the Oppressed* is a manifesto for social liberation, in which the learners emancipate themselves from oppressive power hierarchies through the acquisition of knowledge, including self-knowledge and awareness of the politics of identity. According to the Freirean vision of the future, the possibility of achieving cognitive justice belongs in both the public realm of the social structure and the interior life of the self, which empowers the citizen with agency through knowing themselves and understanding the world they inhabit. It is a project based on building a 'knowledge society', which is very different from the technocratic vision of a 'knowledge economy' informed by the values of wealth creation and competition.

In Freirean thinking critical literacy as a human right is a prerequisite to knowing the world and being empowered (Freire, 1970). This is not simply magical realism. Freire provides very cogent reasoning for addressing cognitive justice as one of the highest policy priorities in a democratic society, because it empowers people, through the acquisition of critical literacy skills, to participate in and understand the world in which they live. This includes the capacity to critically assess mass and social media information and disinformation. It also challenges the welfare state, as an institutionalist response to social inequality, to play a more active part in creating educational equality and promoting a more participative vision of democracy. These are essential prerequisites in maintaining an ethical civil society, as the cornerstone of democracy (Powell, 2013).

Aims, objectives and methodology

The aim of this book is to analyse growing social inequality in the 21st century and how it has created a marginalised class of educationally underachieving citizens, called the 'left behind' in contemporary public discourse, media representation and academic research. This phenomenon is polarising society and threatening democracy. It constitutes a fundamental challenge to social justice, the democratic philosophy that underpins the welfare state. The evidence based on field research shows that the majority of students from disadvantaged communities in one the most prosperous areas of the European Union – Ireland – aspire to pursue third-level studies but fail to realise their aspirations, despite the support of their parents.

The main objectives of the UCC field research were to:

- better understand patterns of higher education participation among young people from working-class backgrounds and minority ethnic groups;

- investigate orientations towards higher education within communities experiencing socio-economic disadvantage and low participation rates;
- identify factors including facilitators and barriers, which impact on young people's decision-making in relation to participation in higher education;
- explore the experiences of young people from socially disadvantaged backgrounds who have progressed to higher education through the HEAR (Higher Education Access Route) widening participation programme.

Policy makers are beginning to comprehend the magnitude of the problem facing society. Widening participation in higher education by the inclusion of marginalised groups is suggested as the policy solution. For example, the Higher Education Authority (HEA) in Ireland, published a consultative paper in 2021 on its National Access Plan 2022–2026, which stated the need for greater social inclusion through tackling inequalities (HEA, 2021: 2):

> Education has the power to transform lives, lift people out of poverty and break down cycles of disadvantage. ... Despite progress made in recent years, we know that our higher education system is still not as inclusive, as we want it to be. There are still communities and parts of our population, who are not accessing higher education. We know that some prospective students simply do not see themselves as belonging to a university, institute of technology or college in the first place. That needs to change.

The HEA (2021) enumerated the challenges in terms of major social inequalities in access to higher education among two core groups: students from disadvantaged areas (10 per cent) and members of the Traveller population (1 per cent). While these statistics are very disappointing, data in relation to access to Irish universities indicates that participation rates for students with disabilities were substantially above their target of 8 per cent, accounting for 12.3 per cent of participants in 2019–20 (HEA, 2021). *The Irish Times* (26 May 2022) announced that a forthcoming report from the Economic and Social Research Institute indicated that migrant children were progressing to higher education in 'astounding' numbers. This commentary was based on data that showed progression rates are broadly the same for Irish-born and migrant children from both English-speaking and non-English-speaking backgrounds. This evidence is contrary to international trends, where migrant children are victims of an 'aspirations/achievement paradox', in which they underperform. This may be due to the fact that many Irish child migrants come from the European Union and enjoy similar rights within its legal structure to their Irish-born counterparts. On the other hand, participation rates for full-time mature students, according to the HEA (2021), are in sharp decline, which may partly reflect the current buoyancy of the labour market, as the consequences of the 2008 crash decline. But, it may also reflect the high costs of higher education in Ireland – €3000 per student per annum – which *The Irish Times* (O'Brien, 2022) estimates to be among the most expensive in the European Union, while modest by UK standards.

This book is about a global educational and social narrative that draws on local narratives from a number of advanced Western democracies, exploring of the emergence of a left-behind class or 'precariat' in an increasingly divided world. It particularly analyses and discusses a field study funded by the Irish Research Council – *Widening Participation in Higher Education* – carried out during 2016 and 2018 by the authorial team from University College Cork (UCC) National University of Ireland on the relationship between DEIS (Delivering Equality of Opportunity in Schools) and higher-education access. DEIS schools are part of the Irish government's social inclusion strategy, which aims to address the educational needs of children and young people from disadvantaged communities. The data presented in the book explores the under-representation of disadvantaged young people in a sample of DEIS schools. There are 884 'disadvantaged' or DEIS schools in Ireland, and another 310 were planned in September 2022. The UCC Widening Participation in Higher Education project was based primarily on in-depth qualitative research which incorporated the views of young people (who were in the senior cycle of secondary school), parents, teachers and youth and community workers. In that way we set out to examine the complex issue of educational disadvantage from three research sites: home, school and community. We also report on data from interviews with 16 undergraduate students from disadvantaged backgrounds who entered university through the Higher Education Access Route (HEAR).

There is a strong geographic and community basis to under-representation in higher education with some areas far below the national participation rate (HEA, 2015). In recognition of this reality, the research project took a case-study approach to explore access in three areas of social disadvantage: two urban locations (Dublin and Cork) and one rural county. These areas were selected on the basis of existing sources, focusing upon: socio-economic disadvantage (such as the Pobal HP Deprivation Index) and areas with low participation rates in higher education (HEA, 2015). Within each case study location, we invited two DEIS secondary schools to participate in the research, providing a total of six schools for the study. Although our research was primarily qualitative, an initial survey of senior-cycle students in the six schools was conducted in order to provide an overview of the students' plans for the future, personal aspirations and orientations towards higher education.

The meta-questions of access inequality

What are the challenges DEIS school senior cycle students face in accessing third-level education, given that our research findings indicate 66 per cent of senior-cycle students aspire to do so? We explore a number of meta-questions in this book: (1) the cultural and economic factors that impact on DEIS school pupils' underperformance relative to their middle-class counterparts; (2) whether there is evidence to support the idea of social class convergence envisaged in the political projects of meritocracy, social mobility and widening participation that are promoted as strategies for achieving greater social equality; and (3) an investigation into discriminatory treatment of ethnic minorities in the education system, with particular reference to Irish Travellers.

These issues raise complex conceptual challenges. The barriers to accessing higher education are ultimately economically driven but they also impact on human subjectivity by reshaping consciousness and expectations. Professor Boaventura de Sousa Santos (2007: vii) in his book *Another Knowledge is Possible* contends that the hegemonic impact of global neoliberalism has 'effected a redefinition of contexts, objectives, means and subjectivities of social and political struggles', questioning the neoliberal belief in 'progress' based upon de-socialising capital and subjecting society as a whole to marketisation. His critique reminds us of George Orwell's prophetic novel *1984*, describing a dystopian post-truth society. As part of the project 'Reinventing Social Emancipation', de Sousa Santos (2007) concludes that among many consequences of these developments has been the extremely unequal distribution of the costs and opportunities between rich and poor countries, as well as between rich and poor from the same country, thus embedding inequality in the system and within citizens' consciousness.

Access inequality has both economic and cultural dimensions. Problems in accessing higher education are clearly not explicable simply in terms of unequal socio-economic structures, however influential. Disadvantage also raises important cultural questions that need to be dialogically posed – about the fairness of meritocracy and the disempowering of human agency in marginalised communities through territorial stigmatisation, endemic poverty and lowered expectations. This involves shared conversations with the key actors on the ground. In our field study we asked students, parents, teachers and youth and community workers for their views and experiences in order to locate the answers to our questions grounded in the social reality of their lived experiences. We seek to elicit these actors' views on the seminal question of what de Sousa Santos (2007: viii) calls 'cultural and cognitive justice and citizenship'.

We start from the theoretical premise that education occupies a contradictory position in society: it is both an agent of class inequality and its social reproduction but also contains the potential for transformative change in social relations between rich and poor through a Freirean epistemological 'conscientisation' (consciousness-raising) strategy. Freire's dialogical approach to empowering communication means in practice enabling the development of critical awareness among disadvantaged people through a dialogical process of reflection and action, reframing social reality and the possibility of changing the world for the better. A dialogical process involves an ethical conversation devoid of domination that is based on a 'consensus theory of truth', as Jurgen Habermas (1987) proposes in his philosophy of cultural action – advocating a commons for public knowledge as a shared democratic activity. The cultural empowerment of the marginalised and democratic participation are advocated by critical and resistance pedagogical theorists as the means to create greater educational and social equality (Friere, 1972; Giroux, 2013; McLaren, 2021). While action was not within the remit of our project, we did, as already noted, encourage participants to engage in 'talking back', based on critical-reflection interviews and focus groups regarding their perceptions of the equity of their social and educational reality.

Widening participation in higher education has become internationally accepted as a key focus of public policy goals since the 1990s. It is a laudable policy objective in its social ambition for citizens' future welfare that requires major investment in universities and student support, particularly free tuition and adequate maintenance grants. Currently, there is a lack of commitment to adequately fund widening participation as a policy initiative, which would involve an intergenerational redistribution of wealth from the old to the young. It also would require greater fluidity in university admissions strategies, accommodating participation on a lifelong-learning basis in order to compensate for disadvantage in childhood and youth. This objective is partly achieved through adult education and mature student access programmes but there is a need for much greater resourcing and creativity in relation to student progression through the third-level education system. Further Education and Training Awards Council (FETAC) pathways are promoting 'opportunity pluralism'. However, many students from disadvantaged communities are being left behind in a merit-based access race. That constitutes a double crisis of underinvestment and structural inequality in the current meritocratic higher education system. It urgently needs to be addressed, if universities are to move beyond 20th-century models of learning and participation.

The 2020 United Nations Human Development Index, which measures quality of life indicators in 189 countries (using the categories of health, education and income) ranked Ireland overall second in the world, behind Switzerland. The UK was overall ranked 13th and the US 17th, with Niger at the bottom of the league table. Ireland has a population of 5 million, with the highest birth rate and lowest death rate of the EU 27 member states (*The Irish Times*, 1 September 2021). This statistical profile and international ranking portray Ireland in a very positive position in relation to quality of life. The social realty is somewhat different, with young people from disadvantaged communities largely excluded from higher education in a divided society, where expenditure on education at every level is fiscally constrained.

An *Irish Times* front-page headline (17 September 2021) announced that the OECD (Organisation for Economic Co-operation and Development) *Education at a Glance 2021* report ranked Ireland in last place out of 36 OECD countries in investment in education as part of GDP. Ireland spends 3.3 per cent of GDP on education compared with the OECD average of 4.4 per cent. This comparative shortfall in investment in Irish education is likely to be a contributing factor to the under-representation of lower socio-economic groups in higher education. DEIS schools are a policy response intended to redress this imbalance through making the education system more socially inclusive.

The research raises fundamental questions about the purpose of access to higher education, which Harvard-based philosopher and public intellectual Michael Sandel (2010: 191) tells us is 'not obvious but contestable', adding: 'Some say universities are for the sake of promoting scholarly excellence, and academic promise should be the sole criterion of admission. Others say universities also exist to serve certain civic purposes, and that the ability to become a leader in a diverse society, should be among the criteria for admission.' He contends that 'sorting out the purpose of the university is essential to determining proper criteria of admission' and raises 'the teleological aspect of justice in university admissions'. Sandel's distinction is essentially between traditional elite universities and civic universities, which are arguably more open to social inclusion and widening participation.

From a perspective of widening participation, there were some very positive findings in our research, particularly in relation to young people's aspirations of going to university. The data also suggests that most working-class parents value education, believe it has become more important over time and want their children to progress to further and higher education. Nonetheless, it was clear that there are still significant barriers to accessing higher education for young people from disadvantaged communities. In line with previous research (such as Forsyth and Furlong, 2003; McCoy and Byrne, 2011), we found that economic factors continue to have an important influence and arguably have become more significant since the recession in 2008. While some economic barriers occur at the point of university entrance (for example registration, fees, accommodation, travel) others reflect deep-seated structural problems, notably poverty and unequal access to educational resources. Teachers and community workers, particularly in city schools, observed that there were different levels of disadvantage *within* disadvantaged communities: some young people lived in conditions of extreme poverty and their families faced an uncertain future, for example due to financial debt or the threat of eviction or of becoming homeless. In these circumstances, education was inevitably pushed down the list of their existential priorities, with knock-on effects on school attendance, academic attainment and career aspiration.

Much of the focus of this book is on the polarity in contemporary education between privilege and wealth on the one hand, and disadvantage and stratification (based on class and race) on the other in determining admissions to higher education. The evidence suggests that these class and ethnic barriers govern access to higher education. Michael Sandel (2020: 155) concludes: 'Higher education has become a sorting machine that promises mobility on the basis of merit but entrenches privilege and promotes attitudes towards success corrosive of the communality democracy requires', for example in the trope of the brilliant student with top grades that dominates media coverage of examination results. While individual achievement rightly deserves acknowledgement, celebration and congratulation, there needs to be an equal focus on those students who succeed against the odds. Their achievements also deserve recognition in a democratic society. The philosophy underpinning this book is that the university is part of an ethical civil society (the associational space between the state and the market) that underpins democracy and, as such, should reflect its humanistic and inclusive social and cultural values, rather than being led by the competitive values of the market that divides society.

Aristotle's curse: educational stratification and the origins of Western civilisation

Educational stratification is an old story, with roots going back to the origins of Western civilisation. The ancient Greek philosopher Aristotle endorsed the principle of human flourishing, meaning the achievement of self-actualisation and fulfilment within the wider community. He did not envisage, however, that human flourishing would apply to most of the Athenian population, if one uses access to education as a human development yardstick. Education in classical society was viewed as the acquisition of both knowledge and the cultivation of civic virtue, which means, according to Fintan O'Toole (2012: 32–33), 'human beings take personal pleasure in trust and decency and collective achievement'. However, in classical Greece the cultivation of civic virtue was limited to the ruling upper class. The poor were cursed with ignorance. In Aristotle's prescriptive vision for Greek society education should be the hierarchical preserve of the male elite composed of free citizens, preparing them for participation in the governance of the public sphere, or in classical parlance 'a life of leisure'. Aristotle's *Politics* (1944) equated education with class privilege, as a higher state of being. He infamously observed 'it is necessary for the tillers of the soil to be slaves'. Slaves were called *helots* in ancient Greece, providing a subjugated class of labourers. For farmers, merchants and tradesmen Aristotle recommended practical training in their vocations. Similarly, women were not viewed as people in need of the enlightened classical virtues essential for governance (wisdom, temperance, justice, courage) – that was conferred on the Athenian male elite by education. In Aristotle's classical world women were (with few exceptions) offered practical training in childcare, weaving and household management. Aristotle's vision of education normalised and legitimised inequality from the beginning of Western civilisation.

Reading Aristotle 2,500 years later reminds us how little has changed in the public sphere in Western civilisation. While slavery has been abolished, society remains fundamentally socially stratified. Social scientist R.H. Tawney (1880–1962) wrote a century ago (22 February 1965) in the *Times Educational Supplement,* on the formative influence of the past on the present:

> The educational system of today was created in the image, of our plutocratic, class conscious selves, and still faithfully reflects them. Worshipping money and social positions, we have established for children of the well-to-do an education lavish even to excess, and have provided for those of the four-fifths of the nation the beggarly rudiments thought suitable for helots who would be unserviceable without a minimum of instruction, and undocile helots if spoilt by more. The result has been a system of public education neither venerable, like a college, nor popular like a public house, but more indispensable, like a pillar box. (cited in Thompson and Ivinson, 2020: xv)

Comparison with the ancient world is illustrated by the current debate about the relative merits of academic education based on knowledge acquisition (humanistic model) versus the economic utility of practical training and skills acquisition (utilitarian model). Whatever view one takes about the purpose of the university, there is undoubtedly a shared public appreciation of the role of higher education in transforming the quality of many people's lives in democratic societies. Education is the key to full democratic participation and inclusive citizenship. In the words of the great Greek philosopher, Socrates, who sought to replace theology with reason as the basis of human understanding: 'There is only one good, knowledge, and one evil, ignorance.' However true this profound philosophical statement (and it is irrefutably correct) is in practice, eradicating educational stratification is a complex and challenging task involving the achievement of basic human rights. It involves achievements, challenges and deficits:

- Widening access to education in the form of mass participation has, according to the OECD *Education at a Glance 2021* report, altered historic gender access statistics governing entry to tertiary education – with females significantly outnumbering males – and is gradually reshaping society's power hierarchies, opportunity structures and social values.
- Higher education is, arguably, influential in empowering citizen participation in democracy by challenging traditional belief systems with common sense and rationality in an era when we are living through the electronic fragmentation of public discourse on multiple platforms, as well as the vulnerability of popular opinion to manipulation by conspiracy theorists on social media and the control of information by political autocrats, religious zealots and media tycoons.
- Large numbers of people continue to be excluded from higher education on the basis of their class, age and ethnic status, leading to social polarisation and spiralling inequality, while others are incapacitated by student debt for life.
- The principle of merit, currently governing access to higher education, is recreating pre-democratic forms of privilege and hierarchy – 'the meritocracy'.
- As a consequence, a disrespected left-behind class is emerging in 21st-century society – discredited, disempowered, demoralised and sometimes demonised, particularly if they are Travellers, Roma, asylum seekers or refugees, who are effectively stateless citizens without rights and so basic freedoms.

Hope and despair form the contents of Pandora's box, along with the two sides of an existential coin we call human experience. Both of these sentiments inform the discussion of educational stratification, its causes and what to do about it, We need to start from the premise that constraining access to education at the end of the second level through the sorting mechanism Joseph Fishkin (2014b) calls 'the Big Test' (SATs in the US, the Irish Leaving Certificate, UK A levels and so on) is a policy for the preservation of class, privilege and wealth. Fishkin argues the case for 'opportunity pluralism', suggesting that there needs to be greater flexibility and more pathways between higher education and further education and training (FET) in the interests of achieving equality of educational outcome. How can this pluralistic vision be reconciled with the elitism of meritocracy? Is equality of condition – treating everybody broadly the same in terms of life chances – the only way of equalising education, or is that pure utopian idealism? Is it possible to imagine such an egalitarian education system in a liberal democratic society? Some scholars think it is possible but contingent on achieving a greater commitment to social justice (Lynch, 2022).

Paulo Freire viewed education as a political and ethical project that enabled human beings to become more 'human' and reach an understanding of the world and its transformative potential to become a better and just place to live. It is a hopeful vision of the future. Peter McLaren (2021: 1) observes in this context: 'Another of Freire's categories, "untested feasibility", was an elaborate philosophy of hope that called for disenfranchised groups to move beyond "limit situations" re: the constraints placed on their humanity by underdevelopment – and transform those adverse conditions, into a space for creative experimentation.' We share Freire's hope and belief in the possibility of transformative change in education and society, while remaining acutely aware of the obstacles.

The democratic challenges of a fair society

It is not easy to democratically agree the basis of a fair society, since we have different ideas about what is fair. For example, *The Irish Times* reported (O'Brien, 2021b) that private schools in Ireland were claiming exclusion from state grants would be 'discriminatory' and may violate parental rights. In reality, 51 (post-primary) private fee-paying schools in Ireland received €121 million in state grants during 2021 to fund teachers, special needs assistants and other supports, which led the state broadcaster RTÉ (2023) to pose the question: 'Is it fair that public money helps to fund private schools?' This state support for private schools compares with €150 million funding targeted at educational disadvantage for 884 DEIS schools (687 primary and 197 post primary), accounting for approximately 20 per cent of the school population in 2021 (Dáil Éireann debate, 2022a). These figures suggest very strong institutional support for private education in Ireland. French researcher, Aline Courtois (2017: 54) observed:

> Another peculiarity of the Irish fee-paying sector is that it is heavily subsidised by the State – which is very different from the British situation. As the [2008] economic crisis unfolded, bringing in its wake drastic public service cuts, their funding by the State came under renewed scrutiny but was only marginally reduced.

In raising the issue of parental rights, this dispute about equity in school funding inevitably touches on children's citizenship. Do children have an individual right to educational equality, or is that right subordinate to the parental right of choice of school in a democratic society? Tormey (2010: 189) has addressed what he calls 'the silent politics of educational disadvantage' in Ireland, which he argues has 'enabled a conservative political perspective to become embedded in public educational policy without debate'. Private schools seek to justify their legitimacy by pointing to their role in cultivating their students' 'moral capital' as future leaders of society (Courtois, 2017).

The philosopher Hannah Arendt (1906–1975), in her 1951 book *The Origins of Totalitarianism*, famously coined the phrase 'the right to have rights', in which she links an abstract concept of citizenship rights to the tangible benefits of citizenship as a member of a democratic community with institutions and social practices that can sustain equality. Arendt understood the value of citizenship, having lived as a stateless person between 1933 and 1951, when she became a naturalised US citizen. Incarcerated in wartime France because of her Jewish identity, Arendt managed to escape to the US in 1941. Her harrowing experiences strongly influenced her political writings. Her relevance to the contemporary world endures and inspires those who value human rights, including the right to access knowledge. The welfare state reflects this philosophical vision of an inclusive society based on a caring moral code, but there are contradictions, notably in education.

The project of meritocracy was at the centre of 20th-century educational reform within the welfare state project. Its critics pointed out that meritocracy rested on a fundamental contradiction – 'equal chances to become unequal'! Meritocracy is not a new concept with its origins in the tests that were required to enter the imperial civil service in China, which led to the emergence of the mandarin class. Similarly, in the 1850s the Northcote-Trevelyan reforms created the modern civil service in Britain, through which recruitment was based on ability rather than hereditary privilege. It both cases meritocracy created new power elites. The closed circle of inequality remained intact and society fundamentally divided, with those at the bottom experiencing disempowerment and social marginalisation. Critics argue meritocracy valorises class hubris and humiliates the poor, the left behind, stoking populist politics of resentment against elites (Sandel, 2020). Real educational equality, known as equality of condition, has remained an elusive policy goal in an increasingly individualised society, where a binary between graduates and non-graduates is creating polarised divisions that are threatening democracy.

We will also engage with what the French intellectual, Paul Ricoeur (1913–2005) – inspired by the critical ideas of Marx, Freud and Nietzsche on the hidden meanings of religion – called 'the hermeneutics of suspicion'. Riceour invites us to look beneath surface meanings of texts in search of deeper policy interpretations and human understanding. In our study we are seeking to expose the repressed texts and meanings in the lived experience of working-class educational engagement that lies behind the policy language and rhetoric. We search for hidden agendas and ulterior motives that influence human societies and human psyche in profound ways. Our policy narrators from below include students, teachers, parents and youth and community workers. We explore normativity in education in dialogue with them, drawing on the counter-stories of their lived experiences and underlying sympathies and antipathies.

Professor Diane Reay, the highly respected British educational authority based at Cambridge University, wrote a remarkable semi-autobiographical book *Miseducation* (2017). On the basis of 500 interviews, she observed: 'The most important thing I found out was that we are still educating different social classes for different functions in society' (Ferguson, 2017). It would seem the legacy of Aristotle's class-based elite vision (where the ruling class had absolute power both symbolic and real) is still at the core of our educational model, despite attempts to make democratic society more equal through the adoption of merit, as the governing principle of access.

Thomas Piketty (2014) in his influential book *Capital in the Twenty-First Century* demonstrates that modern economic growth and the diffusion of knowledge enabled the world during the 20th century to avoid inequalities on the apocalyptic scale originally predicted by Karl Marx. But this may have been a temporary phenomenon because the benevolent influence of the welfare state, which shielded the population from the worst consequences of inequality, is now in decline. Piketty is describing a financial chasm opening up in the 21st century between the rich and the rest of the population as the new normal in capitalist society. The Occupy movement in 2011 gave popular voice to this inequality in the form of public protest (Powell, 2013). Writer Amor Towles wryly observes (Towles, 2021):

> If you look at the 1% dynamic that's happening in the US: extraordinary wealth at such a level that people are sending rockets into space – that's the American Dream gone crazy. And what's happening is your sending a rocket into space and leaving behind all those people who in a society deserve a better shot at fulfilling themselves.

This spiralling inequality represents a return to oligarchy for the rich and powerful at the expense of the poor and powerless. Meritocracy is designed to make inequality fair in the public imaginary but not in social realty. Social justice is the democratic antidote to this toxic society.

Professor Kathleen Lynch (2022) in her important book *Care and Capitalism* argues that the neoliberal capitalist model of the 21st century is neither inevitable nor invincible. She questions the assumption that people are wholly self-interested with little or no regard for the other, advocating affective justice, based on love, care and solidarity as an alternative to market values. She seeks to challenge the logic and ethics of neoliberal capitalism at the gravitational centre of meaning-making in 21st-century society and displace it with an alternative care-centric narrative. As she puts it (2022: 8–9): '*Care and Capitalism* focusses attention on creating an ideological platform for change, by mobilizing new languages and narratives around care, social justice and affective equality in cultural and political discourse, especially by educating people about care and social justice at all levels of society.' It is Lynch's core contention (2022: 21) that 'theories of justice must take cognizance of the endemic inter/dependency and vulnerability of the human condition', adding, 'relationality has both *distributive* and *contributive* implications for justice … being deprived of these experiences individually and collectively is therefore a *distributive* injustice' [italic in original].

Lynch's conclusion is that social justice is institutionally embodied in a 'care-centric society', which during the 20th century was widely called the welfare state in public discourse. Neoliberal capitalism has sought to undermine the ethos of the welfare state and replace it with a competition state and a consumer society. The education system is a microcosm of this strategy of reinventing society in the image of the market. It has produced a left-behind class, victims of a society without a moral compass that has forgotten about human need and vulnerability and the importance of affective justice in sustaining positive human relations. Kathleen Lynch's book offers new thinking on the affective dimension of social justice that encompasses love, care and solidarity.

In this book, we seek to contextualise our social analysis within the institutional conception of the welfare state based on a social contract with the citizen to create a fairer and more humane society, informed by the principle of redistributive justice that supports people in living their everyday lives on the basis of affective equality, including the right to dignity and respect. The welfare state optimally provides free access to healthcare, a right to shelter, guaranteed income security and access to university education. In reality, the welfare state is characterised by many variations and models (Esping-Andersen, 1990). It carefully balances liberty and equality in a democratic society. Merit is the product of this delicate balancing act in reconciling class aspirations; ultimately, in the case of access to higher education, at the expense of the working class. Free tuition helped to legitimise merit. When free tuition was curtailed by austerity policies and in some countries abolished (including the UK, US and Australia) and replaced by student loans, core equity issues emerged more clearly in the system of higher education – notably a problem of student debt, with major implications for social justice.

The metaphoric power of the welfare state in promoting greater social justice has, since the 1970s, been substantially undermined by welfare reform and austerity policies, which have resulted in a major erosion of services through cutbacks, privatisation and the rollback of the state. In response to this project of neoliberal capitalism social inequalities have grown sharply and the Marshallian notion of citizenship as a three-legged stool composed of civil, political and social rights has given way to traditional class divisions, in which the daily immiseration of the poor (such as dependence on food banks) is becoming increasingly visible (Marshall, 1973; Piketty, 2014). On the other hand, the privileged are prospering in an increasingly divided society. For example, in relation to the underlying principle of meritocracy, the middle classes have become expert at gaming the system, known as 'opportunity hoarding' (Friedman and Laurison, 2019: 148).

Social mobility is the objective in the aspirational language of neoliberal capitalism that supports the metanarrative of meritocracy, but the outcomes in social realty are far more complex. Currently, social mobility has stalled and is undermining individual and class morale. This is fuelling the growing demoralisation of those who do not succeed in the meritocratic contest (Reay, 2017). As Sandel (2020: 74) puts it in terms of the moral and social influence of personal responsibility doctrine ('responsibilisation'): 'It [meritocracy] implies that, for those left behind, their failure is their own fault.' This is a bitter message to absorb and reconcile with an individual's self-respect, personal esteem and sense of justice. It puts the anger of the left behind in context in a world where personal responsibility has been elevated to a core principle of social policy at the expense of social solidarity. Sandel's contribution is to reframe meritocracy as a form of elite 'tyranny' imposed by those at the top of the social ladder upon those at the bottom. Nonetheless, the welfare-state legacy has enabled progressive individualism to flourish, notably in the form of increasing gender equality in education and work, reproductive rights and greater sexual freedoms. However, the US Supreme Court ruling in *Dobbs v. Jackson Women's Health Organization* in 2022 (overturning the right to abortion) reminds us that reproductive rights cannot be taken for granted.

In a post-truth era it is important to question the purported fairness of meritocracy, which, as noted above, some scholars perceive as a 'tyranny', effectively promoting a system of social apartheid (Sandel, 2020: 73). Others view meritocracy as the problem because it stifles social mobility and exacerbates inequality. Markovits (2019) views meritocracy as the single greatest obstacle to fairness in the education system. These observations raise seminal questions for researchers. What facts do we choose? Whose subjectivities should we believe? How do we differentiate between theories of causality?

Whatever the validity of these philosophical judgements on the ethical and political value base of meritocracy, it is clear that many working-class people feel, with good reason, a strong sense of grievance with the lack of equality in an education system that disadvantages them and makes social mobility an unattainable ambition. The injunction to students to aspire is not sufficient to enable achievement. For many working-class students, social inequality presents insurmountable structural barriers to accessing higher education, with multiple dimensions (economic and cultural), underpinned by a systemically elitist system called 'meritocracy'. It has created both a left-behind class and a crisis in democracy that is being exploited by populist politicians.

Rethinking social inequality

During the second half of the 20th century the meaning of social inequality as simply a class construct began to be publicly criticised by advocates of a more complex and interconnected understanding of this phenomenon, which they argued should also encompass gender, race, religion, ability, sexuality, age and other forms of minority status, such as the contested position of migrants and refugees. The world is changing in terms of the public debate about social inequality and its impact on civic life. The implications for the reinterpretation of social inequality were profound. The unidimensional concept of equality, based on a traditional materialist paradigm and the principle of redistributive justice that we call 'class' is increasingly challenged by a multidimensional cultural paradigm. It has redefined social equality in an increasingly diverse society to encompass the right to parity of esteem and recognition between diverse social groups. The personal has become distinctly political. Campaigns for equality of respect – called identity politics – increasingly influence public discourse and demands for reparation for past wrongs (such as slavery).

This change in thinking about the meaning of equality adds greater conceptual latitude to our understanding of social and cognitive justice, encompassing gender and race, as well as class. The concept of intersectionality embodies this reconceptualisation of equality. Clearly, there is a high degree of interconnectedness in terms of the experience of these social groups (as well as others, such as people with disabilities, migrants, LGBTQIA+ people, asylum seekers and refugees), who collectively have been subjected to disadvantage, oppression and discrimination.

During a very prolific career, bell hooks (1952–2021) opened up to the world the complexity and interconnectedness of forms of inequality in her wide-ranging corpus of writings. Intersectionality has emerged as a conceptual framework for considering these intersecting forms of disadvantage, oppression and discrimination. The resulting reconceptualisation of the nature and complexity of social inequality in postmodern society as intersectional has considerable implications for sociological analysis and public understanding of educational disadvantage. It is important to note, however, that the influence of class in the explanation of social inequality has remained fundamental in European understandings of social inequality. As Diane Reay sees it workingclass children get less of everything in education – including respect (Ferguson, 2017). Ultimately, we frame our analysis around the intersection of class and race. We view this as a 'double disadvantage'; manifestations of the corrosive dominance of 'white privilege', which Paul Gilroy regards as a product of 'postcolonial melancholia' (Koshy, 2021).

This changing language and meaning of social inequality continue to pose social and political challenges. Robert Wuthnow, in his 2018 book *The Left Behind,* suggested a cultural and political divide was opening up between small-town America and the metropolitan elite. The book caught the public imagination by powerfully evoking the 'moral outrage' of rural US communities in decline – an experience in which: 'Schools are closing, businesses leaving, and jobs disappearing' (Wuthnow, 2018: 6). The political impact of rural decline led many White working-class Americans to vote for Donald Trump in 2016 out of frustration, desperation and despair about the future.

Trump ostensibly gave this left-behind population a political voice through his populist rhetoric, challenging the basic precepts of civility and democracy. It culminated with the attempted coup in January 2021, following Trump's loss of the presidential election. This violent insurrectionary event shook the US and Western civilisation to their democratic roots by its volcanic outpouring of anger and rage against the institutions and values of liberal democracy. The voice of the left behind had registered discontents of the White working class, but was it understood? A near identical coup attempt in Brazil on 8 January 2023, also against the outcome of a lost presidential election, demonstrated that political violence was becoming endemic in democratic regimes, where supporters of defeated candidates were attempting to overturning election outcomes by force.

The working class, educational aspiration and meritocracy

A recent UK survey report, *They Look Down on Us*, from the think tank CLASS (Jesse, 2022: 5) observes: 'Class is not widely nor intuitively understood as a political concept (i.e. a description of power and control, who has it, and who doesn't), nor is it readily talked about in relation to inequality and social justice.' The report found (pp 5–6) that: only one in three people say they know what 'working class' means, and some participants believed it to be a potentially divisive term. Participants in the CLASS survey also distinguished between the employed working class, which they placed at the core of its social identity because of engagement in work, and 'lower class', meaning those in receipt of welfare benefits – put simply, people normally regarded as poor. The report concluded (p 7): 'This study finds that, contrary to what certain politicians and mainstream media say, diverse working-class people across races and other differences share everyday experiences of precarity, prejudice, and a lack of power and of place. They share values, hopes and desires for their families and their futures.'

Increasingly, class polarisation is portrayed as a division between the meritocratic hubris of the college-educated and the resentment of non-degree holders who have failed to adapt to the economic realities of globalisation and automation by upskilling. Michael Sandel (2020: 85) warns that 'the weaponization of credentials shows how merit can become a kind of tyranny'. The purported political alienation of the left behind is often portrayed in the media as sign of a larger cultural apocalypse, or as the symbolic expression of the social and political turmoil of the anomic times we are living through. In reality, the alienation and anger of the left behind are arguably signs of the despair, disillusionment and nihilism evoked among the traditional predominantly White working class in reaction to a loss of relative privilege, growing social inequality and its profound structural injustices (Case and Deaton, 2020). A purported failure of ambition to adapt to industrial change by upskilling through the acquisition of the required educational credentials in order to achieve a sustainable lifestyle is often represented as the root cause of the decline of the traditional working class. Is this true?

The CLASS report suggests that it is a false assumption in the view of the participants in its study: '7 in 10 working-class people believe the system is rigged against them and that wealthy people are wealthy because they are given more opportunities and not because they work harder or have more talent' (Jesse, 2022: 6).

Working-class people do not lack aspiration: they lack opportunity in a stratified society. They understand the importance of gaining academic credentials in post-industrial society, as a route out of poverty. Surprisingly, the CLASS report records working-class support for the principle of merit in the responses of its participants: 'Yet, most participants also strongly believed in meritocracy, that society is structured like a ladder that you climb to a better social and economic position – seemingly defined by higher earnings, material possessions, and crucially security' (Jesse, 2022: 7). Only 15 per cent of the participants in the CLASS study believed the proposition 'that if the working class struggles in our society it is due to its own lack of effort or initiative'.

'The working class' is, therefore, not a monocultural social group of disillusioned White people in a multicultural society: it is defined by its diversity, which devolves on an intersectional axis that is dominated by class and race. In relation to the influence of race, the CLASS report found that participants believed that 'half of working-class people of colour (Black, Asian and minority ethnic people) face more significant barriers to economic success than white people' (Jesse, 2022: 7). This belief rises significantly for Black working-class people, to 77 per cent, and 74 per cent for Asian working-class people.

The importance of student grants

The evidence we have compiled in the UCC study suggests that working-class people do not lack ambition, they are simply confronted with substantial economic and psychosocial barriers. Two-thirds of the Irish DEIS student population we surveyed want to participate in higher education but are shut out by barriers that are both visible (poverty, class and ethnicity) and invisible (cultural capital) – though very real!

Participants in our UCC study identified student grants as being the main factor that would enable them to go on to higher education. Students noted that accessing SUSI (Student Universal Support Ireland) grants to cover tuition fees and living expenses would make the greatest single difference in enabling them to participate in higher education. During focus group discussions the DEIS school students asked several questions in relation to applying for a grant, how much it covered and whether you could really live on what you were given. Several participants observed that they experienced the process as complex and confusing. Working out the costs of doing a degree was clearly challenging, especially if a family was not in a position to significantly supplement the grant. Finance is a major barrier constraining working-class students' participation in higher education (unlike their more affluent middle-class counterparts), which we will return to in Chapter 5.

Community schools

What is a DEIS school? The Irish Minister for Education explained to the Irish Parliament: 'DEIS – Delivering Equality of Opportunity Schools – is the main policy initiative of my Department to address educational disadvantage at school level' (Dáil Éireann debate, 2022b). That is a policy overview that needs to be grounded in the social reality of community life. What is the view from the ground?

A DEIS school principal from our study explains what a DEIS school is from a teaching perspective:

> 'It's a community school and it's very much the ethos of a community school, so we would welcome all students. It's inclusive, so everyone who applies to the school from the community has a place in the school, so we welcome all learners in the school. So, it's very much, we would pride ourselves on being a school for the community, serving the people of the locality and the wider area for the last forty years. It's very much our ethos.'

Community schools provide a broad curriculum for all young people living in a local community, encompassing both academic and vocational programmes. When asked about the profile of the students, including class, nationality and ethnicity the principal replied:

> 'Generally local, we'd have a small percentage of students, maybe about five to eight per cent of students who were born outside Ireland, it would have been higher but that's decreased lately – most of the

students come from the immediate area. It's a DEIS school so you have a significant cohort of one-parent families, I would say around 30 to 35 per cent. You would have a significant cohort of parents on social welfare.'

DEIS schools offer a number of additional supports to disadvantaged students in targeted areas, including: reduced class sizes; additional funding (over €170 million in 2022); access to literacy and numeracy programmes; free school meals and provision of a range of supports in relation to the wider social function of DEIS schools in the community (*The Irish Times*, 21 August 2021):

> Schools are not just seats of learning – for many children they provide security, a structure to the day and a caring environment. In DEIS schools they provide breakfast clubs, lunch and after-school care and activities. Home school community liaison teachers and school completion staff provide an important link between school and home and are often the first to draw attention to child neglect or abuse. The sudden withdrawal of all these supports during school closures [arising from COVID-19] had a devastating effect on many families.

DEIS schools reflect the evolving role of publicly funded schools internationally as community centres, particularly in disadvantaged local areas.

The Irish Times (7 January 2019) reported that research produced by the Education Research Centre in Dublin indicated 'increased confidence' among DEIS school students 'with raised expectations amongst themselves and their teachers', but that they were still 'well below the national norm'. The report also noted girls outperformed boys. Retention rates in relation to senior-cycle students were 82.3 for DEIS students, compared with 93.2 for non-DEIS students. These research findings challenge traditional assumptions that there is poverty of ambition in working-class communities. We seek to understand DEIS students from a position that recognises their experience of discrimination, disadvantage, cultural silence and invisibility.

Structure and content

The book is organised in eight chapters. It is composed of an integrated narrative that devolves on: sociological theory and analysis; civic and democratic values, notably educational equality, social justice and human rights; and empirical research based on the voices and aspirations of marginalised people from disadvantaged communities. The interconnected core themes addressed in the narrative are educational stratification, meritocracy and widening participation.

Chapter 1 – Introduction: Aristotle's curse

This introductory chapter has explored the landscape of educational disadvantage. It contextualises the core conceptual issues underpinning the book and provides an intellectual rationale and overview. The seminal contribution of Pierre Bourdieu to understanding educational inequality is introduced.

The hierarchical origins of education in Western civilisation are explored from its origins in ancient Greece. Aristotle's vision of education as an elite pursuit of 'leisure' and preparation for participation in governance is reviewed in terms of social relations. A binary distinction between education and training is discussed as Aristotle's divisive legacy. Modern class and ethnic hierarchies are discussed as a reflection of these cultural and economic divisions, manifested in the Irish DEIS system that struggles to compete with more privileged forms of education. The changing meaning of social inequality, encompassed in the concept of intersectionality, is introduced to explain how a multitude of intersecting power relations, including class, race/ethnicity, gender/sexuality, ability, age and religion, influence and shape social relations in promoting both privilege and disadvantage.

Chapter 2 – The cultural politics of educational stratification

This chapter offers an overarching analysis of the relationship between class, race and culture and how these influences shape individual educational trajectories for the privileged, while consigning the working class and ethnic minorities to a separate disadvantaged status in a system of targeted community schools (DEIS schools in Ireland) that aspire to pursue a positive discrimination agenda in order to redress the consequences of social inequality. The ideas of Pierre Bourdieu are developed further from Chapter 1: notably his concepts of cultural capital, field and habitus are analysed. Professional and parental perspectives on Bourdieu's conceptualisation of the influence of cultural capital are also referenced from the field research. Social justice is deconstructed into its liberal, institutional, structuralist and critical theory ideological strands.

Chapter 3 – Public education, universities and widening participation

This chapter explores the role of public education and universities in contemporary civil society. Public education is discussed in the context of its role in democratic society, particularly in relation to the function of community schools. The university sector's social commitment to a third mission in the form of civic and community engagement is analysed in all its complexity. We discuss Pierre Bourdieu's view of the welfare state as the institutional embodiment of social justice and the realisation of radical humanism in democratic society. The chapter particularly examines the impacts of adult education and public libraries. It explores the role of affirmative action and access initiatives within the overall context of widening participation. Finally, the chapter, drawing upon the research conducted by the team, analyses student expectations and experiences of widening participation and explores the challenges encountered by non-traditional students from disadvantaged backgrounds in negotiating university life, revealing some very positive stories.

Chapter 4 – The psycho-politics of meritocracy: IQ + effort = merit?

This examines the moral principle of merit and its limitations. We argue that meritocracy provided a metafiction for public policy, based on the philosophy of equality of opportunity and publicly presented as 'a ladder of opportunity'. We suggest it has not succeeded in overcoming privilege or the displacement of elites but arguably has replicated and culturally embedded new hierarchical elites to replace their hereditary predecessors. Alternative models of educational equality that take a more egalitarian and inclusive approach are reviewed and discussed. We explore the impact of the coronavirus pandemic on inequities in exam systems. Social mobility, as an alternative to social justice in an equal opportunity society, is critically analysed as a mythical ladder of opportunity and the consequences of its failures discussed in terms of growing social inequality.

Chapter 5 – Snakes and ladders: aspirations and barriers

This chapter explores aspirations, barriers and facilitators in relation to disadvantaged students' access to higher education. We ask if an aspiration/achievement gap in student performance in the exam system – 'the big test' – is an adequate explanatory model for the stark disparity between social classes and ethnic groups in university access, or is disadvantaged students' failure to progress the product of a poverty trap? Second, what is the nature and social reality of the barriers impeding access to higher education? Third, we discuss facilitators that help students to succeed in achieving their aspirations. In the search for answers to our questions we explore the social and educational perspectives of young people living in disadvantaged communities, their teachers and youth and community workers active in their locality based on the evidence from the team's research.

Chapter 6 – Social class and parental attitudes to education and career choices

This focuses on parental engagement with their children's educational and career choices, and how attitudes to education within working-class communities appear to have changed over time. It draws on the international literature. Despite their own limited experiences of formal education, the parents interviewed in our research valued education and generally wanted their children to progress further than they themselves had done. In line with previous research, we found that parents sometimes lacked the confidence to engage in planning their children's educational and career futures, due to a lack of familiarity with the higher-education system. At the same time, there were notable variations within the group – from parents who took on a strategic role in shaping their children's post-secondary choices to those who played a supportive but less active role. There was little evidence of parental negativity towards students' aspirations.

Chapter 7 – Structural racism and Traveller education

This chapter considers exploratory research carried out as part of the research project in relation to access for young people from the Irish Traveller community. Travellers are Ireland's oldest minority ethnic group but have only recently been recognised as such. The analysis and discussion in this chapter raises fundamental questions about racism and the cultural and human rights of minority people to equal treatment. Travellers and Roma are among the most stigmatised groups that experience the most extreme forms of social exclusion. The research tackles racism through evolving official attitudes and the discursive tensions between interculturalism and multiculturalism.

Chapter 8 – Conclusion: Global lessons

The conclusion also explores the challenges involved in deepening equality within the education system and society at large.

Conclusion

In this introductory chapter we have sought to deconstruct the phenomenon of a 'left-behind' class and how it enables us to make sense of world that is deeply polarised. We essentially view the term 'left behind' as a metaphor that helps us to unlock the experience of a section of the working class who feel like 'ghosts', because of their exclusion from mainstream society. In our view the social and geographical isolation of the left behind is not the product of social pathology, as some commentators suggest, but the result of poverty, social exclusion and discrimination, which undermines human agency and marginalises sections of the population. In the media, policy making and academic representation of the 'left behind' phenomenon, the education gap is attributed to a lack of aspiration and agency among the poor and has been promoted as the causal explanation for this growing social polarisation. Our research evidence suggests otherwise. We argue the explanation for access inequality is to be found in an elitist meritocratic education system that promotes class privilege at the expense of the socially disadvantaged, called 'educational stratification'. It is deeply embedded in the political culture of meritocracy that divides people according to class and race, which we discuss in the next chapter.

2

The cultural politics of educational stratification

The 'college doesn't matter' meme

The meme that 'It doesn't matter whether you go to college' is commonplace among sceptics of the value of widening participation in higher education. It is predicted by historian Peter Turchin (2023) that 'elite over-production' of degrees may cause future social and political instability, because there are not enough high-status positions to satisfy graduate demand. The *Wall Street Journal* reported (Adamy, 2023): 'An overwhelming share of Americans aren't confident their children's lives will be better than their own, according to a to a … poll that shows growing scepticism about the value of a college degree and record low levels of overall happiness.' The abolition of free tuition in many jurisdictions, leading graduates to incur massive debt from student loans, has combined with spiralling mortgage costs, to create a bleak future for many graduates and a challenge to intergenerational justice. Jokes about BA graduates working in fast-food outlets abound and reinforce prejudice against studying the humanities, which, according to US data, is in sharp decline (Heller, 2023).

The financialisation of higher education and the resulting marketisation of degrees, as costly commodities out of the reach of many, has fed this cultural scepticism. It is a long way from the original high-minded humanist mission, advocated by philosopher and founder of the Humboldt University in Berlin, Wilhelm von Humboldt (1767–1835), challenging the university to bring enlightenment to the world. Von Humboldt believed that higher education enabled students to become autonomous individuals and citizens, anticipating democratic society. Undoubtedly, no amount of education can be a substitute for good social skills and common sense. Yet, Socrates' (470–399 BCE) powerful statement 'the unexamined life is not worth living' resonates down the millennia as part of his monumental intellectual legacy to Western humanism.

A primary degree offers a foundation for self-improvement, personal empowerment, intellectual awakening and human flourishing. Education is, as Nelson Mandela (1995: 194) asserted, 'the great engine of human development'. It also brings enhanced self-esteem, career advancement and greater knowledge and social equity. These are the intangible benefits of higher education. It is a gift that keeps giving and cannot be taken away.

Higher education also has transformational societal impacts in developing critical minds (consciousness-raising) and civic values (solidarity, tolerance, empathy and compassion) in the population – the foundations of democracy and the best guarantor of its future sustainability in an era of rising authoritarianism and nativist populism. But are the theorists of alleged 'elite overproduction' correct in terms of a negative impact on graduates finding a well-paid job? Or, is the elite overproduction of graduates a distraction from the social reality that half the population cannot access a university education?

We argue in this chapter that educational stratification is emerging at the core of social inequality in the 21st century, dividing society into graduates and non-graduates. It is producing a profound sense of injustice, resentment and bewilderment among the left behind. Some critics, as noted earlier, have questioned the benefits of higher education, mocking the value of a degree. We demonstrate on the basis of the evidence that their logic is profoundly misguided – most young people and their parents intuitively understand the value of education. For many young people who are left behind, we argue, the real challenge is overcoming a myriad of visible and invisible inequalities that stand in the way of their participation in higher education, notably their class and race. We show, drawing on the ideas of Pierre Bourdieu, that, from childhood, students are challenged in negotiating the educational ladder by a lack of cultural, social and financial capital. Some commentators have sought to explain differences in educational performance in genetic terms but these elitist ideas have been discredited, as we will show, because of their association with social Darwinism and eugenics. In our view, the explanation of educational stratification is to be found in the environment – where young people grow up living on the margins of society. The concept of intersectionality seeks to interpret this complexity, as we will demonstrate. Finally, we discuss the diverse meanings of social justice as the key to unlocking educational stratification.

The benefits of higher education

The evidence is clear: access to higher education brings significant social and economic benefits to individuals and society. The new knowledge economy is simultaneously creating a cosmopolitan class of skilled graduates, who become salaried professionals in information technology, software engineering, medicine, law, finance, scientific research, media, management consultancy, design and so on, and simultaneously a left-behind class of people without qualifications or skills. The latter often lack insight into the causes of their immiseration, blaming themselves for their fate. Populist politicians have exploited their angst and lack of insight into the causes of their deprivation and misery by fuelling racist misinformation and nativist hubris.

During the economic crisis in Ireland between 2008 and 2013, according to the Higher Education Authority (HEA), the chances of a graduate becoming unemployed was half that of a non-graduate. After the crisis, graduates were employed more quickly than non-graduates. There was also a graduate earnings premium. Men with degrees earn 69 per cent more than non-graduate males. For women, the equivalent figure is 90 per cent (HEA, 2015). The Central Statistics Office in Ireland (2023) estimated that where the head of household had an educational attainment of primary level education or below, the nominal median household disposable income was €26,529 compared with €66,811 for those with a degree. The Central Statistics Office's (2021) *Educational Attainment Thematic Report 2021* asserted that higher educational attainment levels in Ireland are linked to higher employment rates. Those aged 25 to 64 with third-level qualifications had an employment rate of 85 per cent, compared with those in the same age category with primary or no formal education qualifications, who had had an employment rate of just 32 per cent. Women were almost three times as likely to be employed if they had a third-level qualification.

Clearly, there are major benefits arising from higher education that promotes individual prosperity and economic development. As the HEA (2015: 14) put it: 'As well as the benefits that individuals derive from higher education, there are also other economic and social benefits – our educated workforce is Ireland's economic asset and we need more people to take up education to drive economic progress.' Manifestly, the graduate overproduction argument does not stand up to critical scrutiny in a modern economy in the 21st century. A degree unlocks the labour market for the graduate, offering opportunity, a decent lifestyle and job stability. Non-graduates conversely face an unstable and precarious future.

Pierre Bourdieu (1997) originally coined the term 'precariat' to describe an alienated generation inhabiting marginalised spaces in French society. His interest in the existence of a *subproletariate* dates from his days as a student in the 1950s and early anthropological research in Algeria during the 1960s (Bourdieu and Wacquant 1992). The concept of 'precarisation' of sections of the working class has had an international impact. Alberti et al (2018: 450–451) comment:

> In Anglophone sociology, debates around precarity have been fuel for a wider Bourdieusian agenda that has become increasingly prominent in debates around class ... inspired by Bourdieu, the precariat appears at the bottom of the new British class structure, being most deprived of access to social, economic and cultural capital. Precarity thus appears as a means of sorting people into categories which become self-perpetuating, leading to entrenched inequality which undermines the liberal pursuit of social mobility.

Guy Standing (2014: 1) elaborated on the concept of the existence of a precariat composed of alienated and rootless people in Western society, which he described as 'an incipient monster'. He was referring to marginalised people reacting to neoliberalism, often living on the edge of society and surviving in a gig economy characterised by casual and unstable employment. The riots in France during the summer of 2023 following the police killing of a 17-year-old youth signify that the precariat is capable of retaliation against perceived injustice by engaging in street protests that challenge the authority of the state. An editorial in *Le Monde* (2023) posed two questions regarding the street protests by alienated youth from precariat: 'How can we make young people believe in republican equality when every contact with the police is seen as an injustice and a humiliation? How can we make the promise of social inclusion credible to teenagers affected by both urban segregation and discriminatory practices?'

Standing (2018) regards the precariat as a diverse set of alienated social groups, which include the left behind. Manifestly, there are major issues in relation to the distribution of wealth in 21st-century society, notably in relation to the intergenerational wealth concentrated in asset welfare (such as home ownership) among the older sections of the population that is alienating young people across the social spectrum, who are being shut out of the property market. Much of this change in ownership has been led by investment capital and vulture funds at the expense of young people, who are being charged exorbitant rents.

Standing (2014: 14) defines the precariat as having class characteristics: 'It consists of people who have minimal trust relationships with capital and the state. … And it has none of the social contract relationships of the proletariat, whereby labour securities were provided in exchange for subordination and contingent loyalty, the unwritten deal underpinning welfare states.' The precariat is distinctive in class terms. For example, the Occupy movement in 2011, while also lacking trust in capital and the state, was very different in social composition, with a different set of discontents. Equally, migrant and refugee people compose another precariat group living in inferior social conditions and political marginalisation, which, according to Standing (2014) constructs them as denizens rather than citizens. The left behind certainly share the experience of alienation with the other groups that compose the precariat, albeit for different reasons. Alberti et al (2018: 450) conclude: '"Precarisation" is thus best used to describe increasing insecurity in both subjective and objective respects, which can be identified across modern capitalist economies, including ostensibly privileged strata.' It particularly impacts on youth. Alex Foti (2017: 9) asserts in his *General Theory of the Precariat*: 'Twenty-somethings and thirty-somethings are the bulk of the precariat, mostly composed of urban youth of mixed race and social provenance.'

Critical pedagogue and educationalist Henry Giroux asserts that education is ultimately about the future of young people. No policy issue could be of greater importance for the future sustainability of society. Youth embody the future. Young people are idealistic about change and often critical of the status quo in their thinking and social attitudes. That is why Socrates was sentenced to death in ancient Greece on the spurious charge of 'corrupting' the minds of young people, which meant subverting or alienating the youth population of Athens against a corrupt city state. Socrates' trial was ultimately about the prosecution of ideas (Stone, 1988). These events, which took place over two millennia ago, remind us of the importance of education as a human and civil right. It liberates and empowers young people to think for themselves and question authority, as evidenced by the student revolutions of 1848 and 1968.

'White is a metaphor for power'

Why is access to higher education in the 21st century still predominantly the preserve of the economically and socially privileged? The evidence suggests that access to higher education is a mirror image of a socially stratified society, where wealth, ethnicity and academic success are closely correlated (Sandel, 2020). We do not tend to see it that way, however, because society is wedded to the idea of merit, as the guiding ideological principle governing access to higher education. The public tends to think about merit as 'fairness'. As a consequence, there is an unwillingness to recognise educational disadvantage (which is deeply encoded in our culture) as a manifestation of social inequality. Michael Sandel (2020) convincingly argues, on the basis of evidence from the US and UK, that merit in practice is essentially a form of tyranny, in effect creating a system of social apartheid.

Writer, poet and social critic James Baldwin observed in the documentary *I Am Not Your Negro* (2017): 'Not everything that is faced can be changed. But nothing can be changed until it is faced.' The film poses a series of questions: How much has changed in Black-White social relations over the past 50 years? How much of our mythologies have we confronted? How far do we still have to go? Baldwin critiques 'the emotional poverty' of US society, in which 'white is a metaphor for power'. He concludes: 'We don't have two different histories; they're the same. Each of us, each nation, each individual, each race, each gender has a role in this history and we need to confront it' (Baldwin, 2017). His powerful words are a siren call to our divided society to face up to social inequality in all its guises. We see the face of privilege all over the media every day in the form of celebrity, but know little about the face of disadvantage – hidden away from public view on satellite housing estates – except when civil unrest erupts in these socially deprived living spaces, as in Belfast in 2021 and Paris during 2023.

The recurring narrative of this book's contents is focused on the complex interplay between privilege and wealth, disadvantage and stratification, and cultural capital and cognitive injustice, in shaping the cultural politics and social reality that governs educational achievement and higher-education access. This process in turn shapes individuals' biographies. James Baldwin (2017) insightfully comments in relation to cognitive injustice: 'It is certain, in any case, that ignorance, allied to power, is the most ferocious enemy justice can have.' He enables us to understand the intricacies and complexities of class and racial distinctions in Western society. Baldwin invites us to face these unpalatable truths with honesty and open-mindedness. We take up Baldwin's challenge in this chapter by examining the relationship between education, class and ethnicity and specifically the problematising discourse that has led to the social construction (cultural invention) of a 'left-behind' class.

Left behind in a changing world: the problem of anomie

The 'left behind' concept is a metaphor for the victims in a world increasingly shaped by spiralling social inequality and political instability. In an era of globalisation, automation and deindustrialisation in the economically developed world, we are living through an experience of major economic and social transformation. It evokes the parallel image of the left behind in a post-apocalypse world conjured up in novels like Cormac McCarthy's *The Road,* Walter Miller's *A Canticle for* Leibowitz and Russell Hoban's *Riddley Walker*, along with a gamut of science-fiction films. There is a shared sense of devastation and destruction in these narratives, with a bleak future outlook.

While these books and films offer fictionalised accounts of the imagined impact of, for example, nuclear war and economic, technological and climatic disasters, after the insurrectionary events on 6 January 2021 in Washington, we know they are possible in social reality. Pankaj Mishra (2017), in his topical book about the history of the present, has called it the *Age of Anger,* in which large numbers of people find themselves cut adrift from modern society. They are widely referred to as the 'left behind'.

Sociologist Emile Durkheim (1858–1917) was one of the first scholars to analyse the social impacts of transformative industrial change. His theories were founded on the concept of 'social facts', defined as norms, values and structures of society. Durkheim explained the meaning of the meta-changes wrought by industrialisation in terms of the social division of labour (the emergence of complex systems of occupational distinctions within the processes of production that were reshaping society). He contended that the social division of labour was gradually replacing the role of religion in promoting social cohesion in the modern world. Durkheim identified the presence of 'anomie' in a section of the population that were not included in the social division of labour, leading to alienation, aimlessness and social pathology in individual, family and community behaviour. According to Durkheim's theory, anomie was causing social disintegration and deviant behaviour patterns and undermining society's value base and social cohesion (Durkheim, 1953).

Durkheim's near contemporary Karl Marx (1818–1883) detected a similar section of the working-class population that he called the *lumpenproletariat* or 'underclass' and which he regarded as venal and potentially criminal. Franz Fanon (1925–1961), the French West Indian psychiatrist and philosopher, revived the concept of *lumpenproletariat* in his last book *The Wretched of the Earth* (1961). He portrays the colonised peasantry, at the bottom of both the class system of social stratification and racial hierarchies, as the 20th-century post-colonial *lumpenproletariat*. Fanon views this oppressed group more positively than Marx, representing them as potential agents of progressive revolutionary change in the developing world (or 'third world' as it was known at the time). His perspective is in sharp contrast to the social pathology approach that has shaped thinking about the *lumpenproletariat* in the developed West. Western sociology has problematised this social group and viewed them as a 'dependent' class without moral or political agency.

The problematisation of some variants of individual, family and community behaviour became influential themes in early 20th-century social thought and policy responses. Distinguished social scientist and advocate of social justice Professor Richard Titmuss (1962: v) noted there was a 'long though discontinuous tradition … of concern about a segment of families in the population supposedly characterised by similar traits, and thought to represent a closed psychological entity – in Ledbetter's phrase a race of subnormals!'. There is evidence supporting Titmuss' concern about the influence of eugenics on social analysis in Charles Booth's 'submerged tenth', discussed in his 1904 London poverty surveys; in the 'social problem group' identified in the *Report of the Joint Committee on Mental Deficiency* (Wood, 1929) and in the 'economic residuum' of the *Report of the Committee on Sterilisation* (Brock, 1934). All of these British commentaries are strongly influenced by eugenicist thought that seeks to attribute human behaviour to genetic factors. While eugenics is today associated with right-wing ideology, there is evidence that some early Fabian social democrats in Britain were also influenced by this socio-biological philosophy (Novak, 1988).

Spicker (1993: 69) detects a paradigm shift at the beginning of the second half of the 20th century: 'After the Second World War much of this philosophy was discredited – not least because of the association of eugenics with fascism – although the idea of degeneracy did survive in the concept of the problem family.' The 'rediscovery of poverty' during the 1960s began to refocus attention on to deprived communities, where it was believed problem families were clustered (Powell, 2001: 57–60). Hughes and Mooney (1998: 59) assert in reference to this development: 'From this period the language of community became firmly established as a means of legitimising state intervention and regulation and, in the process, community was constructed as a site of intervention.' The establishment of community as a site of state intervention took two forms: community development and the targeting of areas of educational disadvantage. The 'War on Poverty' in the US and Community Development Projects in Britain were established to combat poverty in deprived communities by progressive governments, but soon fell foul of conservative critics and were shut down. A smaller-scale poverty programme in Ireland met a similar fate (Powell, 2001 and 2017).

Durkheim's classical interpretation of the relationship between anomic behaviour and social and economic transformation provides an explanation for the contemporary focus in public discourse on changes in the social division of labour, resulting from economic developments in the form of globalisation, automation and deindustrialisation. These transformative economic and social changes have left a section of the working-class population – contemporaneously described as the 'left behind' – marginalised, disrespected and unmoored from the rest of society in an increasingly competitive and conflicted social order.

What the left behind share is a deep and destructive experience of social exclusion. What is meant by the term 'social exclusion'? The association of poverty with a more divided and disordered society has led to the broader concept of social exclusion, which refers not only to material deprivation but also to disrespect and the inability of poorer people to exercise fully their social, cultural and political rights as citizens. Ruth Levitas (1998: 21) has located social exclusion within the discourse of the European Union, observing: 'exclusion is understood as the breakdown of the structural, cultural and moral ties which bind the individual to society, and family instability is a key concern'.

In countries where social thought has historically been influenced by Catholicism, Durkheimian sociology and a concern with moral and social integration, the concept of social exclusion has been very influential on public policy. France has been cited as a classic example (Silver, 1994; Levitas, 1998). Ireland, which has much in common with France in terms of its Catholic social conservative tradition, has also been significantly influenced by social exclusion in its social policy discourse, notably through the adoption of a social partnership model of governance between 1997 and 2008 (Geoghegan and Powell, 2009). Even in traditionally Protestant Britain (then a member of the EU), the Blair government in the late 1990s established a Social Exclusion Unit and Education Action Zones (modelled on the Education Priority Areas of the 1960s), which apparently proved no more successful than their predecessors. However, the change of policy emphasis from the Fabian concern with tackling the structural issues of poverty and social inequality to a more targeted orientation aimed at alleviating the impacts of social exclusion on deprived communities, did not go unnoticed by critics (Levitas, 1998; Buckingham, 2011).

The introduction of austerity policies, following the 2008 financial crash, has undermined the focus on social exclusion and replaced integration with division and class polarisation. Social exclusion in the discourse of British public policy has been replaced by 'levelling up'. The Europe Union continues to pursue an active inclusion strategy. The challenges remain, however. In 2020, almost a quarter (24.9 per cent) of children from the EU at risk of poverty and social exclusion. The *European Pillar for Social Rights* (European Union, 2017) commits the EU to the right of everyone to quality and inclusive education, training and lifelong learning. The realisation of this principle in practice in a divided society will not be easy.

Childhood, education and social hierarchy

In Western society we tend to think in terms of binaries. This thinking mode inevitably divides the world into binary oppositions in the process of meaning-making, for example in relation to class (rich/poor), race (White/Black), gender (male/female) and so on. Traditionally, we have placed class in the dominant explanatory position when we unpack the meaning of systemic inequality. These binary oppositions tend to oversimplify the diverse meanings of systemic inequality – in social reality they are complex. Clearly, there is a high degree of intersection between class, race and gender in terms of a shared history of subordination and domination. Intersectionality enables us to understand the complex nature of systemic inequality, in the highly stratified social and cultural configuration we call Western civilisation. In Europe, class in particular has continued to be at the core of public understanding of systemic inequality, whereas in the US race has played a much more prominent role since the second half of the 20th century, inspired by the 1960s Civil Rights campaign, and in the 21st century by the Black Lives Matter movement.

When we reflect upon contemporary meanings of discrimination and disadvantage, we need to think about their intersectionality with reference to overlapping identities and experiences of prejudice and injustice shared across class, race and gender. Sam Friedman and Daniel Laurison (2019: 233) observe in relation to the importance of intersectionality that equality and diversity issues 'are better understood as being shaped by many axes of inequality that often work together and influence one another, or create distinct types of disadvantage that are experienced in different ways'. We also need to understand that in a stratified society class from childhood plays an overarching role in the lived experience of working-class people by creating a 'them and us' social hierarchy. It has always been thus in Western civilisation since its beginnings in classical times, encoding the normativity of the privilege/disadvantage binary into our social structures and mentalities. Aristotle is the original architectural designer and custodian of these hierarchical values in our Western education system.

The study of childhood is poised to broaden the intersectionality debate about human oppression and exploitation, as the most recent arrival in a series of demands to *know*. Children are both disenfranchised and without agency over their lives. This powerlessness can have serious social consequences. Historic child abuse reports have lifted a veil, revealing a legacy of cruelty and exploitation in charitable institutions across the Western world, frequently managed and owned by Catholic religious orders. Ireland has been at the epicentre of these shocking revelations (Powell and Scanlon, 2015). It is notable that the Catholic Church continues to control almost 90 per cent of Irish primary schools, despite these scandals. This policy inertia constitutes disturbing evidence of the powerlessness of children in Irish society and the enduring power of social conservatism to dictate the political agenda. Writer and critic Fintan O'Toole (2021) has commented in relation to this political-religious conservative alliance: 'Together, these two forces formed the Irish matrix.'

While representation of women and children as occupying the same social and political space dates from antiquity, the liberation of women during modernity has not been accompanied by any change in the marginalised civic and political status of children (Cohen and Rutter, 2007). Childhood has proven to be an even more complex area of study than women, gender and ethnicity. Why? Ada Cohen (with Rutter, 2007: 3) suggests the explanation that 'unlike biological sex the very definition of childhood is unstable, its reality shifting no less than its cultural parameters; in other words, there is no stable pre-existing definition of childhood on which to anchor its evolution'. Within the binary oppositions used to socially and culturally differentiate children from adults, we represent this division as 'natural' in public discourse. We know a child when we see one, or do we? Childhood, after all, can be subdivided into temporal frameworks – infancy, childhood, youth, adolescence, young adults and so on – underlining its cultural and representational complexity (James et al, 1998). Much of our thinking about child welfare and its associated risks is framed within the discourse of failures of parental care and ambition. In traditional society the village raised the child, as the African proverb reminds us. Modernity changed the focus of care to the nuclear family. The child's educational progress became closely connected to the family's aspirations and ambitions for social mobility. Education in modernity emerged as the key to unlocking the future. Sadly, for too many working-class parents and children, it turned out to be an unachievable dream.

The mother in modern society is culturally constructed as being in the central position of responsibility within this discourse of child socialisation, which is linked through the domestic sphere and family life to the school and the public sphere. Care and security are the twin pillars of a socially constructed world of the ideal family. Children are portrayed in modern society as living and flourishing within this family ideal. They are culturally represented as innocent and vulnerable in the adult world of social responsibility (Powell and Scanlon, 2015). Education is at the centre of the child's world. This is a cultural legacy traceable to antiquity, albeit classical culture was largely lost after the fall of Rome in 410. During the barbarism of the medieval European world, between about 400 and 1400, culture, education and childhood as pillars of civilisation partly disappeared, despite iconic architectural landmarks, such as the Cathedrale Notre Dame de Paris. In the words of Kenneth Clarke, in his famous 1969 TV series *Civilisation*, Western civilisation survived the collapse of antiquity by 'the skin of our teeth', holding on at the periphery of Europe in the abbeys of Ireland. How did classical civilisation regard education?

In classical civilisation childhood emerged as a separate social status, differentiated by class. Aristotle, as already noted, is widely regarded as one of the greatest philosophical minds in human history. He was quintessentially a teacher, and for a period tutor to Alexander the Great. He is a seminal influence on the institutional formation of education. Aristotle divided schooling into three stages: primary (ages 7–14), secondary (14–21 years) and higher education, which commenced at 21 years and was open-ended in terms of the period of study. All three educational stages are followed by transitions (often periods of stress and anxiety) as the student negotiates the lived reality of change. Aristotle took a class-based view of education, in which he differentiated between the political and social elite, primarily the free (citizens) and unfree (slaves). In Aristotle's view, the role of education was to equip aristocratic male students for the complex tasks of leadership, in which they were required to participate in governance of the city state of Athens.

Aristotle believed that the ruling class of Athenians needed a humanities education to ground them in the cultivation of virtue (including music, poetry and philosophy) as an essential preparation for the demands of 'noble leisure', meaning, as already noted, governance. On the other hand, Aristotle advocated an 'unleisurely' practical training curriculum for farmers and the commercial class. In the case of subjugated or enslaved people, their role in Aristotle's view was service, which meant unrelenting exploitation and oppression. Aristotle infamously remarked that 'there is no leisure for slaves', which often included *metics* – foreigners or immigrants – culturally regarded as barbarians. For women in ancient Greece, formal education was largely denied except for music, dance, gymnastics and some training in the art of conversation and rhetoric, presumably reserved for the social elite. Learning for women as a whole was mainly restricted to training in household management, weaving and childcare.

The medieval period (400–1400) experiences the disappearance of childhood, which was rediscovered in modernity. The discovery of the printing press and the demand for literacy in industrial society resulted in the introduction of mass education and 'the invention of childhood' (Aries, 1973). The primary school emerges at the centre of the child's life.

Historically – and in many respects up to the present day – education and its benefits has been the closely guarded possession of privileged elites: ecclesiastical, political, military, hereditary, meritocratic, academic, professional and artistic. As Pierre Bourdieu has argued, the possession of cultural capital defines social class and individual identity. That is why access to education is so jealously guarded by social and political elites, who correctly view its acquisition as a prerequisite for prosperity and power in a world polarised by wealth, class and ethnicity. Aristotle understood that education and privilege are interlinked and provided a blueprint for its perpetuation, as the embodiment of class hegemony and human flourishing.

'The great educational ladder': social Darwinism, class and race

Michael Young (1958: 53) commented that 'the educational ladder is also a social ladder'.

In modernity, Fiona Dukelow and Mairéad Considine (2017: 244) observe the popular use of 'the ladder' as a metaphor for social mobility and trace its intellectual origins to the late 19th century. Influential biologist T.H. Huxley (an exponent of Charles Darwin's theory of evolution encapsulated in the slogan 'survival of the fittest') proclaimed 'the great educational ladder', on which every child would find their preordained place on the bottom rung through to the top rung, depending on their genetic characteristics in the 'talent pool'. In this Darwinian scheme of natural selection, the working class were historically positioned at the bottom of the ladder and deemed to require no more than an elementary education (basic literacy and numeracy), with the social elite at the top occupying a small number of places in residential universities, such as Oxford and Cambridge. The social Darwinist assumption was that high intelligence equated with class and racial superiority, with 'exceptional scholarship children' being allowed to progress through the education system.

Socialists, such as the academic R.H. Tawney (1880–1962), challenged the elitism of the social Darwinists' academic selectivity policies based on breeding. Instead, Tawney (1965) advocated the radical theory of equality of condition, which promised to treat all students broadly the same in terms of life chances. The resulting intellectual dispute turned into a polemical debate about the relative importance of nature (genes) versus nurture (environment), the essence of which was dramatically encapsulated in the IQ controversy. At a scientific level, IQ (Intelligence Quotient) tests are open to fundamental methodological and moral critique because these purported measuring instruments: seek to reduce intelligence (in all its complexity) to a number; rank the population hierarchically; assume that intelligence is genetically and biologically endowed; and are ultimately unchangeable. Social philosopher Professor Brian Barry (2005: 117–127) damningly concluded that there was little research evidence to support the validity of IQ tests in measuring potential educational achievement and that they constituted 'an abuse of science'.

The proponents of psychometrics, embodied in IQ testing (notably Hans Eysenck in the UK and Arthur Jensen in the US), linked intelligence to class and ethnicity. Their controversial argument – conducted in the public sphere – was that intellectual ability is endowed unequally in human genes. Others followed, despite public protests about the inflammatory nature of the Jensen-Eysenck thesis. Richard Herrnstein and Charles Murray in 1994 published *The Bell Curve: Intelligence and Class Structure in American Life,* which frankly acknowledged on the cover that the book was likely 'to ignite an explosive controversy'. They adopt the ladder metaphor in their slogan 'steeper ladders, narrower gates'. Herrnstein and Murray (1994: 91) pessimistically conclude: 'Cognitive positioning through education and occupations will continue, and there is not much that a government or anyone can do about it.'

Pierre Bourdieu's analysis (discussed later) suggests that while educational inequality is deeply encoded in modern culture in the form of 'cultural capital', it is also influenced by other more visible forms of capital, notably financial capital (how rich your family is) and social capital (who you know). There is nothing immutable about educational inequality, as the proponents of genetically based eugenic arguments suggest. Environment rather than genes is arguably the ultimate arbiter of performance – a hypothesis the empirical evidence in this book broadly supports.

While the local communities we studied were located within the EU, in Ireland, they might have been located anywhere in Western society. The answer to educational inequality is, in our view, to be found in redistributive justice in a society that genuinely shares opportunities and wealth. Finland, for example, is widely reported in the media as having achieved outstanding progress in terms of educational investment and performance. Education potentially transforms both individuals and society. Bourdieu's advocacy of social justice and the welfare state points towards possible resolution of educational inequality in a fairer society that invests in the education of all its citizens and changes public mindsets about the treatment of disadvantaged citizens in the pursuit of equality of condition. However, inequality, as we have argued, remains one of the most perdurable characteristics of Western society.

There is a long history of eugenicist claims to White racial and upper-class superiority as the natural order of society. Eugenics is widely discredited as a pseudo-science, currently describing itself as socio-biology. Eugenicists' engagement in human-rights atrocities – most notoriously in Nazi Germany, which sought to problematize sections of the population as intellectually and racially inferior and subject them to sterilisation and in many cases execution – had made it academically largely a taboo area for research and teaching (Burleigh, 2000). But clearly this viewpoint remains influential. Writer and columnist Owen Jones (2012: 10–11) critically observed in this regard: 'The plight of some working-class people is commonly portrayed as a poverty of ambition. It is their individual characteristics rather than a deeply unequal society rigged in favour of the privileged, that is held responsible. In this extreme form, this has even led to Social Darwinism.'

The history of psychometric testing, despite its controversial record, continues to shape university admissions in many parts of the world up to the present day. Michael Sandel (2020) notes that the US adopted the Scholastic Aptitude Test (SAT) as the key to developing a meritocratic higher-education access system. He concludes, however (2020: 164): 'The SAT, it turns out, does not measure scholarly aptitude or native intelligence independent of social and educational background. To the contrary, SAT scores are highly correlated with wealth. The higher the family income, the higher your SAT score.' The University of California has dropped the SAT from its admissions system. It would seem on the basis of the available evidence that tests are not a ladder to academic achievement but a barrier to access.

The cultural politics of the class divide and White privilege

Joan C. Williams (2018: 3) compares class perspectives on the world, asserting: 'The central logic of life in the professional-managerial elite centres on self-development.' This is why college-educated progressives care particularly about inequalities that impede opportunity and undercut human rights. Key freedoms – from the availability of abortion and affordable childcare (which protect and support women's reproductive rights and career pathways) to LGBTQIA+ rights (which protect against abrupt loss of employment, criminalisation and other discriminations, formerly suffered particularly by men who happened to be gay) – are part of the equality of opportunity agenda. On the other hand, Williams (2018: 3) attributes a different and more traditional logic to working-class families, whose focus, she suggests is more existential, 'on self-discipline: the kind that get you up and out to an often not very fulfilling job on time every day, without an attitude'.

She further notes in a reference to White working-class culture: 'Non-elites typically place a high value on traditional institutions that aid self-discipline – the military, religion, traditional family life.' These traditional values and attitudes are often rejected by more educated sections of the population, who espouse 'cosmopolitan' liberal values. However, for White working-class people, being a citizen of the White Anglo-Saxon world (for example the US and the UK) is viewed as a symbol of a high-status identity. Williams (2018: 3) views this false ethnic consciousness 'as a salve for the hidden injuries of class', adding, 'to have this national pride written off as racism further fuels class conflict'.

The relationship between working-class culture and political values has been explored in a series of classic studies, Paul Willis's *Learning to Labour* (1977), Joseph Howell's *Hard Living on Clay Street* (1972) and Michele Lamont's *The Dignity of Working Men* (2000). The problem in globalised and highly automated Western societies is that working-class men have lost their status and security (based on solid blue-collar employment), creating a crisis in White male identity. It is leading to a rejection of core democratic values – liberty, equality and solidarity – in political discourse and demands for a restoration of 'White privilege' in the form of a White ethno-nationalist state. The emergence of the alt-right across the Western world, advocating White privilege and conspiracy theories (such as 'the great replacement' of White people by immigrants) embodies the authoritarian nativist sentiments that have driven such manifestations of political and social turbulence.

Kalwant Bhopal (2018: 9), in her book *White Privilege: The Myth of Post-Racial Society*, explores how Whiteness and White identities operate as a form of privilege in society. The concept of White privilege has its origins in the US Civil Rights movement during the 1960s, which sought to challenge its racial dominance in segregation and other types of discrimination. It then became a subject of academic interest before being rekindled in the public sphere during 2014, when the Black Lives Matter movement emerged, utilising social media as a major political platform. White privilege is a societal privilege that advantages, in visible and invisible ways, people of White skin over people of colour. Its roots are in colonialism and imperialism and the slave trade. In many societies race became a proxy for class, but generally both forms of domination and subordination have merged together to 'doubly disadvantage' people of colour (Jack, 2019: 143). The idea of White privilege has produced angry denunciation from White politicians. Conservatives in the US are widely opposed to racial sensitivity teaching (involving topics such as 'White privilege') and critical race theory.

Critical race theory is based on the premise that race is not a natural biological product of physical distinct subgroups of human beings but a socially constructed (culturally invented) category used to oppress and exploit people of colour. Critical race theory became a divisive issue in the 2021 Virginia gubernatorial contest because it invites school children to examine the oppressive and discriminatory side of their history, notably slavery. Opponents of critical race theory in the US object to the endorsement of terms such as 'White supremacy', 'privilege' and 'microaggressions' in educational discourse on the grounds that it is going to disparage one particular race (*Los Angeles Times*, 24 November 2021).

The use of the term 'White privilege' has also raised concerns in the UK. The House of Commons Education Committee issued a report during 2021, *The Forgotten,* which asserted (p 17): 'Our inquiry has shown that poor White pupils are far from privileged in education', advising: 'Schools should consider whether the promotion of politically controversial terminology including White Privilege is consistent with their duties. … The Department [of Education] should issue clear guidance for schools'.

The evidence compiled by the Committee (2021: 3) suggests a complex picture, revealing that the percentage of 4 to 5 year olds meeting Developmental Goals in 2018–19 was as follows:

> 53% of Free School Meals-eligible White British pupils met the expected standard of development, against an average for all FSM-eligible pupils of 55%. This was the lowest percentage for a FSM-eligible ethnic group other than Irish Travellers (29%), Gypsy/Roma (33%) and White Irish (49%). 55% of White other FSM eligible pupils met the expected standard. 67% of FSM-eligible Chinese met the expected standard for development, and 66% of FSM-eligible Indian pupils did. 61% of FSM-eligible Black Caribbean pupils and 64% of Black African pupils meet the expected standard.

The Committee (2021: 3) further noted: 'The proportion of White British pupils who were FSM-eligible starting higher education by the age of 19 in 2018/19 was 16 per cent, the lowest of any ethnic group other than Travellers of Irish heritage and Gypsy/Roma.' In its approach to addressing the challenge of the attainment gap the Committee (2021: 3) decided to target the White working class as the central concern of its investigation, reasoning:

> [T]he large number of disadvantaged White British pupils that underachieve in education remains a significant obstacle to closing the overall attainment gap. We understand the justified anger that many people feel about racism, prejudice and discrimination. It is vital that we work together as a country to address those issues and we commit to investigating this in our future work on left-behind groups.

The term 'White privilege' also began to appear as a significant concern in policy discourse. A BBC news report in October 2020, 'Elitist curriculum not serving white working classes', examined the evidence given to the Education Committee on the reasons for White pupils from disadvantaged backgrounds being left behind in the competition for university places. The

BBC report (Sellgren, 2020) included comments from a number of prominent academics. Professor Matthew Goodwin posed the question: 'What is happening outside the school environment, that's happening perhaps not only within the family but within society, that is sending these kids the message that higher education or pursuing further education is not for them?'. Professor Diane Reay observed that it was important to look at the history of the education system and ask whether the intention was 'to educate and empower the working-class children'. In answer to her own rhetorical question, Professor Reay stated: 'I think if we look at history we can see it was mainly about curtailing and controlling what was seen at the time as an unruly and disreputable group – and I think that history dogs us still in the present.' Professor Lee Elliot Major noted that poverty and disadvantage were key issues in underachievement, declaring: 'What particularly is an issue for some of these white working-class communities is that they live in places where there aren't many opportunities.'

In postmodern society the social and cultural construction of a 'left-behind' or 'forgotten' underclass on the margins of society constitutes a major policy challenge. The inclusion in consumer society of a major section of the White working class during the post-war era led to speculation about the embourgeoisement of the 'affluent worker' (the adoption of middle-class lifestyles), fragmenting traditional class solidarity (Goldthorpe et al, 1967). Deindustrialisation undermined this prosperity, leading to social and economic decline. The emergence of a left-behind class is a potent symbol of economic dislocation in an era of globalisation and automation. Postmodernity has brought with it a sharp decline in the traditional employment base of the working class in manufacturing industries. This has displaced a section of the workforce, resulting in unemployment or low-paid, often casual, employment in the gig economy of the business services sector, such as catering, hospitality and cleaning services. While the publication of Andre Gorz's *Farewell to the Working Class,* in 1982, with its apocalyptic vision of a future in which the traditional working class would be replaced by a 'non-class' of 'non-proletarians' seemed far-fetched at the time. Its dark prophecy has come to pass in many of the so-called rust-belt areas of the Western world.

Owen Jones (2012: 172) argues that, as a consequence, sections of the traditional White working class, once the bedrock of the labour movement, have become a marginalised group on the periphery of society. However, the social construction of the White working class in public discourse as a reactive and reactionary social group motivated by 'racist bigotry' in Jones' (2012: 182–183) view obscures a deeper process of stigmatisation:

> [T]he demonization of working-class people is a grimly rational way to justify an irrational system. Demonize them, ignore their

concerns-and rationalize a grossly unequal distribution of wealth and power as a fair reflection of people's wealth and abilities. But this demonization arguably has an even more pernicious agenda. A doctrine of personal responsibility is applied to a whole range of social problems affecting certain working-class communities – whether it is poverty, unemployment or crime.

Jones' prescient analysis reminds us that the age-old practice of blaming the victim is very much alive in the 21st century. We need to find more sophisticated explanations.

Bourdieu, culture and class

Our conceptual approach is significantly influenced by the ideas and analytic perspectives of the French post-structuralist Pierre Bourdieu – probably the most influential authority on educational disadvantage in post-war society – which as a sociologist he constantly discussed and critiqued. Bourdieu 'developed a philosophy of social science, grounded in the phenomenological tradition, which treats knowledge as a practical ability embodied in skill behaviour, rather than intellectual capacity for the representation and manipulation of propositional knowledge' (Gerrans, 2005: 53). Bourdieu's theory of knowledge has enhanced the understanding of the role and influence of capital and class on educational achievements and outcomes. Essentially, his thesis is that the purpose of education in society is primarily to be found in its contribution to the social reproduction and maintenance of unequal class relations, which it legitimates through the possession of cultural capital. This powerful insight constitutes Bourdieu's seminal contribution to the understanding of the sociology of education.

Bourdieu rose to public prominence during the 1960s as a vociferous critic of the French education system and was a significant influence on the 1968 student revolution. He controversially argued that the education system was essentially a machine that enabled the French bourgeoisie to 'reproduce' itself, since only the scions of that class had the 'cultural capital' – institutionalised in the form of academic qualifications convertible into economic capital (Bourdieu, 1986: 242). Bourdieu further asserts: 'I have analysed the peculiarity of cultural capital, which we should in fact call *informational capital* to give the notion its full generality, and which itself exists in three forms, embodied, objectified and institutionalized' (Bourdieu and Wacquant, 1992: 119). Through this further elaboration, Bourdieu (with Wacquant, 1992) outlines three states of cultural capital: the *embodied* state, in the form of the long-lasting dispositions of the mind and body; the *objectified* state, in the form of cultural goods (pictures, books, dictionaries, instruments, machines and so on); and the *institutionalised* state, such as educational qualifications that guarantee the possession of cultural capital. He had struck a nerve that questioned the core republican values of equality and freedom from elite class domination, underpinning the official ideology of the modern French state.

The official version of the truth about French education was that scholarships (of which Bourdieu was a recipient) served to equalise the system. This was a reference to the merit principle, which in Bourdieusian logic the bourgeoisie had already mastered. Bourdieu argued that the education system should give equal recognition to all forms of competence (Hoffmann, 1986). Despite his egalitarian views Bourdieu was elected to the pinnacle of French academic life – a chair at the College de France. It did not change his critical view of French education and society.

On his death in 2002, Bourdieu left behind a rich legacy of ideas for posterity. He had passionately engaged with his subject matter in search of truth and enlightenment. He had overcome a disadvantaged childhood in France to become a world-renowned academic and public intellectual. Bourdieu never forgot his humble origins in rural southwestern French society, which remained at the core of his identity and consciousness. His seminal scholarship reframed thinking internationally about educational disadvantage and its complex roots, deeply embedded within the culture and class structure of modern society.

The Bourdieusian view of education is strongly influenced by power hierarchies and their capacity to shape and dominate human consciousness, individual agency and social practices that are valorised above all others in public opinion, personal esteem, individual recognition ('success') and social signification (status recognition). Bourdieu has provided an overarching architectural model for analysing social and cultural reproduction of elite education. His critical thinking has enabled us to understand barriers – visible and invisible – that prevent working-class participation in higher education and their location 'within a complex mix of personal, social, cultural, economic and institutional issues' (Archer et al, 2007: 220).

In defining the structure and influence of capital on the education process, Bourdieu offers a dynamic approach to social analysis, expanding its parameters to include both economic and non-economic dimensions that incorporate both tangible and intangible forms. Bourdieu's reconceptualisation of class also presents a more complex construction that takes its meaning as a social phenomenon beyond traditional Marxian materialist approaches. Instead, we are invited to look at class inequality through the lenses of structure and agency in shaping an individual citizen's biography, with a particular focus on the exclusionary cultural power of privilege and social dominance. According to the Bourdieusian perspective, the working class are subordinated to the power of privilege in order to define and legitimate successful educational and career outcomes for the bourgeoisie. It is popularly informed by the public language of social mobility, merit and equality of opportunity.

Pierre Bourdieu's contribution to knowledge primarily rests on the conceptual trilogy of capital, *habitus* and field that define the core of his theoretical approach. These concepts are currently published in *Habitus and Field* (2020) and *Forms of Capital* (2021). We will discuss Bourdieu's trilogy of ideas sequentially. Three points arise. First, Bourdieu posits four distinct forms of capital:

- *economic capital* (wealth and income);
- *cultural capital* (educational credentials, accents, tastes, manners and attitudes);
- *social capital* (social networks, connections, relationships and friendships – who you know);
- *symbolic capital* (the power to establish, reproduce and construct reality).

Bourdieu (2005) contends that these four forms of capital provide the overarching architecture of childhood, which he views as 'the conditions of existence'.

Education is the primary arena in which the privileged middle classes dominate the underprivileged working class. It perpetuates a fundamental cultural and social division known as 'the attainment gap'. Sam Friedman and Daniel Laurison (2019: 14–15) comment on the impact of these forms of capital on the socialisation of the child, arguing that 'this process is straightforward in terms of economic and social capital: upper-middle-class parents are able to directly pass on to their children both financial assets and social contacts. … The inheritance of cultural capital is more complex, because it involves processes of personal embodiment and symbolic mastery'. Bourdieu views cultural capital as pivotal in his conceptual trilogy, but as only comprehensible in relation to its other two components.

We discovered in our UCC research project that Bourdieu's analysis resonated with professionals and parents on the ground. A DEIS school principal we interviewed commented insightfully on this analytic complexity in relation to the impact of cultural capital in shaping students' expectations:

> '[S]elf-belief and confidence and almost entitlement. I would know in conversations with colleagues in other [middle class] schools, there's an entitlement, there's almost expectation that of course they'll be doing higher level papers at Junior Certificate [exam level], whereas we [DEIS schools] can't take that as given; we've to work at that, we've really, really to work hard at that, so, at assemblies, at parent-teacher meetings we're talking about this, we're raising the expectations of students.

> I think mindset, again, it's mindset. It's a sense of once again you speak with some students and it's their sense of entitlement. From the age of when they're in primary school, they're already talking about, "Well I'll be going to university", – this is just their discourse. Like bringing students to the campus for the day in first year – that is, I won't say it's emotionally massaging students, but that's not going to make a significant influence on the student.'

This DEIS school principal also identified class differences in financial and social capital as significant factors in influencing the educational performance of students in DEIS schools: "It's an unequal system really. In terms of social capital, in terms of financial capital – that's where society is at … it's not just one cause and effect there's lots of variables really."

A mother of four students attending a Dublin-based DEIS school observed: "It's good to have a grounding in certain things. So, from primary school, I allow them do whatever they want. I will pay for anything they need, extra curriculum activities, the ballet. … The music, the dancing, the vocal harmony; they are doing as much as possible." However, she was also realistic about the costs of accessing higher education and the resulting financial barriers for her children's progress: "The cost of education may affect [access] because there are four of them. So, I have to look at [them] going in one after the other. … Yeah, oh the cost, yeah." Manifestly, the possession of capital in all its manifestations impacts significantly on educational expectation and the achievement of aspirations.

This brings us to the second issue of *habitus*, involving consideration of what Bourdieu calls 'dispositions'. Sam Friedman (2018: 1) offers an insightful definition: '*Habitus* is a set of dispositions (i.e. long-lasting manners of being, seeing, acting and thinking) that flow from your primary socialisation, and in particular from the social class position of your parents when you are growing up.' Bourdieu (2020: 118) argues that these dispositions generate 'both a sense of the game … and the ability to play the game'. It is where class and culture merge in the deep consciousness of both the individual and the collective, enabling privilege to survive and prosper. In the upper-middle-class family milieu, children are distanced and protected from the everyday struggles of earning a living and putting bread on the table. This privileged socialisation experience creates a set of dispositions that shapes children's relations with cultural codes, society and their expectations of themselves in the world, instilling personal confidence in the upper-middle-class child. Bourdieu also observes that for some individuals from working-class origins (including himself) the social mobility conferred by educational achievement can be personally undermining because their 'conditions of existence' change too dramatically. He called this negative reaction to social mobility *habitus clive,* broadly meaning dislocation from one's roots.

Bourdieu in a personal reflection on his 'miraculous trajectory' observed (Bourdieu and Eagleton, 1992: 117):

> My main problem is to try to understand what happened to me. My trajectory may be regarded as miraculous, I suppose – an ascension to a place where I don't belong. And so, to be able to live in a world that is not mine I must try to understand both things: what it means to have an academic mind-how much is created and at the same time what is lost in acquiring it.

This questioning observation constitutes a profound insight into the role of class in education. An upward social mobility trajectory to the academic stratosphere – in Bourdieu's estimation – is sufficiently rare to be described as 'miraculous'. Not all miracles have happy outcomes is the message – *habitus clive*! Bourdieu graphically represented the working-class student in the academic environment as 'a fish out of water', in contrast to their bourgeois counterparts, who effortlessly swim in the metaphorical pond of privilege by cashing in on their embodied cultural capital. (Bourdieu, 1986) viewed embodied cultural capital as a form of 'hereditary transmission' through the process of socialisation in the family. The result, according to Bourdieu's logic, is that higher education is normal, desirable and attainable for the privileged bourgeoisie. The reverse applies to the disadvantaged and often stigmatised working class.

Third, Bourdieu advances the concept of 'field' (meaning 'space') in preference to the social institution or market because of its lexical and conceptual fluidity. It encompasses the possibility of social conflict and the existence of social worlds that are weakly institutionalised and characterised by underdeveloped boundaries. In Bourdieu's mind, field is an evolving concept in which he envisages the world as being composed of a variety of distinct fields (such as education, art, religion, law) with their own unique rules, epistemologies and forms of capital.

Alienation and young people's perceptions of higher education

A significant body of research – often influenced by Bourdieu's theories of cultural and social capital – suggests that young people and families from disadvantaged backgrounds regard higher education *habitus* as remote and alien from their experience, which in turn effects aspiration. Archer et al (2007: 232), for example, in a UK study, describe:

> the continued dominance of middle-class habitus within higher education, against which working-class students imagine that they do not 'fit'. Higher education does not appear to offer working-class

young people the space to 'feel myself' … and/or to generate value through 'known' mechanisms. Rather, it is seen as an alien space in which they will stand out and 'not belong' in a myriad of ways.

Diane Reay (2017: 153), drawing on her own personal experience in the UK as a working-class student, observes:

> What I want to convey here is far from the university being the beginning of 'a new better middle-class life' for the working classes, as is often implied in the social mobility rhetoric, it is much more often another stage in a difficult and painful struggle to be accepted and included in middle-class contexts.

Lynch and O'Riordan (1998) raise a similar point in their Irish research:

> For second-level students, one of the major social and cultural barriers identified was the sense of education, and particularly higher education, as being remote and alien from the lives of their families. Second-level students noted repeatedly that they knew very little about college life. Not knowing what to expect created fears and anxieties which exacerbated practical difficulties. … They believed college was a very different and unfamiliar place, and they feared isolation.

However, other research calls into question the idea that young people from disadvantaged communities are significantly deterred by perceptions of universities as elitist and 'alien' (James, 2002; Bradley and Miller, 2010; Kettley and Whitehead, 2012; Baker et al, 2014). One large-scale Australian survey (James, 2002) found that most young people (including those from lower socio-economic backgrounds) had generally positive attitudes towards university, even those who were not planning to go there themselves. In addition, a significant proportion of those from poorer backgrounds indicated that, if there were no constraints, they would prefer to go to university. Baker et al, 2014: 532) found that most young people did hold high hopes for gaining further academic qualifications, even though these aspirations 'are running ahead of them being achieved given the current continuation rates into higher education'.

The class divide, the Gatsby Curve and the privileged id

The Great Gatsby, a novel written by F. Scott Fitzgerald and first published in 1925, is one of the classic 20th-century novels, portraying the 'roaring 1920s' in wealthy New York society as the age of excess. The novel focuses on the social life of a mysterious self-made tycoon, believed to have accumulated his fortune bootlegging during prohibition. It has resonated down the generations and fits closely the runaway growth in wealth among a new financial aristocracy and the systemic inequalities of the 21st century. The Gatsby Curve represents the current state of rising social and financial inequality (Piketty, 2014). It is both a metric and a measure of our times, illustrating the connection between wealth and its intergenerational transmission, enabling the next generation to position themselves at the top of the ladder of opportunity. The Gatsby narrative is essentially a metaphor for corrupt wealth and its potential consequences in a careless world of extreme social inequality in which it is possible to indulge the privileged id in a life devoted to pleasure. It also is a reminder of the wider influences of a class system, where the middle class dominates educational achievement and the working class is disadvantaged in a systemically unequal education system.

Lee Elliot Major and Stephen Machin (2018: 12–13) observe that that social class has traditionally been 'broken down into three broad distinctions: working class, middle class and upper class'. They also note that there is increasing immobility at both ends of the class hierarchy. Class is at the core of Diane Reay's (2017: 143) analysis in her book *Miseducation*:

> This monopolising of 'brightness' by the middle-class within state schooling yet again positions the working-class across ethnicity as the lesser other within the educational systems. But this 'brightness' is often cultivated, manufactured, sometimes even coerced by a significant number of middle-class parents who are over anxious and powerfully invested in their children's educational excellence.

In her book, Reay (2017: 11–27) argues that there are myriad reasons why the education system cannot compensate for wider structural inequalities in society, including a growing devaluation of the working class (a decline in respect); the erosion of working-class employment rights in the labour market; and the emergence of abusive language (such as the use of sobriquets 'scum' and 'chavs') enabling society to 'other' working-class students as victims of their own purported deviant subculture.

Professor Kathleen Lynch (2020), in a challenging online opinion piece in *The Journal* argued that social class is a suppressed topic in Irish public discourse, particularly in relation to education, where class dynamics play a central role in influencing examination outcomes and career opportunities in the labour market:

> Things that matter most are often the things we speak about least. They are taboo subjects, kept hidden, and if spoken of are discussed

in euphemisms or metaphors that hide the full truth. Social class is one such subject in Ireland. Unlike in England or Europe where class inequalities are part and parcel of political debate, 'social class' is rarely used in Ireland. … The most obvious place where we speak in metaphors and euphemisms about social class is in education, and one of the prime examples of this is the use of the term 'disadvantaged'.

'Disadvantage/d' is used to classify schools where poorer working class (and increasingly ethnic minorities) attend – and to describe the students themselves. The use of the term 'disadvantage', while intending to be respectful, is also concealing. It does not open up debates about the wealth and power differentials between classes that create inequalities in educational outcomes in the first instance.

Lynch (2020) concludes:

Educational credentials are a positional good in a competitive society: by this I mean their value is always relative to what others have in educational terms. This is not some ideological standpoint – this is the logical outcome of economic inequalities. If we really want to address class inequality in education, then we need to challenge the neoliberal capitalist economic model that generates the growing income and wealth inequalities between households in the first instance. It is these inequalities that feed into injustice in education. They literally 'frighten' the middle classes into working systemically, and sometimes frantically, outside the school to advantage their own children.

We do not dissent from Professor Lynch's criticism alleging the suppression of the term 'social class' in Irish public discourse. The resulting silence, as she suggests, has undoubtedly constrained social analysis. In our view, however, the concept 'educational disadvantage' is not simply an abstraction that conceals the truth about poor people's lives. Rather, it embodies real people with agency over their own story, which they narrate without reticence, speaking truth to power. We also think that our adoption of the concept 'educational stratification' most effectively captures the intersectional nature of social inequality, which encompasses class, race, gender and many other under-represented identities that we feel need to be addressed. This intersectional approach includes a focus on the specificity of children's rights as a distinct social group with arguably equal entitlements to recognition and respect. While we regard social class as central to our analysis, we wish to avoid the limitations of a purely materialist paradigm. As Bourdieu has demonstrated, culture should also be fundamental to our consideration of educational inequality.

Territorial stigmatisation, othering and social discredit

The concept of territorial stigmatisation is linked to the process of 'othering' and 'social discredit' (Crossley, 2017: 1–14). It is culturally constructed by what Erving Goffman (1968), in his classic study *Stigma,* defined as the attribution of a 'spoiled identity' to an individual. Goffman (1968: 11) observed: 'The Greeks, who were apparently strong on visual imagery, originated the term stigma to refer to bodily signs designed to expose something unusual and bad about the moral status of the signifier.' These are the historical origins of the social practice of 'othering', in which blame for human degradation is displaced onto the victim or victim class, such as the 'left behind'. Michel Foucault (1967, 1977, 1980) exposed the power dynamics of othering as a mechanism for legitimating discrimination against 'problem' groups in the population by placing them outside the scope of normality and acceptability. The attribution of a stigmatised identity, arising from these groups' marginalised status, leads to their social exclusion and victimisation. Othering follows the classic lines of discrimination, placing 'us' above 'them'. The power of definition enables the subordination and domination of the stigmatised other.

Goffman (1968: 13) links the attribution of a stigmatised identity to social discredit: 'The term stigma, then, will be used to refer to an attribute that is deeply discrediting but it should be seen that a language of relationships, not attributes is really needed.' He further observes (p 15) that social attitudes towards:

> a person with a stigma, and the actions we take in regard to him, are well known, since these responses are what benevolent social action is designed to soften and ameliorate. By definition we believe the person with stigma is not quite human. On this assumption we exercise varieties of discrimination, through which we effectively, if often unthinkingly reduce his life chances.

In framing his stigma theory, Goffman (1968: 15–16) conceded that it is 'an ideology to explain inferiority and account for the danger he [the stigmatised person] represents, sometimes rationalising an animosity based on other differences such as those of social class'. In a cultural world dominated by binary oppositions in meaning-making, stigma and disadvantage have become intertwined with deeply polarising consequences towards wealth and privilege.

Poor people are the quintessential othered group. They are located at the bottom of the social hierarchy. They are segregated from the rest of society, frequently involving spatial separation. This spatial separation is referred to as 'territorial stigmatisation' because it symbolically reflects the power relations between social classes. Stephen Crossley (2017: 52–55) has applied a Bourdieusian approach to analysing the concept of territorial stigmatisation. He comments on the 'intense focus' on neighbourhoods 'located elsewhere' in political propaganda, popular folklore (fed by soap operas) and tabloid media representations of street life as stigmatised spaces with a cultural life that serves to 'entrench poverty' and 'attract disadvantage'.

This social construction of territorial stigmatisation includes language and words such as slums; ghettos; no-go areas; problem neighbourhoods; mean streets and sink estates that symbolically construct such social spaces as alien and dangerous. These negative cultural representations reduce the residents of territorially stigmatised spaces to the status of a homogenous underclass that lacks aspiration and embraces anomic lifestyles. It is discursively constructed as the 'culture of poverty' thesis that seeks to deny the reality of structural inequality as the root cause of social deprivation. Erving Goffman (1968: 17) argues the problems of the stigmatised are partly rooted in their perceived imperfections that become generalised in explaining their stigmatisation by society at large, concluding pessimistically that this is a shared belief: 'The stigmatized individual tends to hold the same basic beliefs about identity as we do; this is a pivotal fact.'

In a benchmark study of territorial stigmatisation in 1970, Lee Rainwater (then Professor of Sociology at Harvard University) published *Behind Ghetto Walls: Black Families in a Federal Slum*. His book was based on a community study of a notoriously segregated housing estate, called Pruitt-Igoe in St Louis that was subsequently demolished. In the preface to the book Rainwater (1970: vi) observed: 'The research on which this book is based began as a study of problems in a housing estate project, Pruitt-Igoe in St Louis, and ended as a study of the dynamics of socio-economic inequality.' As an introduction to comprehending local rationality, Rainwater (1970: 50) set out 'to examine the system of understandings and meanings that serves to make rational one's relations with those significant in one's life'. He observed (pp 50–51):

> People in social groups acquire complex sets of conceptions that express their sense of what their own lives and the life around them are all about. These 'typifications' incorporate ideas about how lives should develop, how they are most likely to develop, how one should, may and can act in various situations, and what attitudes one should take towards these situations and one's own and other people's behaviour in them. These complex sets of conceptions are 'meaning systems' that embrace what are variously described in sociological studies as norms, values, beliefs, world views, ways of life, prescriptive, proscriptive and permissible guides to life. Such meaning systems incorporate many disparate, often contradictory elements.

Stigmatised territorial spaces, such as Pruitt-Igoe are socially isolated but simultaneously subject to external social control. According to Rainwater (1970: 507), the influence of externally based institutions, such as churches, schools, stores, workplaces and public agencies, help to enforce conventional norms of behaviour: 'What comes across most clearly to the lower-class person in in these settings is that he would be much better off if he were able to live in a conventional way because other people would not "bug" him so much.' Recent conflicts between the police and Black communities in which there have been unprovoked assaults and killings, leading to calls by the Black Lives Matter movement for the defunding of the police, underscores the point. Rainwater (1970: 508–509) pessimistically concluded: 'The lower-class world is defined by two tough facts of life as it is experienced from day to day and from birth to death: deprivation and exclusion.' These undeniable facts of life do not stop the world from 'blaming the victim'.

Blaming the victim: the poverty debate

The publication in 2020 of a landmark study by Anne Case and Angus Deaton, *Deaths of Despair and the Future of Capitalism*, attracted major public interest. This well-researched book linked 'deaths of despair' to low educational achievement. The book alarmingly revealed that the US is experiencing a fall in life expectancy, caused mainly by suicides, alcohol-related deaths and drug overdoses, amounting to 158,000 'deaths of despair' in 2017 – the equivalent casualty rate of three full Boeing 737 passenger jets falling out of the sky every day for a year. Strikingly, Case and Deaton discovered that virtually the entire increase was among non-Hispanic White adults without a bachelor's degree. From the early 1990s, the mortality rate for Americans aged 45 to 54 has declined by 40 per cent, but has increased by 25 per cent for White people without a basic primary degree. In contrast, middle-aged Black people (while still disturbingly more susceptible to premature death rates than their White counterparts) experienced a fall of 30 per cent in mortality. The reasons are both economic and social, as the backstory to the publication of Case and Deaton's important book reveals.

Case and Deaton's research challenged traditional assumptions that blamed the poor for their circumstances, ignoring the role of social inequality and structural poverty. It also posed serious questions about the competitive nature of meritocratic society and the ethics of welfare reform. Globalisation, automation and the 2008 financial crash – which have created depressed 'rust belt' geographical communities – are also a fundamental part of the explanation and almost certainly the main causal factor. The left-behind populations that occupy these depressed areas are being increasingly undermined by structural poverty and personal despair about their lives and futures – which look distinctly bleak. Populist politics has fed the illusions of their despair.

Education is the main prospect of a way out of their despondency, but the barriers are substantial, often involving the accumulation of debt that students can ill afford. Inevitably there is a reaction from those who feel unfairly disadvantaged. Daniel Markovits (2019), in his book *The Meritocracy Trap*, observes that, in the 2016 US presidential election, Donald Trump won the share of White voters without college degrees by 39 percentage points, underlining the connection between underachievement and political anger. When Trump lost the 2020 presidential election, that sense of anger and alienation helped fuel the conditions for the unsuccessful coup attempt on 6 January 2021.

Anne Case and Angus Deaton are economists at Princeton University. Deaton was awarded the Nobel prize in 2015 for his research on consumption poverty and welfare. Yet, according to Gawande (2020: 22), when Case and Deaton tried to journal-publish their findings on White non-degree holders they were unsuccessful. Case and Deaton were confronting mainstream opinion, which tends to locate the explanation of poverty as being rooted in stereotypical images of human behavioural characteristics, traditionally associated with cultural practices in ethnic minorities.

This 'culture of poverty' thesis has a long pedigree going back to Oscar Lewis' bestselling books *The Children of Sanchez* (1961) and *La Vida* (1966), which depicted the lives of slum-dwellers as pleasurable and dissolute. Lewis argued that there was a deviant subculture of poverty that defined slum life. He studied poor families in Mexico, Puerto Rico and India. Lewis describes social worlds characterised by undisciplined work habits, impulsive sex, and child abuse. His research made Lewis the most influential anthropologist of his generation in the US. While professing to be sympathetic, Lewis' depiction of poor people as victims of their own moral choices (which he viewed as adaptive behaviour to adverse social conditions) unsurprisingly made him popular with conservative commentators, who were drawn to 'blaming the victim' analysis in the explanation of poverty. While President Johnson's war on poverty in the 1960s redefined poverty as a structural issue, rather than a behavioural problem, the culture of poverty thesis has had a lasting and damaging legacy for the poor.

The implications of Oscar Lewis' culture of poverty thesis have also had damning consequences for education. It spawned a cultural deficit theory that connected school underachievement to home environment, traditionally linked to minority ethnic status, but latterly (in an ironic twist of fate) to White underperforming males. Parsell (1981: 19) has described genetic and cultural deficit theories, in an article in *Black Studies,* as 'two sides of the same racist coin'. Children from socially deprived homes, where there was little access to books, were, according to this cultural deficit theory, likely to have underdeveloped vocabularies. Public and school libraries are designed to meet this need but are increasingly subjected to cuts and closures in countries such as Britain and the US (see Chapter 3). Socially disadvantaged children were also purported to be less likely to be prepared for school participation and adaptation to school environmental norms. Clearly, in a multicultural society there are language barriers, which need to be addressed by the provision of specialist language support and tuition. It is widely argued by policy makers that the role of the school is to promote the cultural values that assimilate minorities into the mainstream. In a multicultural society, diversity by definition becomes a core component in maintaining social cohesion. That involves including critical race theory in the curriculum.

The influence of 'damaging' cultural issues is evident in the HoC Education Committee report (2021: para 34), which viewed 'a culture of low expectations' as a key part of the problem of White male underperformance at school: 84 per cent of disadvantaged White male British students do not go to university. This has led to a focus on White male underachievement, arguably at the expense of other underperforming social groups, such as Irish Travellers, Gypsies and Roma.

Some educationists have lamented the influence of Oscar Lewis' culture of poverty thesis on teaching and learning. Jennifer Rogalsky (2009: 198), for example, argues that it 'posits that the poor remain so because their lives are determined by and adapted to poverty'. She counters this cultural pessimism with the assertion (p 198) that 'it is crucial to inform educators about the structural causes of poverty. Pedagogical interventions should focus on educating teachers about the influence of deindustrialization, decentralization, classism, racism and disproportionate funding upon their students' educational outcomes'. The debate about the causes, explanations and scale of poverty continues to rage, reflecting deep ideological splits.

The problem with the culture of poverty thesis is that its focus on purported anomic human behaviour and attribution of individual moral failings neglects the structural cause and context of the immiseration of the working class living in endemic poverty, arising from deindustrialisation, the gig economy, automation and, crucially, the decline of the trade union movement that fought for fair wages, economic rights and the dignity of labour. These factors have impacted on job opportunities, wages and working-class people's self-esteem. Employment in well-remunerated blue-collar manufacturing jobs in the US has declined from 19.5 million in 1979 to current levels of 12 million, against a backdrop of a population that has increased by 50 per cent. During this period, wages of high school (second level) qualification holders in the US declined by approximately 15 per cent, while the level of college-educated (third level) degree holders rose by about 10 per cent and those with higher degrees by 25 per cent (Epstein, 2020). The culture of poverty thesis is fundamentally flawed because it problematises poverty, blames the victim and advocates individual and family responsibility.

Case and Deaton offer a different approach to the exponents of subcultural theories of poverty – rooted in purported individual and group deviance – by offering a structural analysis. That makes their contribution to knowledge very important. Case and Deaton argue that growing economic insecurity is at the root of educational disadvantage in the US. They refocus policy on to the structural causes of poverty, and the potential role of higher education in its eradication in President Biden's early social legislation (which he struggled to get through Congress and the Senate) indicates an awareness towards the needs of all poor families, children and young people and ethnic minorities.

Educational disadvantage, intersectionality and the attainment gap

The concept of educational disadvantage provides a revealing perspective on the failures of the Irish education system. The Joint Irish Parliamentary Committee on Education and Skills in its *Report on Education, Inequality and Disadvantage and Barriers to Education* (2019: 5) described educational disadvantage as 'the impediments to education from social and economic disadvantage, which prevent students from deriving appropriate benefit from education in schools' and 'as a situation whereby individuals in society derive less benefit from education than their peers'.

What is clear from these comments is that some children at school personally experience systemic inequality in the form of disadvantage and discrimination because of their class, ethnicity, disability, sexuality, and because of their place of origin, culture and primary language. Frequently, these inequalities are experienced in multiple forms with individual students having their own personal experience of disadvantage and oppression in school.

The term 'intersectionality' emerges in the writings of bell hooks and was included in the Oxford Dictionary in 2015, defined as 'the interconnected nature of social categorisations such as race, class and gender, regarded as creating overlapping and interdependent systems of discrimination and disadvantage'. Intersectionality is a very important concept because it offers an overarching understanding of the interaction between social class and other forms of inequality that devolve on individual identity and culture.

Professor Denis O'Sullivan, an Irish authority on educational inequality, identified six divergent uses of the term 'educational disadvantage', each underpinned by a different political perspective:

1. A focus on the *constitutional limitations* of the person – identifying that people who are educationally disadvantaged are presumed to have a low intellectual capacity.

2. A focus on presumed *personal deficit* in the socialisation of some pre-school children, which leaves them unable to benefit fully from the education offered by the school.
3. A focus on a presumed *cultural deficit* in the environment of some children, which gives rise to them developing anti-school and anti-social attitudes and values.
4. A focus on *schooling practices which are identified as culturally irrelevant,* such as the decision by schools to require particular patterns of speech and behaviour which are alien to some young people, thereby giving rise to a cultural discontinuity for them, which impacts on their learning.
5. A focus on the *material condition* (wealth or poverty) of the pupils' community and on the impact this material condition has on their housing, healthcare and school conditions.
6. A focus on the broader *political economy,* which identifies that the current system of disadvantage exists because those parents who are in a position to do so try to give their children an advantage in society (through education), thereby placing others at a disadvantage. (Cited in Tormey, 2010: 191–192.)

It is notable that the focus of three of these six explanations is on deficits in the individual, family socialisation and community environment, with the final three raising class-related issues including: alienation from schooling, material conditions (wealth/poverty) and the influence of privilege in accessing a higher-quality educational experience. Regardless of the causes, the consequences of educational disadvantage are very serious for both the individual and society.

A report, published by Solas (the Irish state agency concerned with FET), entitled *Adult Literacy for Life,* mapped out the demographic groups, scale and social consequences of educational disadvantage (2021: 4):

> The link between literacy, equality and disadvantage is clear. The groups most at risk of social exclusion are often those where unmet literacy needs are greatest, whether it is early school leavers with negative experience of education; people with a disability; people seeking international protection or other migrants needing language support, or minority ethnic groups which have struggled due to inequality and racism.
>
> However, there is also another 'hidden' group, within the workforce itself, and particularly across all age groups. These are over 300,000 adults in Ireland who do not have any formal education equivalent to the leaving certificate, and almost 900,000 people who have no formal education beyond school level. Many of these struggle with literacy, numeracy, and digital skills, which are essential to sustaining employment in the future world of work.

The report pessimistically concluded (p 18): 'The evidence on numeracy and literacy learning deficits suggests those left behind at school age are unlikely to develop their skills over the succeeding decade.'

The Joint Committee on Education and Skills (2019) observed that, on completion of primary school, children from higher professional backgrounds, such as doctors, lawyers and academics, had a mean literacy score of 43 (out of 50); those of semi- or unskilled manual working-class backgrounds had a mean score of 28; and those from households where both parents were unemployed had a mean score of 25. The Committee further noted the significance of regional inequalities and educational poverty, with 21.9 per cent of young people over 15 years of age in County Donegal not progressing beyond primary level, followed by County Monaghan (18 per cent), Cavan (17.8 per cent), Longford (17.7 per cent), Mayo (17.4 per cent) and Wexford (16.6 per cent). Overall, the Committee concluded that 1,000 Irish children do not transfer to secondary school and 4,500 drop out of school before completing the Junior Certificate Examination, which students normally sit at 14 or 15 years of age. In reference to Dublin, the Joint Committee (2019: 6) commented: 'There are in Dublin communities where progression to higher education has remained below 20 per cent despite 20 years of investment in activities to raise the educational aspirations and outcomes for children from these communities.' Clearly, this is a very disturbing conclusion and raises serious doubts about the effectiveness of equal opportunities initiatives.

The Committee's report asserted that participation in high-quality education benefits both society and the economy, including better jobs and health outcomes. It also helps to address issues such as homelessness, addiction, unemployment, poverty and poor health. The Joint Committee (2019: 6) reached six important conclusions regarding the attainment gap:

1. The Irish education system 'as it currently stands is unfair and unequal' and 'the current structure, where there is unequal distribution of income and wealth, is being legitimised through ideologies of meritocracy, and is acting to reproduce social class-related inequalities'.
2. Educational disadvantage is intersectional – 'class, community and family, policy and school, individually and intersectionally impact on outcomes'.
3. There are key transitions, including from primary to secondary school and at the point of access to higher education.
4. There are specific groups that particularly experience the education system as 'unfair and unequal' including Travellers, lone parents, people with disabilities, homeless people, children in care, asylum seekers and people in poverty.
5. Educational disadvantage occurs both horizontally, 'whereby policies and practices do not speak to each other and/or negatively impact upon

each other, and vertically, where the broad meso-structures and policies influence the macro systems of schools and universities, which impact with individual capacities, including finances and family status'.
6. There are shared challenges among vulnerable groups (provision of support, finances and understanding) and specific challenges, which are not adequately understood.

These observations raise fundamental issues regarding the connection between educational disadvantage and social justice.

Educational disadvantage and social justice

Disadvantage means being placed in an unfair position relative to others. It implies hardship (economic) and disempowerment (personal and political constraint) that reduces the chances of social inclusion and participation in the world for an individual, group or community. At a normative level, disadvantage in the language of social policy means structural inequality and disempowerment. Social scientist and human-rights advocate Professor Jim Ife (2002: 61) identifies the primary structurally disadvantaged groups in society in terms of: class (the poor, the unemployed, low-income workers and welfare claimants); gender; and race/ethnicity (indigenous peoples, ethnic and cultural minorities, asylum seekers and refugees). Ife adds several other disadvantaged groups: the aged; children and young people; people with disabilities; the LGBTQIA+ community; and the isolated geographically and socially. Finally, Ife includes on his list, what he calls 'the personally disadvantaged' (those experiencing grief, loss and personal and family problems). His classification highlights the complex nature and extensive scope of disadvantage in modern society.

Ultimately, Ife (2002: 61–69) argues that empowerment of the disadvantaged is a struggle for social justice based on social need and human rights that are foundational concepts in empowering the poor and marginalised. The UK Commission on Social Justice (1994: 1) defined the values of social justice as 'equal worth of all citizens, their equal right to be able to meet their basic needs, the need to spread opportunities and life chances as widely as possible, and finally the requirement that we reduce and where possible eliminate unjustified inequalities'.

Margaret Ledwith (2005: 42) elaborates on what social justice might mean practically in terms of equalising respect and recognition: 'Social justice embraces a range of ways of being in the world that are not seen as deviant from the norm – young, old, disabled, single, lone-parent, lesbian, gay, all faiths and none and so on', adding: 'If a just society is one in which people are treated with equal dignity and respect, where different cultures are embraced, where different abilities are valued and where everyone is enabled to reach their full potential, then injustice can be seen as a violation of these values.' These insightful observations raise seminal philosophical questions about the meaning of social justice, which has a broad variety of ideological strands: liberal, institutional, structural and critical theory.

First, the liberal concept of social justice is rooted in the work of the philosopher John Rawls (1921–2002). Rawls' theory of justice is set out in his best-known work *A Theory of Justice* (1971), in which he equates justice with fairness in a liberal democratic society composed of citizens with equal basic rights. He believed a society regulated by a public commitment to social justice is inherently stable. One of Rawls' core principles – the difference principle – defines the regulation of rights, powers and privileges in a just society in terms of equal opportunity. It implies an obligation to redistribute wealth in a manner consistent with the values of modern democracy – liberty, equality and solidarity. Rawls based his political philosophy on the values of reciprocity, fairness and mutual respect. He embraced the concept of the welfare state, but later despaired of its acceptance of social inequality and contraction under the influence of the New Right during the 1980s and 1990s. Rawls' theory of justice logically led to support for a fairer distribution of educational resources (Beattie, 1982: 39–50). Rawls argued that those who have the same innate qualities and share the same level of motivation should have the same opportunities for success regardless of their natural and social condition (see Chapter 4 for a discussion of equality of opportunity). The problems with the Rawlsian theory of social justice are who gets to decide what constitutes redistributive justice and why it is individualised. Such problems entail major democratic limitations on constructing a just society in a contractarian individualist polity. The US is the classic example. Its current social, cultural and political divisions reflect the limits of liberal individualism and Rawlsian social justice.

Second, the institutionalist concept of social justice is reflected in the historic edifice of the welfare state, which sought to adapt the classical ideal of civic virtue to modern society. The inadequacies and divisions in society were viewed by early social reformers, such as Sidney and Beatrice Webb, H.G. Wells and George Bernard Shaw, as a reflection of the quality of its institutions. Advocates of an institutionalist approach to achieving social justice argued for the extension of citizenship to embrace social rights, encompassing: health, housing, education and social security. Social rights extend the scope of citizenship beyond civil and political rights to provide, what T.H Marshall (1973) called a 'three-legged stool', which completed the architecture of modern democracy. Unfortunately, the contradictions of the welfare state – in seeking to socialise the state in a capitalist economy – arise from its values rooted in humanistic democracy and public altruism, which are fundamentally in conflict with market values – driven by private ownership, profit maximisation and serving the economic interests of corporations and shareholders (O'Connor, 1973; Gough, 1979; Offe, 1984). The resulting conflict between oligarchical capital and democracy has resulted in deep welfare cuts and harsh austerity measures that have shaken the foundations of democracy and undermined the pursuit of social justice in a post-socialist world order.

Third, the structural concept of social justice is rooted in the view that social inequality is part of the fabric of a capitalist, racially divided and patriarchal society that is based on unjust and oppressive policy regimes. The view is ideologically shaped by Marxist, feminist and critical race theories of power. Advocates of a structural perspective locate social inequality in the subordination and domination of working-class people, ethnic minorities, women, marginalised gender groups, Travellers and Roma, and increasingly asylum seekers, migrants and refugees, through a combination of social and political oppression, institutional racism and patriarchy that undermine democracy, social justice and human rights. Poverty is the most visible expression of social inequality in society. Child poverty is undoubtedly its most disturbing manifestation of structural inequality. The structural analysis and prescription for social justice advocates the replacement of capitalism by democratic socialism, and equality of respect and dignity regardless of gender, race, ability, age and sexuality in a multicultural society that embraces diversity. It seeks fundamental equality in society, both in terms of redistribution of wealth and the promotion of dignity and respect. For this reason, it does not find favour with power elites, leading to public critiques in the media that suggest its prescriptions for an egalitarian society are unrealistic, at best, and tyrannical, at worst. Jeremy Corbyn's failure to convince the electorate in the UK is a good illustration of the problems involved with advocating anti-capitalist political solutions based on social justice. The structural perspective on social justice is a classic illustration of the debate within the social sciences about the relative importance of social structure versus human agency in achieving change. Educational disadvantage versus embodied privilege captures the essence of this debate. How do you 'level up' educational inequality without eroding traditional privilege based on family rights, wealth and individual achievement?

Finally, there is the critical theory / poststructuralist perspective of social justice, which is both illuminating about the nature of power (arguing that all relations are power relations) and pessimistic about the possibilities of social and political change. Critical theorists maintain that reason and truth are social constructs used to support power hierarchies. The thinking behind critical theory is shaped by a number of intellectual influences, including the Frankfurt School of Marxism in Germany (and later the US), French postmodernists, radical feminists and Black Studies. Critical theorists challenge Enlightenment universalism and its political value base – located in equality, liberty and human rights – as a system of domination and subjugation that excludes oppressed groups from the social and political order and has historically defended imperialism, colonisation and slavery. Language and identity, rather than the Marxist concern with material conditions, are at the centre of the critical theorists' social analysis, which replaces objective reality with subjective experience in its analytic approach. George Packer (2021: 76) insightfully comments: 'The focus on subjectivity moves oppression from the world to the self and its pain-psychological trauma, harm from speech and texts, the sense of alienation that members of minority groups feel in their constant exposure to a dominant culture. A whole system of oppression can exist in a single word.'

The critical theory perspective is particularly embodied in the scholarship of the post-structuralist philosopher, Michel Foucault (1926–1984). In his philosophical writings, Foucault explored the nature of power and its uses and abuses in objectifying human subjects and ordering society. However, he also recognised the reality of human resistance to oppression. Postmodernists, such as Paul Ricoeur, are primarily concerned with discourse and language in the cultural construction of truth and meaning in society. As discussed, a seminal intellectual influence on critical theory was Pierre Bourdieu, whose ideas have fundamentally reshaped our understanding of educational inequality in his symbiosis between class and culture, which he called 'cultural capital'. The critical theory perspective of social justice has enabled us to understand how oppression and disadvantage are discursively rationalised and legitimated in society. Critical race theory has emerged in recent years as a broader application of this approach to popular democratic discourse. The deconstruction of oppressive power structures in society becomes subjectively possible through the interrogation in the classroom of meanings and symbols of history to incorporate issues such as slavery, imperialism and colonialism and their reconstruction as critical discourses of power that challenge the dominant social and political order. Critical literacy is essential to unlocking the hidden meanings of power and promoting individual freedom. That is at the core of Freire's theory of education.

Conclusion

We have explored the influence of hierarchical thinking and the use of ladders of opportunity as a metaphor for every citizen achieving their full potential. The latter prospect, however, rests on illusionary thinking and distortions of the truth. It is not supported by the evidence. This chapter also began to analyse inequalities located in class, race and other forms of disadvantage that deny social justice to large sections of society. We have sought to outline and explain the variety of interpretations of social justice that exist and will draw on this rich intellectual diversity in our discussions of educational disadvantage throughout the book. All are useful and important in understanding the interplay between disadvantage and privilege in shaping the lives of human beings. The chapter introduced the ideas of Pierre Bourdieu as a seminal thinker regarding the understanding and explanation of educational inequality. Bourdieu unlocked the deeper meanings and social constructs underlying educational disadvantage in his theory of cultural capital. Our book seeks to examine the challenges to social justice, which were discussed in this chapter. As George Packer suggests, a whole system of oppression can exist in a word, such as slavery. The language of oppression is important to any understanding of educational disadvantage as a product of social inequality, thinking about it and finding answers for changing it. We suggest that the answers are to be found deeply embedded in our culture, where meanings and opportunities are generated and power elites reproduced.

3

Public education, universities and widening participation

The university in the knowledge economy

Pierre Bourdieu (in a televised conversation with the writer Gunter Grass) described the complexity of the times we live in and the challenges involved in unravelling their political meaning:

> Yes, but there is a connection between this sense of having lost the traditions of the Enlightenment and the global triumph of neoliberalism. I see neoliberalism as a conservative revolution – as the term was used between the wars in Germany – a strange revolution that restores the past but presents itself as progressive, transforming regression itself into a form of progress.

Later in their conversation, Bourdieu dismissed his critics as 'dinosaurs' (Bourdieu and Grass, 2002: 65). Where does public education and the role of the university in civil society fit in this changed neoliberal cultural landscape, called the 'knowledge economy'? The Irish president, Michael D. Higgins, a distinguished public intellectual and social scientist, has pondered the future role of the university: 'Are the great universities of the world, rather like the stones of monastic sites visited today, to become like them in time, merely tourist attractions of the future' (*The Irish Times*, 8 June 2021). We are living through challenging times for higher education in the 21st century that will test the institutional sustainability of the university.

Public education encompasses education funded by the state, democratically accountable to the public and free and accessible to everybody. It is normally secular in ethos. As a cornerstone of an ethical civil society, public education is an embattled concept in a neoliberal society, where culture wars – between secular and traditional religious values – increasingly threaten the independence of schools to teach about diversity (for example Black history) and human rights. Books in school libraries are being banned – reminiscent of past cultural intolerances in Europe, such as book burnings in Nazi Germany. The American Library Association has stated that, in 2022, a record 1,269 demands were made to restrict or ban books and other materials in schools and libraries, up from 156 in 2020 (*Los Angeles Times*, 23 May 2023). Florida has passed the Stop Woke Act, seeking to curtail instruction in historic human-rights violations against minorities, such as slavery.

In June 2023, Texas governor Greg Abbot signed a bill that will ban diversity, equity and inclusion offices in public universities across the state and terminate activities that seek to promote the participation of under-represented groups of individuals over others based on race, ethnicity and gender – historically known as 'affirmative action' (*The Guardian*, 15 June 2023). Then, on 29 June, the US Supreme Court struck down affirmative action based on race, which had benefited Black Americans for nearly half a century through opening up admissions policies to universities. The ruling does not apply to gender. But it may have unintended consequences. Naomi Schoenbaum (2023: 1), in a legal opinion on the consequences of the decision, concluded: 'The Supreme Court inadvertently instituted affirmative action for White men.'

Other policy changes are also reframing the mission of the university along more utilitarian lines. Universities are increasingly influenced by the reorientation of public policy towards neoliberalism, embodied in the concept of the 'knowledge economy', meaning a system of consumption and production that is based on building intellectual capital in the workforce and replacing or displacing traditional forms of industrial activity that employed manual labour – now increasingly redundant. Deindustrialisation is part of the futurist vision of the knowledge economy. For those left behind in the race to build personal intellectual capital, the future looks bleak, and for many, participation in higher education a remote possibility. The future of the university as an institution built on humanist values is also in crisis.

The modern university faces a conundrum in reconciling the utilitarian demands of neoliberalism to commodify higher education with its original humanist educational mission. It has always straddled the public and private spheres of social life, but the balance is changing in favour of the latter. Some commentators think this simply a reflection of a market-oriented society. Neary and Winn (2017) argue that the distinction between public and private in higher education is a 'false dichotomy'. They point to the introduction of student loans in England as evidence of the increasing role of private markets, while the state simultaneously takes on a greater regulatory role. In Ireland – where tuition fees (abolished in 1996) were reintroduced in the 21st century – a similar restructuring of the state's relations with the universities has occurred, with the state taking on an increasing regulatory role. How do we explain this apparent paradox? Neary and Winn (2017) conclude that in a market society the private and public spheres are not antithetical but complementary in a shared capitalist productive project of economic growth. While this argument is logical in a neoliberal economy, it is also important to consider the democratic role of the university as a cornerstone of civil society. The purpose and role of public education in a democracy is about a lot more than building a knowledge economy to meet its material needs. Public education is at the core of maintaining the structure and institutions of an ethical civil society as the cornerstone of democracy.

The university stands at the apex of the education system. It takes a variety of forms: the elite research university model, primarily dedicated to scientific enquiry and discovery; the civic university model, emphasising teaching, learning and community engagement in both the humanities and sciences; and what Clark Kerr (President of the University of California during the 1960s) called the 'multiversity' model, combining all these forms and functions.

In this chapter we discuss a number of interconnected topics that inform education policy in relation to the promotion of civility and social inclusion. First, we explore the contested meaning of public education at all levels of learning in civil society. Second, we analyse a complex web of civic and community engagement initiatives as the third mission of the university. Then we examine the role of adult education and public libraries in the cultural empowerment of civil society through the public availability of knowledge to all citizens. Finally, we address the empowering strategies of widening participation, affirmative action and university access initiatives and analyse the expectations and experiences of students on the HEAR programme at UCC interviewed by the research team.

Civil society, public education and humanist values

Civil society is defined by the right to associate, organise and freely exchange ideas as the basis of democracy. It includes the private sphere (families, clubs and churches), the civic sphere (voluntary and community organisations, charities, NGOs) and the political sphere (mass media, political parties and social movements). In an uneasy triangular relationship with the state and the market, civil society defines the normative basis of our world within the rule of law, toleration and democratic engagement, which is the basis of Western civilisation (Powell and Guerin, 1997). Public education is located in this contested space. For example, it has recently been reported that schools in Florida have banned textbooks as part of the culture war against alleged 'woke indoctrination' (*The New York Times*, 16 March 2023). Civility in public discourse is under strain and tolerance at risk.

Public education is by far the most common form of provision in democratic societies. It is by definition open and inclusive, providing the vital and accessible knowledge base for most citizens in their local communities. Public education is generally free at primary and secondary levels, but may be subject to fees at tertiary level, which are prevalent in English-speaking countries but less so in Europe and many other parts of the world. Private education, which is by definition closed and exclusive, coexists with its public counterpart for the benefit of a privileged minority of wealthy citizens or religious or ethnic groups. Furthermore, public education may also be subject to encroachment by the private sphere such as: English 'public schools' (in reality private institutions part funded by the state); religious control of most schools in Ireland; and neoliberal initiatives, such as academies and 'free schools' in the UK that subject educational institutions to market principles through 'a philosophy of commercialisation and marketing rather than anything to do with education' (Reay, 2017: 48).

The civic university shares the democratic and ethical framework underpinning public education in its value base through: the protection of academic freedom to speak truth to power; its civic engagement mission that reaches out to disadvantaged communities; and widening participation strategies that promote access across the social spectrum as a core objective. Nathan Heller (2023), in a *New Yorker* article on the decline of the humanities, provides an example of a state university and its civic role and 'democratic promise' in society:

> Arizona State University, which has more than 80,000 students on campus, is today regarded as a beacon of the democratic promise of public higher education. Its undergraduate admission rate is eighty-eight percent. Nearly half of the undergraduates are from minority backgrounds, and a third are first in their families to go to college.

The robustness of these democratic elements of academic policy in constructing the architecture of a knowledge *society* are constantly in tension with the disruptive advocacy by both state and market of the competition agenda of a knowledge *economy*. Heller (2023), in his analysis of the state of higher education in the US, observes: 'In 1980, on average, state funding accounted for seventy-nine per cent public universities revenue. By 2019, that figure was fifty-five percent.' He concludes that this cut in funding has pushed public universities towards operating a private business model. The impact of neoliberalism on the civic role of the university, according to Heller (2023), has been detrimental:

> Everyone agrees that the long arc of higher education must bend towards openness and democratization. And universities in an imperfect but forward-inching way, are achieving the dream. ... Although the university funding arc and the university opening arc once grew in happy parallel, intensifying the value of humanistic cultural capital while expanding access to it, those curves have now crossed.

Reading Heller's analysis of the crisis in US universities is not simply a narrative of declining access to higher education. It is also about the much-diminished influence of humanities education on the universities' purpose and mission. Humanism is at the core of the value-base of the Western democratic system. Democracy, increasingly challenged by populist autocrats, ultimately depends on 'enlightened understanding' in making political choices (Dahl, 1956). In the knowledge economy, universities are being repurposed to the market by a reorientation to STEM (Science, Technology, Engineering and Mathematics) subjects, with the consequence that 'enrolment in the humanities is in free fall ' (Heller, 2023).

As modernity recedes into historical memory, real concerns have been raised about a loss of hope in the possibility of social progress. The metanarrative of modernity, institutionally embodied in the Keynesian welfare state based on human rights, social progress and redistributive justice, has been displaced by a global neoliberal narrative of economic development and wealth creation. This libertarian political ideology not only reshaped systems of government but also impacted on the political economy of schools and higher-education institutions, undermining the concept of a broader public good rooted in the civic humanist tradition. Two leading advocates of civic engagement, John Saltmarsh and Mathew Hartley (2016: 24–25), observe in a US context that the impact of neoliberalism is undermining the ethical base of the university as a civic institution with larger democratic and social goals:

> Instead, education becomes part of the commodification of everything, and its larger democratic and social goals were either discarded or redefined in market terms. …
>
> As colleges and universities adopted prevailing neoliberal principles, higher education became viewed as a private benefit, hence the effects of defunding public postsecondary education, rising tuition costs, increasing student debt, the proliferation of on-line for-profit providers, and the dominance of contingent-faculty labour. Philanthropy also shifted funding strategies away from higher education. …
>
> The civic engagement movement was often on the defensive, reasserting the democratic purpose of higher education, countering the reductionist trends sweeping across the landscape of higher education, and attempting to counteract neoliberalism's effects on the university.

Resistance to neoliberalism has been strongest in states with social democratic traditions in the form of an organised labour movement, social rights and a developed welfare state. Pierre Bourdieu (1998: 33) observes:

> The process of regression of the state shows that resistance to neoliberal doctrine and policy is that much greater in countries where state traditions have been strongest. And that is to be explained by the fact

that the state exists in two forms: in objective reality, in the form of a set of institutions such as rules, agencies, offices etc., and also in people's minds.

The zeitgeist of the welfare state is resonant with symbolic power because it represents the triumph of civic virtue (democracy) over market values (oligarchy). That is the humanist yardstick by which the welfare state is measured in the popular imaginary, as a product of democracy embodied in social citizenship, equality and human rights. However, there remain significant problems with social inclusion and civic engagement in contemporary democratic society that may be undermining its foundations. Higher education has a particularly onerous responsibility in regard to fostering the civic humanist vision of democratic society that seeks to embrace all of its citizens through greater access to knowledge.

Pierre Bourdieu was very clear on the influence of social structure in shaping civil and political society in the contemporary world. He makes a persuasive case for the welfare state as the embodiment of social justice and civic humanism in a modern democratic society. The first wave of the welfare state emerged in late-19th-century Germany, with Bismarck's pension and insurance reforms, quickly followed elsewhere in response to the democratic expectations of the newly enfranchised working class. A further, much more comprehensive, 'second wave' of the welfare state social reform agenda emerged in post-war society, embracing: health, housing, social security and education. Bourdieu understood the philosophical meaning of the welfare state as a democratic step-change in social relations between classes, based on a new social contract. His analysis equated the welfare state with the classical ideal of civic virtue.

Bourdieu (1998: 24) describes the welfare state, in his book *Acts of Resistance,* as a bulwark against 'the destruction of civilization, associated with the existence of public services, the civilization of republican equality of rights, rights to education, to health, culture, research, art and, above all, work'. This is a powerful civic humanist endorsement of the purpose and ethos of the welfare state, one which defines it as a set of institutional provisions – including public education – that are designed to meet the social and economic needs of citizens in an ethical civil society. Social policy, which frames the objectives and institutional system of public education, is not simply another area of governance but also constitutes the moral framework for civilised life in modern society. The ethos that underpins public education is the modern expression of civic humanism in a secular world, governed by democratic norms and expectations. It is the link with our past in classical civilisation but also our moral compass for the future if we are to protect ourselves from another Dark Age in which we begin to witness 'the degradation of civic virtue' (Bourdieu, 1998: 4).

The French welfare state – the primary target of Bourdieu's critique – has been one of the most comprehensive in the world. During the first year of the coronavirus pandemic in 2020 the French government spent 62 per cent of GDP, 27.3 per cent of which went in funding social protection programmes (McAuley, 2022: 59). France managed to avoid the Anglo-Saxon conservative movement's frontal assaults on the welfare state during the 1980s, embodied in Thatcherism and Reaganomics. France did, however, experience welfare reform during the conservative era of President Sarkozy, when the generous Socialist welfare programme *revenue d'insertion* was replaced in 2004 by *revenue de solidarité*, which is based on much more restrictive conditionality principles. In France, like many other Western countries, there has been a paradigm shift from welfare to workfare, designed to sharply reduce welfare expenditure and force the poor into low-paid employment. President Macron's 'Third Way' – *ni gauche ni droite* – centrist programme promises further drastic cuts in pensions and welfare expenditure – indicating the direction of travel in French social policy, as his second term shifts to the right.

French public education has meanwhile become the theatre of culture wars. In September 1989 three Muslim students were suspended from school in an act of cultural intolerance because they wore the traditional headscarf hijab in the classroom. This event provoked a showdown between France's hallowed secular values as the basis of its republicanism and the multicultural society that has emerged during the post-war era. It was known as *l'affaire des foulards* and threatened to undermine the universalist philosophy of the French welfare state, and brought cultural politics into the classroom. 1989 was a momentous year, with the bicentennial of the French Revolution and a fatwa proclaimed against Salman Rushdie for his novel *The Satanic Verses,* depicting the prophet Muhammad. The novel was viewed by its religious critics as blasphemous because of its public representation of Muhammad (McAuley, 2022: 61). It led to an assassination attempt on Rushdie in New York in 2022 that left him with life-changing injuries. Cultural tensions also grew in France involving incidents of intercommunal violence, ultimately leading in 2020 to the beheading by Muslims of a school teacher in a Paris suburb. The clear lesson from this tragic event is that cultural politics should have no place in schools. In accordance with the French model of universalist citizenship, minority ethnic people are entitled to equality of respect. France has nonetheless recently reiterated its secular stance in sending home students wearing abayas.

Social justice is at the core of the ideal of the welfare state, which strategically seeks to redress poverty and social inequality. The welfare state and public education normatively promotes community and solidarity by supporting the building of an ethical civil society around its population, encompassing all its citizens regardless of ethnicity or religious affiliation. It also enhances economic development through an active state, supporting and regulating the market, while simultaneously providing the necessary resources for social and economic development, infrastructure (roads, wi-fi, environmental protection and so on) and strategic planning. The welfare state politically represents a set of socio-cultural values based on the principles of redistribution and reciprocity that in turn embody the democratic struggle against the acquisitiveness of self-regulating markets. It reflects a profound conflict, according to Karl Polanyi's (2001: 80) 'double-movement' theory – premised on a tension between the push of self-regulating markets (oligarchy) for autonomy from the state and a push back for social justice from the citizens (democracy) – in the pursuit of social justice through the social contract embodied in the welfare state.

Neoliberalism is inspired by the ideas of the economist Friedrich Von Hayek (1899–1992), which, during the 1970s and 1980s reshaped political economy in the direction of small-state, trickle-down economics, privatisation and low taxation. It was a libertarian policy shift towards what Bourdieu calls regression under the mask of progression, in which markets and wealth once again became self-regulating oligarchies, seeking to impose recommodification upon society. The 2008 financial crash undermined public confidence in this neoliberal project of Hayekian economics. It resulted in bailouts of banks at the expense of taxpayers in several European countries. In Ireland, during 2010, the state was bailed out by the 'Troika' composed of the European Commission, International Monetary Fund and the European Central Bank, with Irish banks receiving major infusions of capital. The loans will not be paid off by the public until 2053. There followed austerity policies with major impacts on public expenditure, including funding for schools.

A DEIS school principal interviewed by the UCC research team explained the impact of public expenditure cuts on the school in terms of growing demands on staff and greater support needs from the students:

> It's been cut back pretty significantly. Pretty significantly, and that has had an impact in every sense on educational attainment, wellbeing; people are being asked to do more and more with less and less. Yeah, the needs are getting greater and more profound. You see, Joe Public won't see that because, as far as you're concerned, school opens at nine and closes at four, so schools continue, right, but all schools would feel the pinch in terms of a lack of investment by the Department [of Education and Skills]. … Now teachers are wonderful, teachers invest huge personal and professional time in to management and minding the kids. I mean we have a very strong caring ethos in this school – it's really strong – but I don't know if that's sustainable in the long term.

The principal's insightful remarks highlight the complex educational and social roles schools play in the community and supporting civil society.

A *New York Times* opinion supplement (Kamenetz, 2022) posed the rhetorical question 'What is school for?'. Its answer was that schools had been undervalued by the public in terms of their civic and social contribution:

> When schools shut down abruptly in March 2020 [due to the COVID-19 lockdown], many Americans realized for the first time the essential roles these institutions play. Yes, they teach students to read and write, but they also provide child care for working families, food for hungry children and a sense of community cohesion for neighbourhoods. As we rebound from years of disruption to education, we have an opportunity to think anew about what our schools do and what we want them to be.

Public education through the schools system is at the core of civil society in many disadvantaged communities, where its role goes well beyond providing access routes to higher education. Schools in disadvantaged areas, such as DEIS schools in Ireland, are evolving into community centres that teach children to read and write, feed children, provide care and support for children and their parents and interact with youth and community services. Student volunteers increasingly play a part in bridging the gap between the university and the school. The emphasis in these schools is increasingly on enabling children to thrive. This institutional development goes well beyond the traditional academic role of the school in its community orientation and is likely to have major social benefits in the long term. This enlightened policy development requires major investment if it is to be sustainable.

Anya Kamenetz, in a core contribution to the *New York Times* feature, describes the origins of public education in the middle of the 19th century. She notes that prior to this enlightened development the rich were home tutored or sent abroad for their education, while literacy for slaves was outlawed – 'those who learned did so by luck, in defiance or in secret'. Kamenetz (2002) views schools as 'the crucible of democracy'. But she is pessimistic about the current state of public education in the US. She concludes (p 4):

> This country has seemingly never had a harder time embracing a shared reality or believing in common values. The parents who are showing up at school boards yelling about 'critical race theory' and pronouns are trying to get public schools to bend history, reality and values to their liking.
>
> Without public education delivered as a public good, the asylum-seeker in detention, the teenager in jail, not to mention millions of children growing up in poverty, will have no realistic way to get instruction they need to participate in democracy or support themselves.

If we lose public education, flawed as it is, the foundations of our democracy will slip. Not only the shared knowledge base but also the skills of citizenship itself: communication, empathy, and compromise across differences.

Professor Naoíse Mac Sweeny (2023: 295), in her recent book *The West: A New History of an Old Idea*, comments on growing warnings of 'the suicide of the West', reflecting concerns among White conservatives that social liberalism is undermining Western civilisation. Culture wars against a supposed 'woke' ideology has created a deep fracture in society. Schools are at the epicentre of this conflict because they shape the vision and values of future generations.

Civic and community engagement: the third mission of the university

The concept of civic and community engagement seeks to locate the university within the public sphere, where democracy is practised as a basic human right to associate and engage in debate about ideas and the nature and meaning of power (Saltmarsh and Hartley, 2011). In Ireland Campus Engage is based at the Irish Universities Association, which seeks to coordinate civic and community engagement across the university system. Its principles are set out in the Campus Engage Charter for Civic and Community Engagement, signed by university heads in 2014 at a landmark event in Dublin Castle, endorsing a 'third mission' for the sector. The ten principles in the charter define the meaning and scope of civic and community engagement, as it is nationally and internationally understood, including in Principle 6 a commitment to widening participation and lifelong-learning agendas promoting civic and community engagement.

Higher education is unique because it is based on the free choice of adults, who voluntarily engage in the pursuit of knowledge. That makes the university a creative space that inspires people to think and understand. The pursuit of knowledge is the professed goal of the university. Arguably, the university is one of the greatest gifts to humanity, which empowers citizens through knowing. Plato regarded education as the means to achieve justice, both individual and social. Civic and community engagement seeks to broaden the university's mission to encompass and connect with civil society in all its complexity and possibility. That has given rise to the civic engagement movement within universities led by publicly engaged scholars (Saltmarsh and Hartley, 2011).

Civic and community engagement is a dualistic and integrative concept, encompassing both community-based learning (CBL) and community-based participative research (CBPR). Civic and community engagement are dependent on bottom-up initiatives in civil society that are both precious and fragile. The scope is wide as is clear from the Campus Engage Charter, including: student volunteering, adult education, diversity initiatives and widening participation in deliberative processes at local, national and global levels. In practice, civic and community engagement is a loose organising concept that provides an umbrella under which local activists, academics and volunteers can find common purpose with the university. It offers the university democratic legitimacy at a point when it faces a potential tsunami of criticism for its perceived elitism from an increasingly sceptical public. For citizens living in marginalised communities, civic and community engagement offers a bridge to knowledge acquisition and democratic participation in civil society.

A democratic epistemology based on critical enquiry (as advocated by critical pedagogues), in which communities become co-creators of knowledge, has become a challenging new frontier – a borderland between the university and civil society, where cooperative models of knowledge meet and join the citizenry in a form of intellectual levelling. The citizen science research model (epitomised by the EU Science Shops programme) opens up new epistemologies in a wide variety of disciplinary areas, such as public and environmental health, conservation and biodiversity, 'volunteer' geography and archaeology and public sociology. The harnessing of 'citizen sensing' becomes a valid data collecting tool in the production of counter-discourses to elite sponsored research models. It reflects the power of local knowledge in a globalised world to challenge expert knowledge systems, often funded by corporate interests. Citizen journalism also offers members of the academic community an opportunity to contribute to the public understanding of truth and to critique corporate power in the best Socratic tradition of questioning the world around us.

Civic and community engagement represents a bold hermeneutic step in changing the way academics think about scholarship and research and its dissemination in the public sphere. A core focus for its advocates is the relationship between the university and the community in a shared democratic learning environment. The practitioners of civic and community engagement are intellectually inspired by a critical epistemic, in which the citizen community takes centre stage in the process of thinking. That represents a step change in in postmodern democratic epistemology, led by critical pedagogical thinking and practice, catalysing transformative action. Publicly engaged scholarship is not rocket science: it is more complex because it is about people as opposed to machines. It requires a different kind of *verstehen* that transcends positivism and is grounded in the lived experience of citizens, reflecting back to them their power to shape truth and the emancipatory possibilities of knowledge and discovery. Paulo Freire's seminal contribution to knowledge has been to translate this philosophical vision into a manifesto for practical pedagogical action among the oppressed in society.

Ultimately, the civic and community engagement movement in 21st-century higher education is a narrative of shared agency, in which academics, students and citizens in communities become co-creators of knowledge in an act of deliberative engagement that both challenges and potentially changes the academy. This third mission of the university is informed by the dual objective of democratising the university and the democratisation of knowledge. Civic and community engagement depends on a mutually beneficial collaboration between the university and civil society, in which knowledge is shared with the public. It is also a reciprocal process of shared understanding, open enquiry and knowledge, based on mutual respect. That is the acid test of the universities' democratic commitment to promoting social justice.

John Saltmarsh and Matthew Hartley, in their edited book *"To Serve a Larger Purpose": Engagement for Democracy and the Transformation of Higher Education* (2011), broadly interpret civic and community engagement as 'democratic engagement', which means seeking the public good *with* people rather than *for* people. It is based, in their view, on a genuinely dialogical relationship with communities, as opposed to a public relations exercise. The realignment of reciprocal processes is at the core of the 'democratic engagement' vision. However, Saltmarsh and Hartley pessimistically conclude that the paradigm shift towards more innovative practices, new epistemologies, changed pedagogies and curriculum reform required to realise a third mission for the university is not supported by the institutional norms and staff recognition required to implement civic and community engagement. Yet, arguably, this systemic change is necessary to negotiate the social conditions of the postmodern world, in which the university is challenged by multicultural society to adapt to a new social and cultural reality that embraces ethnic and gender equality and deindustrialisation that is undermining the economic conditions of the traditional White working class.

Of a discussion in the US between 31 academic leaders in civic and community engagement, known as the Kettering meeting, Saltmarsh and Hartley (2011: 5) reported that 'while not everyone at the meeting characterized civic engagement in higher education as stalled, there was general agreement that the movement has unclear goals, fragmented efforts, and is met with a predominant ideology in the academy that acts contrary to overtly civic aims'. There is a wide variety of activities involved in civic engagement, which encompass student volunteering, diversity initiatives, adult education and widening participation. A key institutional challenge is that these civic engagement activities are 'highly fragmented and compartmentalised' (Saltmarsh and Hartley, 2011: 6). On the other hand, the spontaneity and independence of these activists give them strength, vitality and authenticity. It also empowers civic-engagement actors to explore democratic epistemologies because they are from the university but not part of its corporate reality.

During recent decades universities across the world have embraced civic and community engagement as a strategic priority in order to increase their social impact and tackle challenges that matter to local communities. In Ireland the potential benefits of civic engagement have been highlighted in a series of policy documents, including the *National Strategy for Higher Education to 2030,* known as the Hunt Report. This innovative report identifies civic and community engagement as one of the three core functions of the university, in addition to teaching and learning. In the era of the elite 'research university' this was an important statement of democratic values. The Campus Engage Charter signed by all the Irish universities provided an institutional commitment to the implementation of this additional or third mission. The Irish Universities Association through its National Steering Committee on Campus Engagement has overseen the implementation of the Hunt Report's recommendations on civic and community engagement. Student volunteering became a central focus of the civic and community engagement third mission in Ireland.

Some commentators have worried about 'civic apathy' on campuses, notably among students (Bok, 2006). At UCC we carried out the most comprehensive survey of student volunteering in Ireland to date, involving an online survey of over 2,000 students, as well as in-depth interviews and focus groups with 11 students. Most of the survey respondents (71 per cent) were female, and women made up the majority of both volunteers (73 per cent) and non-volunteers (69 per cent). The report, entitled *Making a Difference* (Powell et al, 2018), set out to explore students' experiences of volunteering. We looked in particular at how students find out about volunteering opportunities; patterns of volunteering during term time; the areas in which students volunteer; the motives and benefits associated with volunteering; and the challenges that student volunteers encounter. We also set out to identify barriers to student volunteering. The key findings of the research on student volunteering at UCC included the following:

- 46 per cent of the 2,038 students surveyed said they had volunteered in the previous six months.
- Over 58 per cent of the students surveyed reported that they volunteered on an 'occasional basis', while 37 per cent volunteered for 'occasional or one-off events'.
- Over the previous month, 21 per cent volunteered for 1–3 hours and 36 per cent for 4–9 hours.
- 'Word of mouth' is the primary way students find out about volunteering opportunities.
- Student volunteers are engaged directly with people across youth work (40 per cent); sports/exercise/outdoor activities (29 per cent); and tutoring/supporting learning (22 per cent).

- Comparatively few students are involved in conservation and environmental causes (7 per cent) or animal welfare (6 per cent).
- Most students became involved in volunteering before they came to UCC.
- Altruistic motivations are commonly cited as the reason why students volunteer (85 per cent) – the desire to 'give something back' and 'help others'.
- Time commitment is the main challenge to participation in volunteering. Academic work, part-time jobs and, in some cases, a lengthy commute to and from the university make volunteering challenging and can curtail participation.
- Offering 'more one-off volunteering opportunities' and increasing 'publicity and awareness of volunteering' are the most important means by which the university can encourage volunteering.
- The majority (63 per cent) of student volunteers were 'very satisfied' with their experience and one-third 'somewhat satisfied'. Only 1 per cent of respondents said they were dissatisfied.

Student volunteering is clearly a vibrant activity in terms of community engagement. However, participation is very much skewed towards female students (73 per cent in the UCC survey). Its orientation is significantly directed at children and young people. There are real barriers that constrain student volunteering, including the need to engage in part-time work and long commutes due to high city rents. It suggests that concerns about 'civic apathy' among the student population may not be as severe as imagined, but student volunteering is unlikely to alter the dynamics of social exclusion and endemic poverty.

Cultural empowerment, adult education and public libraries

At the beginning of a new millennium in which Europe and America are being transformed into multicultural societies, the culture-blindness of a purely economic paradigm – embodied in the concept of the knowledge economy – has become increasingly obvious. The decline of social democracy is symptomatic of the complex challenges that confront the welfare state in the 21st century, where the politics of redistribution is being challenged by identity politics based on gender, ethnicity, disability, sexuality, age and so on, that reflect the world of accelerating diversity. These citizens are seeking greater respect and recognition. In this context a new paradigm in progressive politics has emerged, which conceptualises social justice in cultural and symbolic terms. It is grounded in social patterns of representation, interpretation and communication. The social philosopher, Nancy Fraser (1997: 71), cites, by way of illustrating its discursive meaning, several examples of the cultural and symbolic dynamics of social exclusion:

- Cultural domination – being subjected to patterns of interpretation and communication that are associated with another culture and are alien and/or hostile to one's own.
- Non-recognition – being rendered invisible via authoritative representational, communication and interpretative practices of one's culture.
- Cultural disrespect – being routinely maligned or disparaged in stereotypic cultural representations/or everyday interaction.

Manifestly, in a multicultural society, neither an economic nor a cultural paradigm is in itself adequate in terms of explaining social injustice. The rise of the far right, advocating White, Christian and nationalist values, reflects a worrying challenge to democracy tolerance and civility. Multiculturalism and immigration are at the top of the right's professed agenda of concerns. Clearly, social justice needs to be pursued in both economic and cultural forms, simultaneously augmenting greater redistribution and recognition in society.

Education, which operates in the cultural rather than the economic domain of society, has much to contribute to the promotion of remedies to injustice and intolerance through empowerment and greater cultural respect and social recognition for minorities. Arguably, in postmodern conditions, social citizenship, as the axis of the welfare state philosophy (Marshall, 1973), is increasingly influenced by educational participation based upon a generative lifelong strategy that empowers and informs simultaneously.

Education meets the liberating needs of the socially excluded through the process of empowerment. Cultural empowerment is per se the antidote to social exclusion and is closely associated with adult education and critical pedagogy. Paulo Freire has offered a model. It has four basic characteristics, according to Denis O'Sullivan (1993: 195–196):

- *instrumental* – knowledge, communication and literacy skills;
- *expressive* – confidence, assertiveness, freedom from dependency;
- *critique* – the capacity to question the society in which one lives and engage in a critical reading of reality;
- *activist* – the motivation to take action to change society in the light of critical awareness.

Paulo Freire, as discussed earlier, views what he calls 'conscientisation' as the core of cultural empowerment. He defines conscientisation as an activity through which oppressed people develop critical consciousness, expose myths and ideologies that disempower them, and act according to their own new critical awareness so that they can attain their rightful positions in the world from which they have been unjustly excluded. Conscientisation and empowerment are, therefore, essentially one and the same thing. However, it is a complex process, as Drudy and Lynch (1993: 272) have noted:

> The empowerment of oppressed groups, however, is not by adult educators to those who are oppressed. Rather, it is a more subtle, and indeed slower, process whereby people come to an awareness of their oppression and develop the ability to do something about it. … All that an adult education process can do is to give people the opportunity to develop the critical capacity that generates empowerment.

Empowerment-based adult education initiatives are not new. The have been practised for many years. Professor Tom Lovett (1989: 42) in a seminal essay summarised the history of adult education and the working-class:

> Attempts to reach the workers, the working class, with relevant education forms is part of the social history of the 'common people' and reaches across nations and back into the beginnings of the industrial revolution. … Those involved in this 'movement' were committed to removing the social, cultural and economic barriers to a more just society. They believed that adult education had a vitally important role to play in this process of peaceful social change. However, although many of these historical initiatives were concerned to break down the barriers between education and 'real life', between education and action, they maintained very different ideologies, very different views about the nature of injustice, poverty, oppression and the means to remove it.

The origins of adult education are diverse. In Italy, for example, the Societa Umanitaria de Milan, founded in 1893, was among the leaders in Europe. It convened the first European conference on unemployment, created a large People's Theatre, established the first adult-education unions, created the Italian People's Universities, promoted People's Libraries, all before 1910 (Lovett, 1989). The Italian Marxist philosopher, Antonio Gramsci (1971: 330), was supportive of the People's Universities' 'enthusiasm and strong determination to attain a higher cultural level and a higher conception of the world' among the working class, but critical of the philosophical and organisational limitations of the of People's Universities initiative.

Public libraries also became a major information and knowledge source for the general population, often locked out of elite universities. Moira Donegan (2022), in a paean of praise for the public library asserts that:

> the majesty of library buildings is matched only by the nobility of their purpose. The public library does not make any money; it does not understand its patrons as mere consumers, or even as a revenue base. Instead it aspires to encounter people as minds. The public library exists to grant access to information, to facilitate curiosity, education, and

inquiry for their own sake. It is a place where people can go to pursue their aspirations and their whims, to uncover histories or investigate new scientific discoveries.

Robert Putnam and Lewis Feldstein (2004: 4) have described local libraries as 'the heartbeat of the community'. An official Irish report entitled *Our Public Libraries:* Inspiring *Connection and Empowering Communities* (Government of Ireland, 2022: 7) observed: 'A modern and well-resourced public library contributes to the social, economic and cultural well-being of communities. The public library supports people and communities through its civic presence. It provides information, supports learning and culture and is the focal point for a growing number of public services.'

Support for public libraries varies between countries. Some, including the US and UK, have imposed severe cuts on public libraries in recent times. Others have enhanced the role of public libraries, notably Norway, Finland and Ireland; targeting reading, musical learning and digital literacy, while promoting the library's role as a public space (Government of Ireland, 2022). The new Oodi Central Library in Helsinki is a testament to Finland's commitment to put libraries at the cultural centre of Finnish society. *Our Public Libraries* (Government of Ireland, 2022) outlines the values of public libraries as promoting: trust and integrity; equality; creativity; quality and excellence; innovation and flexibility; inclusion and democratic dialogue.

Local populations, from children to senior citizens, over generations have been able to avail of free access to books and latterly digital sources of knowledge in the public library system. This is a major democratic achievement. Unfortunately, as noted, some Anglo-Saxon countries' austerity policies have particularly targeted libraries, many of which have been forced to close in recent decades, as the welfare state is gradually dismantled. This is a cultural tragedy, denying many citizens the opportunity to educate themselves through free access to knowledge. It also diminishes the availability of cultural spaces for self-improvement, interpersonal connection and the empowerment of communities essential to an informed civil society.

Donegan (2022) laments the enforced decline of public libraries in the US as victims of austerity cuts that undermine access to knowledge and public information, which are essential to the exercise of democracy:

> If the public library did not already exist as a pillar of civic engagement in American towns and cities, there is no way we would be able to create it. It seems like a relic of a bygone era of public optimism, a time when governments worked to value and edify their people, rather than punish or extract from them. In America, a country that can often be cruel to its citizens, the public library is a surprising kindness. It

is an institution that offers grace and sanctuary, a vision of what our country might one day be.

In an era in which social media has enabled anti-democratic politicians to create a 'post-truth society', the public library remains a repository for citizens to inform themselves objectively about what is true and what is false.

There are, clearly, countries where libraries still prosper. In Ireland there are 330 local public libraries and 31 mobile libraries serving a population of 5 million citizens, 800,000 of whom are library members. These members borrowed 10,756,742 items during 2022, ranging from books to musical instruments and equipment, newspapers, wi-fi and musical recordings (Government of Ireland, 2022). The local public library is both a cultural centre and a place to meet, to work, learn and play (Hunt, 2023). Ireland's Public Library Strategy 2018–2022 aims to ensure a free library service across society – empowering, connecting and informing citizens with access to information and cultural products and skills. Public libraries are vital forms of cultural empowerment that connect with local communities. Adult education shares this community outreach agenda that seeks to incorporate all sections of society.

In Britain the association between adult education and the working class was championed by the National Council of Labour Colleges (NCLC) founded in 1921. According to Lovett (1989: 45), the NCLC had strong ties with social movements and pursued a 'rigid Marxist teaching approach'. In contrast, the more liberal Workers' Educational Association followed a pluralist philosophy and continues to be a highly successful organisation, offering 8,000 courses in 1,800 community venues in 2015/16. However, a recent policy brief compiled by the UK-based Institute of Fiscal Studies (IFS) concluded that, excluding higher education: 'Total spending on adult education and apprenticeships fell by 38% in real terms between 2010–11 and 2020–21, with a 50% fall in spending in classroom-based adult education' (Sibieta et al, 2022: 2). The IFS policy brief noted that, despite commitments to restore funding by 2024/25, the total spend will be 25 per cent lower than 2010/11. This policy will also include the development of 'skills bootcamps', which suggests an authoritarian emphasis on 'tough love' (Sibieta et al, 2022: 21). The British government has pledged a 'new' Lifelong Loan Entitlement to cover all adults over 18 years for four years' education, which was primarily an attempt to make the existing system more transparent (Sibieta et al, 2022: 28–29). The philosophical approach adopted by 21st-century policy makers in the UK is very different from the empowering agenda of adult-education pioneers, notably the introduction of 'skills bootcamps', which has a penal resonance.

Ruskin College, Oxford, was founded in 1899 with the objective of providing educational opportunities for the excluded and disadvantaged. The college has a strong personal and social transformational agenda and continues to prosper. It is a model for good practice. Many universities established adult-education departments during the 20th century, offering certificate and diploma courses that manifestly benefited working-class communities. Social justice provided the philosophical framework, sometimes leading to accusations of Marxist sympathies, meaning they were regarded as social heretics. At a practical level, adult-education initiatives also clearly need to be underpinned by pathways towards participation onto degree-level programmes through effective credit accumulation and transfer (CAT) systems, funded tuition, part-time study, evening classes and significant financial support from universities as alternatives to direct entry from school.

In reality, a paradigm shift in thinking about the university as a social and cultural construct is required. This has been culturally resisted because it could potentially change the composition of the university student population and reverse social inequality, which is currently shaped by the meritocratic system of elite university admissions based on school examination results that is widely, if paradoxically, viewed by the public as fair. A civic university model by definition belongs to civil society and is engaged in the life of its locality. However, a meritocratic culture embeds social elitism. It also puts up barriers with local communities. Mature student participation (as noted earlier) has gone into decline in Ireland, falling well below its targets. Similarly, the impact of an elitist meritocratic model in the UK has resulted in the number of (mostly mature) students on sub-degree courses or enrolled in apprenticeship training plummeting by almost 47 per cent from around 2.8 million in 2010 to 1.5 million in 2020, resulting in a net decline of 30 per cent in the number of adult learners starting qualifications in 2020 (Sibieta et al, 2022).

Adult education arguably needs to be fully financially resourced by universities if it is to avoid accusations of tokenism and bad faith as opposed to genuine civic engagement. The civic university is defined by the authenticity of its engagement with the community that exists beyond its walls, which are both physical and psychological. Its mission arguably needs to be transformative in the interests of achieving social justice, drawing upon the adult-education initiatives of the past to forge a democratic future. That involves building on the shoulders of giants from the past – whose philosophical beliefs were diverse but driven by a shared passion for social justice and civil rights – as the basis of an egalitarian society. Knowledge in the view of these enlightened adult-education activists belonged to everybody in a democracy, however heretical that proposition appeared to social conservatives and economic elites. Adult education in the spirit of Paulo Freire promised to set the oppressed free. It provided an alternative to meritocratic values and elitist higher education. That is its inspirational legacy. Its liberating influence was not restricted to Europe.

Key examples of adult-education initiatives in North America include the Antigonish Community in Canada and the Highlander project in the US, which played an influential motivational role in the development of the Civil Rights movement in the 1960s.

The Antigonish movement in Nova Scotia was based on the principles of adult education, co-operatives, microfinance and rural community development. It was philosophically influenced by the British Workers' Education Association, Danish folk schools and Swedish study circles. Founded in the late 1920s, the Antigonish initiative was led by two dynamic Catholic priests, Fr Jimmy Tompkins and Fr Moses Coady, and associated with the Department of Extension Studies at St Francis Xavier University. Several of the earliest community educators in Ireland were trained at the Antigonish Community. The Highlander Folk School in Tennessee was founded in 1932 by activist Myles Horton, educator Don West and Methodist minister James A. Dombrowski. It is now called the Highlander Research and Education Center. The Highlander Folk School was hugely influential in shaping adult education in the American South, notably in the disadvantaged Appalachian region. It was the target of violence and suppression by anti-communists and opponents of civil rights.

Both the Antigonish and Highlander projects have been influential in shaping international thinking and practice in relation to adult education and empowerment (Lovett, 1989). In the 21st century, as neoliberalism transforms the educational agenda increasingly in the image of welfare productivism, support for transformative adult education initiatives has waned because these humanistic projects challenge market values and the hegemony of corporate capitalism in a polarised world.

Widening participation: policy, practice and voices of disadvantaged students

The policy context of widening participation: a silver bullet?

The post-war expansion of higher education can be viewed as one of the great achievements of the welfare state that opened up higher education to mass participation. In 1999 the then UK prime minister, Tony Blair, launched the widening participation agenda, which aimed to increase the university participation rate to 50 per cent by 2010. In a subsequent speech on 23 May 2011, Blair asserted: "Our top priority has always been education, education, education." It was, on the face of it, not just a rhetorical mantra of aspirations but a far-sighted policy initiative. The UK Universities and Colleges Admissions Service (UCAS), in a report entitled *What Happened to the Covid Cohort?*, defined widening participation and access as being about ensuring future generations have equal opportunities to access and succeed in higher education. UCAS views its role in widening participation as supporting students in their aspirational choices. However, UCAS (2020) notes in relation to the Conservative government's levelling-up opportunities agenda that at the current rate of the progress required to deliver social justice, the gap between advantaged and disadvantaged students will not be closed for many decades.

At the core of the widening-participation agenda is the objective of achieving equality of access for students who come from disadvantaged backgrounds with their more affluent peers. At least that is the theory. Successive British administrations have continued to support this expansionary policy of widening participation. In 2020/21 there were 2.66 million students attending UK higher education institutions, which were record numbers, despite the negative impact of Brexit on EU students' participation (Bolton, 2022). Widening participation in England and Wales, however, is now constrained by very expensive student loans and fees of £9,000. 2012 saw a decline in student applications due to the cost of fees, but numbers rebounded in 2013 (Bolton, 2022). In 2016 maintenance grants were scrapped by the Conservative government. Student accommodation costs have reportedly risen by 60 per cent (Hall, 2021). The problem of high costs is compounded by questions of value for money. Diane Reay (2017: 123) observes: 'The new opportunities for the working class have diminished value because they are studying at low-ranking universities with too many students like themselves who are perceived to be low status.' She concludes (p 125): 'Widening access to a very unequal, hierarchical field is a very crude response to an intractable problem that requires a much more sophisticated, morally informed solution.' In 2022 the Conservative government announced that it wanted to introduce minimum entrance requirements to prevent students who do not pass English and maths GCSE from entering university. This would likely further restrict poor, ethnic minority and migrant students' participation in higher education in England.

Widening participation is clearly a social and moral imperative. Many worry about traditional academic standards as grade inflation has taken off. Some traditionalists blame widening participation for lowering academic standards, but it is hard to deny that the commodification of degrees, financialisation and chronic underfunding of the university system from the public purse is at the root of the problem. Competition does not work as an organisational model for humanistic institutions, including universities, hospitals, charities, cooperatives and cultural organisations.

At a human level, the commodification of knowledge is open to serious criticism. Jonathan Zimmerman (2020: 36), in reference to the US, regards marketised 'for profit' developments in higher education as a 'scandal' that has widened the gap between the privileged elite and the disadvantaged, who face spiralling debts: 'America's overall student debt burden recently topped $1.5 trillion, exceeding our collective debt on credit cards.' He further estimates that 22 per cent of student loan borrowers in the US are in default, which he calculates is higher than the rate among home owners. Zimmerman (2020: 36) goes on to say: 'The debt burden falls most heavily on people of colour, especially women. Four out of five African Americans graduate college with debt; on average they carry 70% more debt than white students do.'

In the era of Black Lives Matter, this intersectional form of discrimination and disadvantage highlights the structural inequalities of the US higher-education system and the perils of engaging in widening-participation initiatives without adequate support from the welfare state. In a welcome initiative President Biden's Higher Education Relief Fund is investing billions of dollars in historically under-resourced colleges and universities. If this is followed up with debt relief on tuition fees for students attending these institutions, which President Biden has sought to enable in law, it will represent a big step forward in terms of widening participation.

Tressie McMillan Cottom (2018: 11) in a study of the higher-education sector in the USA, ironically entitled *Lower Ed: The Troubling Rise of For-Profit Colleges in the New Economy*, argues that the 'education gospel' is encouraging more people to pursue higher education, involving 'personal sacrifices' and financial risk-taking, as a 'moral choice':

> Based on the education gospel, we increasingly demand more personal sacrifices from those who would pursue higher education: more loans, fewer grants; more choices, fewer options; more possibilities, more risk of failing to attain any of them. We justify that demand by pointing to the significant return in higher wages that those with higher education qualifications enjoy. And we imply this wage premium will continue in a 'knowledge economy', where twenty-first-century jobs will require everyone to have some post-secondary education to do highly cognitive work. The gap between the education gospel and the real options available to people – those who need a priest but instead get a televangelist – is how we wind up with *Lower Ed*.

McMillan Cottom critiques the expansion of requirements for more and more credentials in a changing labour market – 'the new economy' – where 'cognitive work' has geometrically expanded, with costs being displaced from the welfare state onto individuals and families. She views 'Lower Ed' as an organised widening-participation strategy designed to commodify participation by the poor in higher education and entrench social inequality between the privileged and the disadvantaged.

Writing in a British context Lee Elliot Major and Stephen Machin (2018: 87–90), in *Social Mobility and Its Enemies*, reach a similarly pessimistic viewpoint: 'The education system has expanded and upgraded with the aim of widening opportunities and developing talent from all backgrounds. Yet at every turn the privileged have found new ways to distinguish their offspring in the academic stakes' – including cheating in admissions, relocating their home to neighbourhoods with high-performing schools and private tuition. They call these 'middle-class manoeuvres'. Major and Machin (2018: 88) conclude: 'Widening inequalities in income and inequalities in education reinforce each other in an endless feedback loop from one generation to the next.' This dismal observation is undoubtedly not unique to the UK, given rising social inequalities in an increasingly globalised world.

The coronavirus pandemic has normalised online learning in higher education, compounding social inequalities and throwing them into sharper relief. Some students were made homeless. Others returned to homes that lacked computers and wi-fi, or simply the space to study (Zimmerman, 2020: 36). This is the pandemic experience of educational disruption that is particularly impacting on disadvantaged students and debasing their learning opportunities at an unsustainable cost for the individual. The intersectional nature of the relationship between discrimination and disadvantage highlights the experience of social and ethnic groups, particularly exposed to the coronavirus. The mounting of debt that lies behind the coronavirus disruption of the education system is a salutary comment on the shortcomings of the widening-participation strategy that lacks adequate investment. If widening participation is to succeed it will need more investment by the welfare state targeted at the poor and marginalised. It also involves affirmative action that positively discriminates in favour of under-represented social groups.

Public education, desegregation and affirmative action

In 1903, sociologist and civil-rights activist W.E.B. Du Bois (1868–1963) predicted that the most important issue in the 20th century would be the 'color line'. Segregation and desegregation have convulsed US society during the 20th and 21st centuries. In a landmark decision in Brown v Board of Education in 1954 the US Supreme Court declared, 'in the field of public education the doctrine of separate but equal has no place'. This judgement represented in principle the outlawing of segregation in schools and universities. The reality was very different in terms of integration, with 'busing' children between districts becoming highly contentious. In practice, Appiah and Gates (2005: 711) have commented:

> most schools remained segregated, not because the law required it, but because the neighbourhoods they served were racially homogenous. In the South, racial segregation increased when whites removed their children from public schools in response to court ordered integration.

As a result, in Southern communities the public schools were legally integrated, but often only blacks attended them, while whites attended private schools.

The reality was Black students remained segregated because they lived in racially segregated areas, known as ghettos. Multicultural society remains an elusive ideal in many societies (Goldberg, 1994; Willet, 1998). Diversity, affirmative action and access initiatives have emerged in higher education as strategies for promoting greater representation from minority groups.

The origins of affirmative action date from the US in the 1960s. It was a multicultural initiative in positive discrimination intended to enhance the rights of under-represented minority groups in higher education and employment to remedy the effects of past discriminations, particularly in relation to race, ethnicity and gender. From the start, affirmative-action policies were controversial and contested by some who viewed them as a threat to White people – White males in particular. Critics argued that it was unfair to compensate for past discriminations against minority groups by discriminating against other groups in the present. They dubbed affirmative action as 'reverse discrimination' in order to emphasise that it was 'unfair'. Proponents of affirmative action countered by arguing the only way to achieve a just and inclusive society was through affirmative action based on equal rights of participation that seek to address the wrongs of the past. The campaign against affirmative action was successful, initially in California where both the University of California and the state were forced to abandon this social inclusion policy (Appiah and Gates, 2004). In 2023 the US Supreme Court ruled against affirmative action programmes at Harvard University and the University of North Carolina, which it is feared could lead to a sharp drop in Black and Latin American students.

Widening participation in practice: disadvantaged students voice their experiences

Anthony Abraham Jack (2019: 38–39), in his widely acclaimed book *The Privileged Poor,* argues that the struggles of disadvantaged students continue long after their arrival on campus:

> [T]he sense of alienation and difference often started before they arrived on campus. And even after they had unpacked their suitcases, found shortcuts to different buildings, and gotten to know their classmates, it did not always go away, or even diminish. For many it grew. In my conversations with them, they highlighted the differences – cultural, racial, and socio-economic – between themselves and their fellow students.

Access, in Jack's view, does not equate with acceptance of diversity and the right to equality of recognition on campus. Jack (2019: 11) declares: 'I call these students, who are both poor and unfamiliar with this new world, the *doubly disadvantaged*.' Financial issues and needing to work are constant pressures experienced by disadvantaged students, who often have families at home that they need to care for, further eroding their time for study. Is Anthony Abraham Jack's pessimistic vision universal or is it specific to the exclusionary value systems embedded in the campus cultures of elite third-level institutions? Are civic universities more inclusive? We sought to find out by asking HEAR students at UCC about their expectations and experiences. Students were asked a series of questions about their hopes and fears before starting their studies, their experiences and impressions of higher education, and how they felt now. Their responses often centred on social and personal issues, academic transitions and pedagogy.

Transitions to university: social and personal issues

Making new friends

Most of the young people in our study did not know anyone at university when they first arrived and were worried about the prospect of making new friends. Previous research suggests that, while making new friends may be a concern for all new entrants, it is likely to be more so for students from under-represented groups because many are not accompanied by friends from school or their wider social circle (Keane, 2009). One participant in the interviews, now a second-year student, recalled her anxiety about going to the orientation day on her own and her relief at meeting someone she recognised from her neighbourhood. Her determination to not let him out of her sight during the day was recounted with a touch of humour, but nonetheless indicative of the social anxiety that many students experience even before they start their studies at university: "He was on my course for the orientation day and I was like, 'Stay with me. If you move out of my sight you're dead! Just stay with me!'" Another HEAR student described his unsuccessful attempts to induce his friends to apply to his choice of university so he would not be on his own: "I didn't know anybody – none of my friends came here. I tried to get some of them to come to UCC just so I wouldn't be the only one there. There was a friend who was interested in it, but he didn't get the points, so I ended up being the only one."

Once at university, HEAR students initially felt a sense of isolation and of 'feeling lost'. Some felt disorientated by the size of the campus and the distance between different lecture rooms. Moreover, the number of students in the lecture halls made it difficult for young people to forge connections with their fellow students. This was particularly the case for those in larger faculties, such as arts or science.

While trying to make new friends was seen as a daunting prospect by some HEAR students, it is important to note that there were variations within the group. A few young people we interviewed from the HEAR group said they had looked forward to meeting new people at university and made friends quickly and easily. In the following example Teresa attributes this social success to her outgoing personality:

> 'Well, I settled in really fast. I made friends pretty fast. But I'm pretty outgoing and I would talk to anyone. I wouldn't be afraid to go over and start a conversation with somebody and say, 'I don't know anyone …' so I think that kind of makes life a bit easier for me … I love meeting new people anyway. I'm a bit of an adventurer. I like going to new places and I'll make friends wherever I go.'

For most students the process of making friends was more gradual. Participants found the HEAR programme orientation event – whereby participating students spend three days on campus before term begins – to be very helpful in meeting other students. They also made friends and got involved in student life through clubs and societies. By the end of the first year all of the students we interviewed had developed a group of friends, although it was clear that these networks varied, both in size and stability. John, for example, had made a large group of friends through his course and participation in a range of extra-curricular activities, particularly sports. On the other hand, Joanne commuted from her family home into the university every day and had fewer opportunities to participate in non-academic activities.

Fitting-in to higher education

The issues of 'fitting-in', identity and personal agency are recurring themes in the literature on widening participation. British scholars have examined the challenges faced by working-class students in the *habitus* of the university campus (Reay, 2017; Coulson et al, 2017). In her personalised account described in *Miseducation,* Diane Reay (2017: 153), asserts: 'What I want to convey here is that, far from university being the beginning of "a new better middle-class life" for the working classes, as often implied in the social mobility rhetoric, it is much more often another stage in a difficult and painful struggle to be accepted in middle-class contexts.' In similar vein, Coulson et al (2017) recounted the negative experiences, such as anxiety, encountered by working-class students in their relationships with their middle-class counterparts. Reay (2017: 153) concludes that there is a complex intersectional dynamic involved in these encounters: 'Relationality raises issues not only about the relationships between classes but also of how different aspects of identity coexist within class. ... Social classes are intersected not only by gender, ethnicity, sexuality, and dis/ability but also by differing class fractions.'

In the UCC research into non-traditional students at university, participants spoke about coming from poorer families and communities, and the challenges they faced coming to college. Their expressions of surprise and delight that they had actually made it ("It was such an honour to even be here coming from where I live") indicate that they did not experience the sense of 'university entitlement' often found among middle-class cohorts (Crozier et al, 2008; Reay, 2017). At the same time there was little to suggest in the interviews that students felt in some way excluded on grounds of social class. Indeed, some enthusiastic exponents of student life were those from the most disadvantaged backgrounds. Significantly, several participants in the UCC study mentioned feeling out of place in their *own* communities and schools because of their interest in education and career aspirations. Annemarie, for example, recalled her sense of frustration at her school friends' lack of interest in education and their disruptive behaviour in class:

'My friends, none of them were interested in study whatsoever, they just about did their Leaving Certificate. But ever since first year they knew I really enjoyed school and I love studying. They knew it. And I remember in history class – loved history –everybody would be talking and stuff and I'd sit down the back at my own table and like, "Everyone keep away from me, I am doing my own work". They'd all be talking in history and I'd stand up to them, like, "Shut up. I'm actually learning something", so they knew I was learning and there was nothing they could do to change my mind.'

Another student described herself as "standing out like a sore thumb" at home because her 'ambitions and dreams' were different from those of other young people she had grown up with. Moreover, several students said that one of the positive elements of university life was meeting with others who shared their aspirations and interests. For one student, issues of fitting in and identity were particularly complex. However, this arose not so much as a result of socio-economic background, but ethnicity, although the two are often interlinked. As a young woman from the Traveller community, Mary comes from one of the most chronically under-represented groups in higher education (HEA, 2015). Her family initially opposed her plans to go to university on the grounds she could face discrimination or she would lose touch with her Traveller roots. While her parents eventually came to terms with her plans – on condition she lived at home – other members of the family continued to have reservations. Despite a difficult start, Mary continued with her course and by the end of the first year had made a few friends and was enjoying her studies. From Mary's descriptions, however, it was clear that the different parts of her life were kept strictly separate. At university, Mary had not told her fellow students that she was a member of the Traveller community. Although she felt that students would be accepting, past experiences of discrimination had made her wary.

One of the interesting paradoxes emanating from the UCC research was that, while students initially missed their homes and communities, they also spoke favourably about the sense of anonymity experienced at university. Away from their familiar surroundings, some students reported a feeling of liberation whereby they could be themselves. Rachel, who described herself as coming from a "strict home", explained that, although she sometimes felt alone at university, she also felt she had developed as a person because of the experience. At home her sense of identity was very much bound up with those of her family and friends:

> 'You just get to develop and grow as a person ... I think sometimes when you are with family and you're with friends, you know it's about conformity. There's certain ways: you act a certain way all the time. Moving away from home, no one knew me here. I could do whatever I want and no one would actually know that 'oh that is out of character' or whatever. So it was a completely brand new slate. I could just be myself, you know. That is one of the best things about university, I think. And the independence is good as well: you get to grow as a person, completely separate from everyone else.'

In other instances, students described the liberating feeling of moving away from a small community to a city and university where no one knew them:

> 'Where I am from, it's like, you walk down the street, and if you are wearing a new pair of trousers there would be ten people talking about you, where here, no one cares. Do you know, you could walk down in a big yellow suit and no one would care – do you know? Everyone is just so accepting and I love that; it's brilliant.'

The point was reiterated by another student: "No one actually kind of cares. When you live in a small village, everyone just knows everything about everyone. When you're here no one cares and you can do what you want and no one cares."

Academic transition from school to university

So far, we have looked at the social and personal issues raised by students, in terms of their expectations and experiences at university. Another recurring theme concerned issues relating to the academic culture of the university – including class sizes, level of contact with teaching staff, focus on independent learning, systems of assessment and so forth. Previous studies suggest that non-traditional students have particular difficulties in transition to independent learning in higher education and reduced support from teaching staff, relative to school. According to Read et al (2003), students who come from backgrounds where there is little history of participation in higher education can find the culture particularly bewildering, and can lack the support and guidance that comes from having friends or family that that have been through the experience of university. Moreover, students from disadvantaged backgrounds often lack confidence in their ability to meet academic standards at university (Keane, 2011). In our UCC research we discovered that participants found some aspects of the academic transition challenging, particularly in relation to independent learning and reduced support from teaching staff, but they also welcomed the opportunity to focus on subjects at which they excelled (compared with the Leaving Certificate) and a system of assessment that was not focused on one final exam.

Concerns about academic standards at university versus school

Previous research suggests that non-traditional students in higher education are often unsure about their academic abilities (Reay et al, 2009). Even earlier experience of academic success may not compensate for the self-doubt 'that inevitably emerges when confronted with a totally unfamiliar educational field' (Reay et al, 2009: 1112). Our findings are broadly in line with earlier studies in this regard: for many students, uncertainty about their own ability was one of their main concerns before enrolling and during the first months at university. For example, one student (who regularly received high marks in school tests) told us: "I think my fears were maybe not being able for the information. Not being able for the classes." In a few cases, students who were accustomed to being at 'the top of the class' were nervous about competing with students from other schools, where they feared the standards might be very different:

> 'In my school I was top of the class, in most of my classes. And then when you come to university you have people from all over the country, even outside the country. And you don't know the standards. … Is the educational level that I am taking [at school] the same as everybody else? Because different schools have different levels, you know?'

Our findings here resonate with Reay et al (2009: 1103–1112), who reported that nearly all young people in their study experienced a 'crisis of confidence' on arriving at university and had to adjust from being 'academic stars' at school to being 'just one of many academically able students' at university. Although some of the students in our UCC study initially found the academic transition from school to university challenging, in the course of the first year they gained in confidence. Successfully completing coursework and exams provided an important boost to their academic confidence, as one student explained:

> 'You are jumping from a Level 5 [Leaving Certificate] to Level 8 [primary degree] and that was an immediate worry – the course would be a lot harder and the expectations a lot higher, and all that. But after I got my first few assignments back … they were all fairly good. So that kind of built up my confidence. That would be the only thing now that, before I came here that would have worried me – that there's a big gap between school and university. I realise now, if you put in the effort … you can bridge that, no bother. You have to put in a lot more work all right. But if you have an interest in it, you don't really mind.'

One of the most positive aspects of the transition from school to university, which is indicated in in the preceding extract, is that students can concentrate on subjects that interest them and for which they have an aptitude. A recurring theme in our UCC research was that, while the work may be more challenging at university relative to school, this is mitigated by the fact that students can focus on the subjects they enjoy. Rachel compared her experiences of study in school and at university: "[At university] you get to do something you love every day. I love science. I remember at school I hated maths, I absolutely detested maths. … Now you're just doing what you love. I love to wake up every morning, go to college and study science, so that is great."

In addition, some students commented that the system of continuous assessment at university – including a higher proportion of graded assignments and coursework, and modularisation (where exams are held at different points of the year) – was a far less stressful experience than the Leaving Certificate Examination, which is held at the end of secondary school. As one student pointed out: "I think the continuous assessment – you know, doing projects, doing assignments, presentations and things like that – they add up to a certain per cent of your overall grade, helps as well. It's not all solely based on one exam. … The Leaving Certificate – it's all on that exam."

Class sizes and contact with teaching staff

Similarly to Read et al (2003: 270), we found that some students were initially disconcerted by the focus on independent learning at university and the lack of supervision by lecturers compared with school or a further education college. (This change was particularly experienced by those students who had experienced a great deal of support and motivation from teachers.) Other students missed not only academic support and supervision but also the pastoral care of teachers who knew them at a personal level, as one student commented:

> 'Yes, it can be quite lonely. … You know, in secondary school, people actually cared about you. You could tell that teachers actually wanted you to do your homework, or, wanted you to succeed and talk to you. And if you got into an altercation at home, you had someone to talk to … you know, they'd care enough to be like, "You don't seem OK?" But I feel [at university] no one really gets to know you enough to come and talk to you. If you are a student that is getting [100 per cent] and then one day you get 30 per cent, the lecturer wouldn't come to you and say, "OK, what is wrong?", do you know what I mean? A teacher back then would have been like, "OK, it's not your usual. What is going on? Is everything OK?" But a lecturer, they just put it through a machine, they don't really care what you get. So you kind of feel sometimes kind of, "Ugh, I'm just by myself. It's me against the world".'

While some students reported that their lecturers were friendly and approachable, there were nonetheless restrictions on the level of contact, given the class sizes. Overall, our findings are in line with Reay et al's (2009) research at one English university, where students found it easier to fit in to the higher education ethos than they did at school.

Conclusion

Public education is a democratic process rooted in civil society. Schools are at the centre of many communities, providing vitally needed services as community facilities that go well beyond their educational remit. Schools are not simply pathways to higher education, where success or failure is defined by the competitive yardstick of access to university. They are community and cultural hubs that need to be fostered in order to empower local populations. Many universities also have a civic role as part of their defining mission through civic and community engagement and student volunteering. Adult education and public libraries have been a mainstay of public education in many societies, but are increasingly threatened by austerity policies, notably in the US and UK, where many public libraries have been shut.

Affirmative action emerged during the 1960s to redress the discriminations against excluded and oppressed citizens who have suffered discrimination and disadvantage over many centuries, notably ethnic minorities. It was struck down by the US Supreme Court in 2023. The outlook for diversity on university campuses looks bleak in the US. The court decision raises broader equality questions about diversity initiatives and social inclusion policies in the future across the Western world. What is fair? Does widening participation really open the higher-education system to equal participation by all students? Or is widening participation a policy chimera based on a jaded political slogan? Why is access to higher education more difficult to achieve for working-class students, minority ethnic people and people with disabilities? Is widening participation still politically feasible in an era when civil rights are under threat? What is the experience of students from disadvantaged backgrounds?

We found, on the basis of our interviews, participation by working-class students in higher education to be both empowering and liberating. However, it is important to note that students' impressions of social and academic culture at university were quite varied, and included both positive and negative comments. For, example the students often missed the level of support provided by teachers, but they appreciated being with students who shared their academic interests and career aspirations. Moreover, while many students initially experienced loneliness, by the end of the first year they had all formed a network of friends, though these appeared to vary in size and stability. In line with previous research, we found that students who lived on or near campus had more opportunities to socialise and participate in clubs and societies. None of the students raised concerns about 'fitting in' because of their socio-economic background, but issues were raised around ethnicity. Significantly, some students indicated that in certain respects, they felt more at home at university!

4

The psycho-politics of meritocracy: IQ + effort = merit?

The paradox of education and freedom

Paulo Freire (1972), in *Cultural Action for Freedom*, addresses the relationship between the oppression of the poor and the domination of power elites in society. In Freire's mind, education is freedom. *Cultural Action for Freedom* raises fundamental questions about the meaning of freedom and the role of education in the cultural empowerment of the silent masses of oppressed people in a divided world. Education in Freirean theory and praxis is a narrative of personal, cultural and social liberation. But there the complexity begins, as we have noted already in relation to access inequality, affirmative action and widening participation. Non-financial forms of wealth, available to the privileged affluent citizens in a meritocratic society – through unequal access to the acquisition of cultural capital and education credentials – empower individuals, define personal identity, promote self-esteem and embed in the public mind the myths of equality of opportunity and social mobility as truths. In a democracy we call it freedom.

Freedom is not available to everybody, however, at least not equally in democratic societies. In authoritarian regimes, such as present-day Afghanistan, there is little or no freedom for women, which includes the denial of education. Afghanistan is a traditional society under religious hegemony that favours gender separation at great cost to women's rights. Access to education for Afghan women is highly constrained because it potentially liberates women to be free citizens with equal rights and opportunities to their male peers. We are reminded of Freire's dictum about the importance of critical literacy as a guarantor of freedom. At the core of this political struggle about women's access to education, labour-market participation and civic activism in Afghanistan is the right to think and express an opinion of one's own, which is as important as the right to breath and food security for all people as human beings.

This chapter explores a competitive education system, where class, culture and wealth largely control access and progression on the ladder of opportunity in a meritocratic society, and asks who gets up the ladder, who is left behind and why. What are the implications for democratic and personal freedom? Is the popular belief in social mobility valid? The chapter argues three points. The first is that the contemporary narrative of meritocracy, based on equality of opportunity, is fundamentally undemocratic in political and social terms. We demonstrate that there are alternatives, which potentially are fairer in achieving educational equality. The second argument is that meritocracy exists because of its ideological utility. It promotes parental choice and traditional values, while enabling affluent families to advantage their children through private markets. But there is a fundamental cultural and social paradox. The metafiction of meritocracy continues to inform policy and has widespread public support because of its perceived fairness and objectivity even after its factual basis has been thoroughly discredited. The third argument is that a meritocratic society facilitates social mobility. We argue that social mobility is a myth that needs to be replaced by social justice in the interests of positive freedom.

The dark side of meritocracy and the hermeneutics of suspicion

The word 'meritocracy' was introduced into the political vocabulary in the late 1950s by the sociologist Michael Young in his book *The Rise of the Meritocracy*, which warned readers of the potential danger of a dystopian society built on the principle of merit. Meritocracy promotes the political fiction that, however humble your origins, with sufficient effort you can become part of the elite. Jo Littler (2018) regards meritocracy as one of the most prevalent cultural and social tropes of our time. It has purported to bring scientific methods of measurement to bear on social equality. Modern society had, it was claimed, learned how to measure children's intelligence through IQ tests and age-related tests (such as the UK 11+), enabling the stratification of children in schools according to their measured cognitive ability. Future opportunities for higher education and ultimate placement in the labour market was largely predetermined by these testing regimes – unless a private (fee-paying) pathway was available. Michael Young succinctly explained the meritocratic norm through an equation: IQ + effort = merit.

Pierre Bourdieu's intellectual contribution has challenged the concept of meritocracy on several grounds. The deconstruction of the meritocratic political fiction that IQ + effort = merit will enable working-class students to overcome the barriers that they confront and achieve the results they deserve is contained in Bourdieu's conceptualisation of inequality, as possessing both visible and invisible forms. The possession of cultural capital plays a vital role in facilitating students' progression through the education system. For example, students from disadvantaged backgrounds are severely impacted during the socialisation process in terms of academic development, in comparison with their more affluent counterparts, through different styles of parenting – middle-class 'concerted cultivation' versus working-class 'accomplishment of natural growth' (Lareau, 2011). Social capital enables students to make the connections that privilege them in entering and navigating the education system. Financial capital enables better-off parents to access education for their children in fee-paying schools and take grinds that enhances students' chances of getting into the university and onto the course of their choice. Postgraduate studies have become increasingly necessary in students' career progression. Fees are very high at this level, as universities seek to maximise revenue. Money is very important in gaining entry to a postgraduate degree, which often includes a vocational qualification. Finally, symbolic capital frames the learning project of schooling that advantages the better off, who are benefitting from 'concerted cultivation'. There is a very clear class divide underpinning educational opportunity in a meritocracy that other distinguished scholars and commentators have also critiqued.

Michael Sandel, celebrated Harvard philosopher and global public intellectual, powerfully critiques meritocracy in his influential book *The Tyranny of Merit* as a major policy failure of centre-left politicians, such as Bill Clinton, Tony Blair, Barack Obama and Hilary Clinton and their many Third Way imitators. He castigates them for championing a policy chimera and advocates the 'dignity of work', as an alternative. Sandel is concerned about the falling living standards of the working class and the resulting loss of self-esteem and public respect. Sandel (2021b) contends that the deceitful moralised rhetoric of meritocracy assumes the 'moral deservingness' of the privileged: 'What makes merit a kind of tyranny is the way it attributes deservingness to the successful.'

Michael Sandel concludes that 'meritocracy, like any "ocracy" is a mode of rule, a way of distributing income, power, wealth, opportunity, honour and social recognition. The principle of meritocracy, simply put, says that if chances are equal, the winners deserve their winnings'. In this revelatory interview (2021b) Michael Sandel is very concerned about the social and political consequences of meritocracy as a divisive influence:

> The growing awareness of the problems with meritocracy in recent decades is a direct result of the deepening divide between winners and losers. The divide has poisoned our politics and set us apart. This is partly to do with widening income and wealth inequality. But it has also to do with changing attitudes toward success. In this way, a seemingly attractive principle – that if chances are equal the winner deserves their winnings – by implication comes to mean that those who struggle and fall short don't.

Sandel's essential argument is that meritocracy has a built-in negativity that is both corrosive of the common good and social solidarity. In the *Harvard Gazette* Sandel (2021a) declares: 'In an unequal society, those who land at the top want to believe their success is morally justified. In a meritocratic society, this means the winners must believe they have earned their success through their talent and hard work.' He concludes damningly: 'Besides being self-deluding, such thinking is also corrosive of civic sensibilities. For the more we think of ourselves as self-made and self-sufficient, the harder it is to learn gratitude and humility. And without such sentiments, it is hard to care for the common good.'

Michael Sandel is challenging the atomisation and individualisation of society, originally promoted by Ronald Regan and Margaret Thatcher during the 1980s and subsequently adopted by the centre-left as a result of their acceptance of globalisation, neoliberalism and political abandonment of the traditional working class. The age of merit is an entrepreneurial world built on human agency, imagined in the language of 'winners' and 'losers' and the moral basis of 'success' built on individual effort, arguably at the expense of the disadvantaged other, inhumanly requiring the latter's acknowledgement of both personal and moral failure. This narrative of human progress largely ignores the structural challenges of globalisation, deindustrialisation and social inequality on poor people's lives and personal freedoms. Unsurprisingly, the working class subsequently moved their political allegiances to populist right-wing politicians espousing protectionist rhetoric, such as Donald Trump's 'Make America Great Again'(MAGA) campaign and the Brexit movement led by Boris Johnson in the UK.

Sandel (2020: 4) reminds us that the coronavirus pandemic has once again made us aware of our shared vulnerability and need for community and society as the foundations of a sustainable way of life, ironically dependent on the contradiction of 'social distancing'. We are assured that 'we are all in this together' because social solidarity has been embraced by the majority of citizens. However, Sandel (2020: 4–5) concludes it is a faux solidarity that rests on a 'moral paradox' of a toxic society deeply divided between the 'hubris' of winners and the 'resentment' of losers, observing 'if opportunities are truly equal, it means that those who are left behind deserve their fate as well', adding 'it helps explain why those left behind by globalization would become angry and resentful'. This resentment was illustrated by the emergence of sovereign citizen movements in 2022, involving protests in Ottawa, Paris and Wellington led by truck drivers, ostensibly against mandatory COVID-19 travel passes and public health measures, including vaccinations. It reflects a deeper libertarian sense of disillusionment with the hierarchical culture of state regulation, expert knowledge and scientific advice and guidance by an alienated minority, who do not feel they belong in a meritocratic world.

In an interview with *The Guardian* (Conman, 2020), provocatively entitled 'The populist backlash has been a revolt against the tyranny of merit', Sandel offers appropriately philosophical remedies suggesting a step change in society, policy and politics that envisages a new respect for those who lack higher-education credentials and a belated humility from the winners.

He comments: 'Humility is a civic virtue essential at this moment because it's a necessary antidote to the meritocratic hubris that has driven us apart.'

But is meritocracy really changing the world for the worse? George Packer (2021: 70) thinks so in relation to the American experience of meritocracy, commenting:

> After the 1970s, meritocracy began to look more and more like Young's dark satire. A system intended to give each new generation an equal chance to rise created a new hereditary class structure. Educated professionals pass on their money, connections, ambitions, and work ethic to their children, while less educated families fall further behind, with less and less chance of seeing their children move up. By kindergarten the children of professionals are already two years ahead of their lower-class counterparts, and the achievement gap is almost unbridgeable. After seven decades of meritocracy, the lower-class child is nearly as unlikely to be admitted to one of the top three Ivy League universities as they would have been in 1954.

Meritocracy, an intuitive concept based on the belief that the highest achievers in a competitive system should be entitled to the greatest rewards, has dominated Western thinking as a metanarrative of educational equality for over half a century. Is this elite hubris, as suggested by Michael Young, a dystopian satire of our times? What happens to those left behind, who lack affirmation for their achievements? They are made to feel shame for their purported individual lack of success in a meritocratic world and largely forgotten by society. Packer (2021: 7) comments: 'But it's this idea of fairness that accounts for meritocracy's cruelty. If you don't make the cut, you have no one and nothing to blame but yourself.' The social reality is that the decline of the trade-union movement and workers' rights, globalisation and automation have introduced fundamental precarity and uncertainty into working-class lives that is threatening democracy. As Donald Trump put it in a speech to the 2016 Republican National Convention: "These are the forgotten men and women of our country, and they are forgotten. But they are not going to be forgotten long. *I am their voice*."

However originally well-intentioned by the architects of the welfare state in terms of promoting social justice in modern society as an alternative to traditional hereditary elites, it is hard not to question meritocracy's aspirations in practice as a Sartrean form of 'bad faith' (self and group deception). We need to fundamentally question the 21st-century relevance of principle of merit as a policy instrument that purportedly enables upward movement on the metaphorical ladder – known as 'social mobility' in contemporary policy discourse. Diane Reay (2020: 405) comments on 'the damage the illusion of meritocracy inflicts on children and young people, but particularly those from working-class backgrounds'. She damningly argues: 'The consequences of the pretence of democracy are to be found in everyday practices' within the school and beyond the classroom in the designation of working-class schools 'as rubbish schools for rubbish learners'. The import of Professor Reay's analysis is that meritocracy is a dangerous illusion that undermines disadvantaged children by inventing a fantasy world of expectations. Young's satirical equation IQ + effort = merit captures the essence of Reay's point regarding the cruelly delusionary logic of meritocracy.

Meritocracy has also become the subject of public comment in Ireland. For example, Professor Kathleen Lynch (2020) published a thought-provoking article in *The Journal* entitled 'Class and wealth, not merit, are rewarded in Ireland's education system' in which she argues that 'merit is a myth':

> Because those from privileged schools and social backgrounds dominate the entry routes to elite programmes year-on-year (leading ultimately to elite jobs), inequalities are normalised; we take no notice of the patterns, they seem to legitimate. There are numerous studies that show that getting high grades and good degrees is heavily dependent on the money invested in a given child/adult over time. The educationally successful are disproportionately drawn from wealthier backgrounds because they have both the economic capital (money) and cultural capital (knowledge of how the education system works, and how and where to maximise competitive advantage for their own children).

Matthew Stewart (2018) accuses meritocracy of creating a new aristocracy in the US, encompassing 9.9 per cent of the population. Meritocracy was conceived at a time in the post-war years when approximately 5 per cent of the population entered higher education. Now up to half the population participate in some form of tertiary education, but the system has once again become stratified. That is the meritocratic paradox. Daniel Markovits in *The Meritocracy Trap* (2019) questions how a system intended to widen opportunity has achieved the opposite by creating a self-perpetuating elite. Meritocracy is arguably a version of what is called Plato's 'noble lie'. Plato propagated the concept of the 'noble lie' in ancient Greek society, which means a myth or untruth (often of a religious nature) promoted by elites in order to maintain social hierarchy.

Sam Friedman and Daniel Laurison (2019: 88), in their book *The Class Ceiling*, observe in relation to the seminal issue of myth and untruth contained in the meritocratic principle:

> The main principles of 'meritocracy' are often formalised by academics through the concept of 'human capital'. This is normally measured by calculating the sum of the individual's credentials, experience and

training, and is seen by many, especially in economics, as the key determinant of a person's productive capacity and, therefore, their earning potential. But one of the biggest problems with the human capital thesis is that it implies people operate in a vacuum, that their work life is cut off from outside influences and their career progression is driven only by their own skills, merits and actions. In other words it implies we live in an era of meritocratic individualism where success and failure are solely matters of personal responsibility.

The binary cultural code of meritocracy is to either succeed academically in a competitive society or submit to a life of uncertainty and precarity. It is each citizen's personal responsibility. Or is it? Libertarians regard this choice as the quintessence of freedom. Unfortunately, this individualistic vision of society decontextualises opportunity, abstracting it from the social reality of living in an unequal society.

Meritocracy is arguably the product of an asymmetric war of media and cultural representations belonging to the domain of a new 'semiotic democracy' (Buckingham, 2011: 33) in which the working class lose out to the more privileged middle class, who dominate the opportunity structure and its entry routes. In the UK, for example, a headline story in *The Guardian* (Adams, 2021) reported: 'The gap between private and state school A-level grades has grown to its widest in the modern era as part of a record-breaking set of results that also saw Black pupils and male pupils outperformed by their peers.' Why? The OECD report *Education at a Glance 2021* estimates that 'across the OECD countries, 20–24-year-old students are most commonly enrolled in tertiary education, typically long-cycle programmes, but not entirely. On average across the OECD countries, 29% of the male population in this age group and 37% of their female peers are enrolled in tertiary education'.

Clearly, a gender gap is opening up in relation to access to tertiary level education and this is an international trend. Increased participation by females is manifestly a positive development in terms of greater gender equality. However, this achievement is offset by structural inequalities constraining access for working-class people, frequently because of a lack of financial resources. Similarly, Black students, as referenced above by *The Guardian*, experience severe educational disadvantage. Other ethnic minorities, notably stigmatised groups such as Irish Travellers and Roma, are highly marginalised in the education system. Travellers are a particular focus in this study (see Chapter 7).

The parable of normal people

Sally Rooney is acclaimed as a voice of the millennial generation through her successful novels, *Conversations with Friends* (2017), *Normal People*

(2019) and *Beautiful World, Where are You* (2021). *Normal People* was adapted into a highly successful television series. Rooney is not just another talented Irish novelist, her political philosophy provides a radical cutting edge to her writing, sometimes controversially. She explores a world riven by social divisions between asset-poor youth and their asset-rich elders, renters versus landlords, workers versus bosses and rural versus urban life. Set at the beginning of the financial crash in 2008, *Normal People* narrates the cruel realities of contemporary capitalism in terms of personal biographies. It is a bleak time to come of age and make the transition to university. Yet the starkness of the lives of peers left behind in the desolate landscape of the west of Ireland illustrates the existential necessity of gaining a degree for survival (economic and psychological) in the 21st century.

The story is about a young woman, Marianne, from a rich background and Connell, a young man from a council estate in the rural west of Ireland. Connell's mother works as a cleaner in Marianne's affluent home. Marianne seamlessly makes the transition from school to an elite university, Trinity College Dublin. Connell obtains a place, based on his prodigious academic talent. The romance ends with Connell emigrating – the fate of many young Irish people during the economic crisis between 2008 and 2013. In Connell's case the future is less bleak because he has won a scholarship to study abroad.

Normal People is a counter-hegemonic narrative that challenges class assumptions about university access and the meaning of educational opportunity. The uncertainty and precarity of the novel's two central characters provides a penetrating critique of contemporary capitalism and its accelerating immiseration of young people's lives and futures, with elegant and brutal clarity. Class, as the principal mediator of opportunity, overshadows and ultimately destroys Marianne and Connell's millennial romance.

Models of educational equality

There are distinct ways of seeing the relationship between education and equality. All of them reflect divergent perspectives on the world. First, the dominant view in a meritocratic society is equality of opportunity, which devolves on the principle of merit and the notion of systemic fairness, in which everybody is in principle given an equal chance to succeed in a competitive process for a place in the social hierarchy. Second, there is the concept of opportunity pluralism, which advocates more diverse career pathways as an alternative to academic education. Third, there is the equality condition model arguing that everybody should be treated broadly the same in terms of life chances.

Equality of opportunity

The concept of equality of opportunity in education envisages a society where everybody has fair and equal access to education to the highest level commensurate with their ability and performance, regardless of their class, race, gender or religion. This anti-discriminatory principle is enshrined in Article 26 of the United Nations' *Universal Declaration of Human Rights* (1948), which asserts that 'everybody has a right to education … education shall be free at least in the elementary or fundamental stages … education shall be directed to the full development of the human personality'. Clearly, equality of opportunity in education is linked to the wider considerations of equality of opportunity in society, which makes its meaning in reality very complex and sometimes disputed. It also raises fundamental value issues in relation to how society views childhood itself, upon which society is broadly agreed in social policy objectives: the care and protection principle in welfare, and equality of opportunity in education.

Shields et al (2017: 1), in *The Stanford Encyclopedia of Philosophy* assert: 'It is widely accepted that educational opportunities for children ought to be equal'. This axiomatic democratic truth follows from two observations made by the article's authors about education and children. First, that education significantly influences a person's life chances in terms of labour market success, preparation for democratic citizenship, and general human flourishing. Second, children's life chances should not be fixed by the morally arbitrary circumstances of their birth, such as social class, race or gender. The authors revealingly add an important clarification that the principle of equal opportunity is the subject of substantial disagreement.

The ideological architects of the concept of equal opportunity linked it to the policy goal of creating a meritocratic society, theoretically based on fairness achieved through competitive entry into membership of the elite group in society. However, the philosophy of equality of opportunity has proven to be problematic in practice because of its lack of specificity, which its many critics view as an 'atmospheric ideal' that does not demand the fundamental redistribution of wealth and resources required to equalise society. Instead, the philosophy of equality of opportunity has replaced the hereditary aristocracy based on blood ties with a new aristocracy based on merit. Only the semiotics have been changed by meritocracy, according to its many critics (such as Sandel, Markovits, Reay, Littler and Lynch).

The semiotics of respect are, arguably, the key to unlocking the hidden socio-cultural meanings shaping the equality of opportunity debate. It is, as Bourdieu argues, essentially a class issue manifested through cultural discourse and social practice. Merit, normatively representing the ideal of fairness, arguably camouflages the interplay between privilege and disadvantage in a competitive race for positioning in a pyramidal social structure. The justificatory rhetoric of 'merit' obscures the social reality of privilege from the public view in what is an unequal competition. Diane Reay (2017: 11–27) identifies a growing devaluation of the working class in terms of rights and respect as a root cause of educational underachievement. A decline in economic rights is linked to an increasing lack of respect in the public sphere. Stereotypical images of class embodied in pejorative descriptions – such as 'chavs', 'scum', 'knackers', 'losers' – enables society to 'other' working-class students as the victims of their own culture of deviance – the 'precariat'. This exclusionary social language results in working-class students living in disadvantaged communities becoming stigmatised in ways that undermine their capacity for educational achievement.

There are also fundamental conceptual problems involved. Joseph Fishkin (2014a: 4), in his influential book *Bottlenecks: A New Theory of Equal Opportunity*, observes that 'the overall problem of equality of opportunity in modern society is almost too vast, too overwhelming to wrap one's mind around'. According to Fishkin (2014b), there are two ideal types of society: unitary and pluralistic. In a unitary society, social roles and purchasing power are allocated according to a few select criteria, notably social class origin and educational achievement. On the other hand, in a pluralistic society, there are multiple criteria for measuring achievement and routes towards human flourishing. The implication of Fishkin's argument is that the focus on equalised opportunity is currently too narrowly academic and socially exclusive, and needs to be made more pluralistic by broadening access to the opportunity structure.

Despite its demonstrable flaws, equality of opportunity is essentially a popular concept. It is in harmony with liberal democratic values shaped by progressive individualism that regulates access to higher education, addressing discriminatory barriers based on gender, ethnicity and religion. The system is founded on the principle of competitive entry, using school terminal exam results (such as the Irish Leaving Certificate and UK A levels) or other tests (such as SATs in the US) for acceptance onto the most sought-after courses in the most prestigious universities. It has facilitated mass participation in higher education and the opening of new universities. On the face of it, equality of opportunity in theory has been a very constructive policy in terms of opening up of opportunity but, in practice, it has reintroduced hierarchy into the system in the form of the emergence of a new meritocratic class largely drawn from private schools, attending elite (normally older) institutions attracting greater esteem and added value to their degrees and enhanced career outcomes in lucrative professions. This is the contradiction at the core of the equality-of-opportunity philosophy that undermines its meaning, integrity and coherence as a policy designed to achieve equality.

In summary, equality of educational opportunity as a policy concept has a popular rhetorical appeal because it suggests fairness in a system based on the principle of individual merit. Its weakness, however, is that equality of educational opportunity does not fully take into account the complex interplay between social structure and individual agency, which is circumscribed by personal circumstances, class positioning and family resources. For example, while laudably proclaiming every child's right to access higher education, equal-opportunity theory does not adequately allow for the impact of child poverty on educational achievement in practice. In social reality, educational achievement is heavily contingent on the possession of wealth and cultural capital to surmount qualification bottlenecks, in what Fishkin (2014a and b) calls 'the Big Test Society'.

Professor Brian Barry, in a philosophical critique of the concept of equality of opportunity, observed that it was not compatible with institutions such as private education and private healthcare. He argued that real equality of opportunity exists only when outcomes depend exclusively on people's choices and decisions, not on factors that are shaped by social class, race and family background (*The Telegraph*, 2009). Barry's damning critique highlights the limitations of equality of opportunity. However, Barry (2005) was no mere sceptic. He forcefully argued that effects of unequal cultural capital and financial resources are by no means beyond the interventive reach of social policy to rectify by a more personalised and flexible view of educational equality. In Barry's (2005: 47) opinion 'equal' should not be understood rigidly as 'identical'. It simply means attainments should be 'equivalent'.

Opportunity pluralism

Fishkin (2014a: 1–2) posits an alternative theory of equal opportunity, which he calls opportunity pluralism:

> The way of thinking, which I call *opportunity pluralism,* involves a shift in focus. Instead of focusing on questions of whose opportunities are equal or unequal to whose, opportunity pluralism requires us to look in a more structural way at how opportunities in our society are created, distributed and controlled. This shift brings new questions into view. In part, it prompts us to scrutinise the *bottlenecks* in the opportunity structure: the narrow places which people must pass if they hope to reach a wide range of opportunities that fan out on the other side. Thus, in addition to questions about discrimination and group-based exclusion, we ought to ask why our society allows people to pursue certain paths only if they have jumped through particular hoops or passed particular tests at particular ages. In a situation of intense competition and scarcity, opportunity pluralism prompts us

only to focus on the question of fairness in who will win the desired and scarce positions, but also what features of the opportunity structure are causing this degree of competition and scarcity in the first place.

What is most striking is that Fishkin (2014a: 2) has dropped the word 'equality' from his vocabulary (which he frankly acknowledges), arguing that 'opportunity pluralism is a conception of equal opportunity in the broad sense'. Fishkin's logic is based on the premise that equal opportunity is ultimately about freedom and ergo 'expands the range of paths open to us', thereby enhancing our freedom. But, Fishkin's emphasis on opening up more diverse career pathways beyond higher education options to include FET options such as apprenticeships, internships and work experience, does little to address the class divide or equalise personal developmental opportunities.

On the other hand, FET can also provide a bridge between higher education and FET in terms of providing lifelong-learning opportunities. Clearly, FET provides a very important entry point into higher education. A DEIS school principal we interviewed had a positive view of opportunity pluralism:

> 'I think … thanks to a very strong education progression team in the form of guidance counsellors (they work really hard at developing career paths for the students) my expectation is that every student will be placed, be that in an institute of technology, a university or FET. I would see a considerable number of them considering further education routes, and I think that is a great option for a lot of them because the beauty of that is that it opens up avenues for them later on as well, and we have had students in the recent past who went down the further education route and accessed university after that … I think we will have students going into apprenticeships again. There are very few kids who we don't know where they are placed.'

While the concept of a more diverse set of pathways in a complex system that we generically call third-level education is demonstrably positive in theory in terms of opening up wider career options, opportunity pluralism will only work in practice if it is well funded and the boundaries between higher education and FET become more flexible, porous and negotiable in terms of access and admissions policies, free tuition and the provision of maintenance grants over the life cycle. Without these essential rights, resources and supports, and the availability of integrated pathways between FET and higher education, Fishkin's pragmatism arguably could represent a step backwards into the traditional Aristotelian dualism between education and training that will appeal to educational elitists and traditionalists, as well as social and political conservatives, but will not enhance democratic participation in higher education. In a democratic society we need a model of educational equality that can be reconciled with its humanistic value base, avoiding false nostrums such as the principle of merit or, in a skills-orientated 'knowledge economy', simply becoming a tool of capitalist production.

Equality of condition

Equality of condition envisages the entitlement of all citizens to the same life chances. Political philosopher John Baker observed: 'Once you endorse any kind of equality, there is a logic that pushes you to endorse equality of condition', which he defines as meaning 'people should be relatively equally well off in terms of the social conditions of their lives' (*The Irish Times*, 16 May 2014). The social impact of inequality has been exposed by a number of important studies, notably one by Richard Wilkinson and Kate Pickett, *The Spirit Level,* published in 2009 and Thomas Piketty's *Capitalism in the Twenty-First Century,* published in 2014. These important studies have reset public thinking about the negative consequences arising from growing social inequality and how it impacts on people from different social classes. Equality of condition increasingly poses a moral and social challenge to the concept of equality of educational opportunity.

The problems of applying the model of equality of educational opportunity in practice are becoming increasingly visible in terms of selection and stratification in both the labour market and society. As already discussed, we have witnessed the emergence of a left-behind class, reflecting the decline of the working class, who feel angry, disrespected and socially excluded. This anger, as already noted, has fed the populists' politics of grievance and resentment that currently dominates the electoral landscape as a clear and present danger to democracy. Equality of condition arguably offers a better and fairer way of achieving educational equality because it seeks to equalise life chances. It is important to note that equality of condition is sometimes used interchangeably with equality of outcome, but the focus on condition is arguably preferable because it is broader in scope and avoids accusations of advocating an Orwellian version of tyranny.

Professor Kathleen Lynch, in a seminal contribution to the debate about educational equality, commented to the Irish Joint Committee on Education and Skills (2019: 15) that 'an equality of opportunity, which is based on individual merit is inadequate insofar it is about promoting fairness in the competition for advantage. It implies there will be winners and losers, people who do well and people who do badly. An opportunity in this context is the right to compete, not to choose among alternatives of equal value'. In her submission, Lynch recommended as an alternative approach equality of condition, which she defined (p 15) as:

a belief that people should be as equal as possible in relation to the central conditions of their lives, particularly in terms of their material conditions and the exercise of power. It is not about trying to make inequality fairer, nor is it about giving people a more equal opportunity to become unequal; it is about ensuring that all of humanity's citizens have roughly equal prospects for a good and decent life. The current approach to policy reinforces stratification by attempting to supplement gaps rather than making conditions equal for all.

Kathleen Lynch and John Baker (2005: 131–164) have identified five dimensions in theorising equality of condition. First, Lynch and Baker identify resources, including the possession of economic capital in the form of wealth and income, social capital, encompassing family and social networks and affiliations, and cultural capital, such as educational credentials. They also identify high-quality healthcare and a clean living environment as important resources. Second, they cite equality of respect and recognition, not simply in terms of equal rights but also an end to the educational segregation of minority groups, such as people with disabilities, Travellers and Roma, asylum seekers and refugees. The third dimension that Lynch and Baker discuss comprises love, care and solidarity, which they view as vital to individual emotional and mental well-being and human development. They particularly mention the care and well-being of vulnerable people, especially in institutions, as part of the community. Kathleen Lynch, as already noted in Chapter 1, makes these principles of affective justice a central theme in her 2022 book on *Care and Capitalism*. The fourth dimension in Lynch and Baker's requirements for equality of condition focuses on reductions in power inequalities in society. This is clearly a fundamental step in unlocking inequality. Finally, the fifth dimension addresses working and learning, where Lynch and Baker advocate major restructuring of the division of labour and the availability of more inclusive and diverse forms of learning.

Brian Barry (2005: 58) has also sought to explain what equality of condition means in terms of social justice:

> The first demand of social justice is to change the environment in which children are born and grow up so as to make them as equal as possible, and this includes (though by no means confined to) approximate material equality among families. The second demand – which is more pressing the further society fails to meet the first demand – is that the entire system of social intervention, starting as early as possible, should be devoted to compensating, as far as possible, for environmental disadvantages.

What does Barry's prescription mean in practice? First, it means a major redistribution of wealth and opportunity in society. Second, it means adopting Paulo Freire's philosophy of praxis, empowering the poor to move beyond their 'limit situations' into creative experimentation with their human potential. Third, it means the rethinking of the project of education into an inclusive humanistic practice of transformation.

These three models offer an overview of the diverse understandings of educational equality. What is clear from this philosophical diversity is a lack of agreement in how we conceptualise and address inequality in our schools and opportunity structure. Members of more-affluent socio-economic groups seek to use their wealth to enhance their children's prospects through the use of private educational markets. This practice is widely accepted as the legitimate assertion of parental rights and responsibilities, but it has detrimental consequences for less-privileged students' chances. It begs the question: 'Is parental choice in education compatible with social justice?'

Private markets, opportunity hoarding and parental choice

Abigail McKnight (2015: 1) observes:

> [S]uccess is considered to be a just reward where it has been achieved on the basis of merit and effort but a social injustice where it has been gained as a result of parental wealth and status. A society in which the success or failure of children with equal ability rests on the social and economic status of their parents is not a fair one. Not only is it unfair but it is a waste of talents of those from less advantaged backgrounds; damaging for the individuals, the economy and society.

McKnight's assertion is the opening statement of the paper *Downward Mobility, Opportunity Hoarding and the 'Glass Floor'*, commissioned by the UK Social Mobility and Child Poverty Commission. What McKnight is describing is the social phenomenon called 'opportunity hoarding', originally identified in the US by Charles Tilly in his book *Durable Inequality* (1998). Major and Machin (2018: 197) in the UK have observed, in relation to opportunity hoarding:

> Those at the top devote incredible resources to ensure their offspring do not fall through society's glass floor – even if they are missing the natural talent or work ethic that their lofty positions would have required otherwise. In societies with high inequality, the loss in income from slipping down the hierarchy is more severe, making parents anxious about children's futures. It is an example of the powerful incentives of loss aversion.

The concept of opportunity hoarding explains how privileged families invoke their natural rights to allegedly game the system to prevent their children from falling down the social ladder and being overtaken in social mobility terms by children from less-advantaged backgrounds. Critics argue that the intention behind the practice of opportunity hoarding is to put in place a 'glass floor' through the utilisation of 'unmeritocratic' means to achieve educational advantage in a competitive system. Major and Machin (2018: 197) contend, for example, that the consequences of opportunity hoarding result in 'high-attaining children from less-advantaged backgrounds … unable to climb the social ladder, since there was no space on the rungs above to advance on to'. They accuse opportunity hoarders of serious unethical behaviour asserting 'opportunity hoarding tends to be at its ugliest at the highest apex of society, where resources are plentiful, places are few, and competition is fierce'.

Opportunity hoarding is in social reality a practice that is embraced by a wide section of the population. In Ireland, for example, a survey indicated that 52 per cent of parents supported private education, ranging from grinds (private tuition) outside school hours (often compensating for learning deficiencies or poor teaching) to attendance at prestigious fee-paying institutions that confer substantial advantages in academic performance and access to the most competitive courses (*Irish Independent,* 21 August, 2008). A DEIS school principal we interviewed observed:

> Obviously you have to respect parental choice, but then again the system is driven by market forces. Market forces are points, hence you have the proliferation of grind schools and as long as you have the points system we have at the moment we're feeding into that system; so were feeding into a system whereby grind schools will have a market of students who'll go to those schools because it's a points driven system.
>
> It's an unequal system really. In terms of social capital, in terms of financial capital – that is where society is at. It is very broad really in terms of kids getting to [higher education]. It is not just cause and effect, there are a lot of variables really. I'm coming back to my original premise – every parent wants the best for their kids. Some have more capacity than others.

A recurring theme from the teachers we interviewed during our research was that middle-class students have a competitive advantage over their working-class peers because they can afford educational resources and services, notably 'grinds' and 'grind schools'. Private tuition is now a significant part of exam preparation in Ireland, with nearly half of Leaving Certificate students taking grinds (Smyth et al, 2009). Clearly, this parallel system is likely to add to the disadvantage experienced by students from poorer backgrounds.

One teacher interviewed by the UCC research team pointed out the performance advantage that could be gained by middle-class students, particularly in the year before exams: "There's money there [in middle-class homes] as well as which can buy extra help. There isn't the money in this community for extra help, you know. … Someone doing their final year in a grind school; they're going to do very well, let's face it."

Grind schools have developed as a response to the points system, conferring advantage on those who can afford to avail of private markets, further exacerbating the existing inequalities within the education system. It fundamentally calls into question the framing of the Leaving Certificate as an objective test based on individual merit.

The issue of principle at stake with opportunity hoarding is that, in a system that purports to be meritocratic, the class status quo is maintained by the better-off parents using their superior financial, social and cultural capital to advantage their children in society. While this is a parental natural right there is a clear case for compensatory measures to level up the opportunities of those children who are disadvantaged by social inequalities, notably poverty and discrimination. Also, there is a strong case for terminating exchequer supports for private schools, unless they can provide a rationale for their existence that is morally and socially justified.

Overall, opportunity hoarding is arguably morally and socially injurious to societal well-being and cohesion. Diane Reay (2017: 131) comments that:

> although the upper and middle classes benefit from an educational system that historically has been set up to serve their interests, they are also, to an extent, damaged by the invidious workings of an inequitable system that emphasises divisions and hierarchy at the expense of commonalities and what different groups in society share.

There is clearly cognitive dissonance involved in our thinking about equality of educational opportunity that enables us to deny its negative consequences and compensate for them.

The COVID-19 pandemic and schooling

The New York Times reported (Mervosh, 2022) that the Coronavirus pandemic had 'erased two decades of progress' in maths and reading for 9-year-old children, especially the most vulnerable. It was part of an international story. The UK House of Commons Education Committee (2022: 10) in a report on the impact of the coronavirus epidemic on schooling, *Is the Catch-up Programme Fit for Purpose?*, dramatically concluded: 'There is no doubt that school closures had a devastating effect on children's education.' The Committee stated that there was research evidence that 'children locked down at home in the UK spent an average of only 2.5 hours each day doing schoolwork, and one fifth of pupils did no schoolwork at home, or less than one hour a day' (UK Education Committee, 2022: 3). In reference to disadvantaged children, the Committee estimated (p 3): 'By the summer term 2021, the gap [in learning] between disadvantaged pupils and their more affluent peers in reading was around 0.4 months for primary aged pupils and around 1.6 months for secondary pupils.' Clearly, study habits were seriously undermined, especially in disadvantaged households. What was the impact on assessment?

Coronavirus had a major impact on student examinations. Student assessment became a politicised issue. The adoption of modified assessment systems resulted in the public perception of a lack of fairness in being assessed by new and sometimes impersonal methods, notably the use of algorithms, which made the assessment process appear opaque and depersonalised. It seemed to protesting students as if robots had taken over the system. There were also challenges arising from the introduction of remote online learning, in terms of disadvantaged students' lack of engagement, suggesting alienation from the school system.

Carl Cullinane (2020) of the Sutton Trust has critiqued the UK's exam response to the coronavirus, in which algorithm was employed to standardise crude statistical data on student performance in England, Scotland, Wales and Northern Ireland. The algorithm exposed significant inequities in the UK exam system that normally would be overlooked, offending public opinion. It was dubbed by the media 'the calculated grades disaster'. What happened, according to media reports, that stirred up public anger of AI bias?

First, UK students' grades were allegedly assigned on the basis of national distribution informed by historic data of their school's achievement record rather than individual merit. This led to an immediate sense of personal injustice and class bias. It was amplified by media exposure into a national collective outcry against the perceived 'unfairness' of UK A level results in 2020 that were reportedly based on historic data and allegedly favoured elite fee-paying schools. Second, the algorithm, was widely viewed as the product of a statistical formula that was wholly impersonal. Third, the algorithm allegedly did not take into account 'outliers': high-performing students from disadvantaged schools. This seriously undermined in the public mind the notion that the higher-education system is based on the principle of individual merit that rewards individual hard work and ability. Fourth, private fee-paying schools were allegedly further advantaged by their low numbers protecting them from closer scrutiny, while, in contrast, the algorithm allegedly rounded down the results of students from the state sector, where larger classes are more open to statistical analysis.

Finally, the palpable sense of algorithmic injustice raised in the media arising from the 2020 exam experiment raised profound questions about decision-making in a democratic society. A system of exams based on statistical variables and algorithmic logic is clearly not easily open to public challenge, even if it is completely fair in its calculation of results. The individual is allegedly lost in a system of prediction based on logic, where the parameters are already set by the system designed to ration the availability of places in line with university capacity in terms of a finite number of places. Disappointed students vented their anger in public demonstrations, reportedly declaring that the algorithm 'stole' their futures. In the end, as Daan Kolkman (2020) wrote in an LSE blog in August 2020: 'Faced with protests, the UK government retracted the grades. Students will now receive grades based on their teacher's estimate of what their grade would have been, had the exams gone forward as planned.'

The controversy surrounding the UK 'calculated grades' experience during the pandemic and its negative impact on public opinion was to significantly shape Irish policy in relation to the crucial issue of equity in the standardisation of results. The Irish government came under intense pressure to ensure students from DEIS schools would not be unfairly disadvantaged by the calculated grades standardisation process.

When the Irish Leaving Certificate results appeared – based on calculated grades, including teacher estimated marking – DEIS schools improved their performance with record results, with many more DEIS students progressing to higher education (O'Brien, 2021a). More places in third-level institutions needed to be created. It seemed like a rare victory for both common sense and social justice. However, this convergence in schools' performance has not been sustained. Nor is there agreement about the causal factors. The *Irish Independent* (19 December 2022) explained the change in results as the product of 'grade inflation':

> In 2020 and 2021, when Covid forced alternative Leaving Certificate assessment arrangements; pupils from DEIS schools benefited most from the use of calculated grades/accredited grades, based on teachers' estimated marks.
> There was significant grade inflation, extra college places were opened to manage expectations and it led to record CAO acceptances in 2021, particularly more registrations from DEIS schools.

The lockdown and school closures resulting from the pandemic also raised widespread public concern about the impact on student well-being, mental health, food poverty and learning regression arising from remote learning. There was also a public perception of a digital divide likely to impact on student engagement. A study on the impact of the school closures on children and young people suggested that it had disproportionately affected students from disadvantaged socio-economic areas (Bray et al, 2021). Low student engagement was shown to be particularly prevalent in DEIS schools. The study also reported that, in addition to significant barriers arising from material deprivation, social and motivational barriers had an even greater influence on hindering student engagement, suggesting alienation from schooling.

The myth of social mobility

Major and Machin (2018: 4), in their UK study *Social Mobility and its Enemies*, observe: 'Social mobility tells us how likely we are to climb up (or fall down) the economic or social ladder of life. And whilst some people are upwardly and downwardly mobile, too many of us are destined to end up on the same rungs occupied by our parents.' They conclude (pp 4–5):

> Figures we have compiled reveal that the low levels of income mobility in Britain are due to stickiness, or immobility, at the bottom and top of the income spectrum. Children born into the highest-earning families are most likely themselves in later life to be among the highest earners; at the other end of the scale children from the lowest-earning families are likely to mirror their forebears as low earning adults.

In 2018, the OECD posed the question whether social mobility had become a broken elevator. Its influential voice identified a key problem in contemporary society – the limited capacity of individual citizens to move up the social ladder. In the post-war era the welfare state enabled citizens to be upwardly socially mobile in absolute terms, even many of those at the bottom of the social and economic ladder were better off in what came to be known as the 'affluent society'. US President John F. Kennedy famously captured the meaning of *absolute* social mobility in the aphorism 'a rising tide lifts all boats'. This 'rising tide' metaphor was to become a poster for the success of post-war development. Assisted by major state investment (notably Marshall Aid), mass third-level education was made available to the population for the first time in post-war society, facilitated in many countries with welfare states by free tuition and maintenance grants.

This enlightened social policy altered the social structure. While the size of the traditional working class in blue-collar positions in manufacturing industries sharply declined there was a major increase in absolute social mobility through the creation of new white-collar positions in the service economy. Many of these newly created positions were occupied by women. The welfare state on the face of it, had created an equal opportunity society. Or had it?

The answer resides in the concept of *relative* social mobility, which compares the movement of people from different social origins in terms of the social distribution of opportunities. While many citizens were benefiting from the 'golden age of the welfare state', others were not – the social elevator for them was either not moving or going downwards. The OECD (2018: 4–5) contrasted this negative correlation between social-elevator 'sticky floors', preventing working-class people from moving up, with the top of the social elevator where 'sticky ceilings' enable the privileged classes to maintain their elite dominant position, often assisted by opportunity hoarding. What we are witnessing is a 'double bind' for young people at the bottom of the social spectrum, who are being turned into a socially marginalised 'precariat', while those at the top intergenerationally dominate the opportunity structure.

Sam Friedman and Daniel Laurison (2019: 209) lay educational privilege bare in *The Class Ceiling*. They argue that social mobility is a strategem invented by politicians to counter the challenge of rising social inequality: 'Amid rising inequality, and growing public unrest it has generated, social mobility has emerged as the key rhetorical tool through which politicians are staging their response.' They conclude: 'It quite literally pays to be privileged', noting that, even when individuals from working-class backgrounds in contemporary Britain manage to enter elite occupations, they earn on average 16 per cent less than colleagues from more-privileged backgrounds.

Friedman and Laurison's book *The Class Ceiling* is primarily based on a qualitative study that draws upon Bourdieu's theoretical framework to expose the micro-processes (often unconscious) that enable individuals from more-privileged backgrounds to climb the ladder of opportunity. They contend that 'embodied capital – widely valued tastes, categories of judgement and bodily self-presentation – is primarily inculcated via a privileged upbringing and therefore acts as a powerful (yet hidden) means through which those from upper-middle class backgrounds secure advantage in elite occupations' (Friedman and Laurison, 2019: 187). Bourdieu's contribution to unravelling understanding of social inequality and how deeply it is embedded in culture is of fundamental importance in interpreting the stickiness of social mobility.

Major and Machin (2018: 87) pessimistically conclude that the levelling-up pretensions of social mobility are simply a myth:

> Many of us cling on to the hope that education can act as a great social leveller, enabling children from poorer backgrounds to overcome the circumstances they are born into. But evidence gathered over a number of decades and for a range of countries, shows that for most children education has failed to live up to these expectations.

They add with dramatic effect (p 87):

> In no developed country for which we have data is there evidence that early-years centres, schools or colleges consistently reduce attainment

gaps, and life prospects, between rich and poor. The education system at best acts as a counter-balance to the powerful forces outside the school gates driving bigger education gaps between advantaged and disadvantaged.

They then sombrely deliver a very damning verdict on social mobility (p 87):

> The pattern is an ever-escalating educational arms race in which poorer children are hopelessly ill-equipped to fight, and where the increasingly rich rewards go to the offspring of social elites. Far from acting as a leveller, the education system has been exploited to retain advantage from one generation to the next. Individuals from wealthy backgrounds acquire higher qualifications that pave the way for higher earnings. Existing inequalities are transmitted and magnified across generations.
> Social mobility falls.

This searing analysis offered by Major and Machin leaves the concept of social mobility and its egalitarian pretensions in tatters. Both the intellectual and moral failings of social mobility as a principle of social justice are fully exposed as largely false. Fact and fiction are in profound conflict in the theorisation of social mobility, which would appear to be largely a myth, that diverts attention away from the democratic struggle for social justice.

Conclusion

This chapter has explored the socially destructive effects of meritocracy as an ideology that purports to be fair and objective but in practice divides society. That is its cruel reality and the cause of its political failure because of the popular perception that meritocracy means elitism in practice, polarising society. It has turned education into competition with winners and losers. Yet societal denial obscures the underlying political and social consequences. The widening education achievement gap is creating a segregated society in which non-graduates feel stigmatised as a 'left-behind' class.

Competition drives the education system in the form of a culture of performativity, league tables and exam results. It shapes social behaviour and family aspiration for their children's success. The accompanying culture of opportunity hoarding reflects the moral dilemmas that underpin the sanctity of parental rights as a traditional cornerstone of family values in a liberal democracy. It raises profound value issues. What about children's rights in a democracy? Aren't children's rights supposed to be paramount in law in a purportedly child-centred society? Is this hallowed legal principle of paramountcy in practice reserved for the regulation of the lives of the working class through child protection services, or should it be a universal human right that informs educational equality for children from all social and ethnic backgrounds?

Sadly, equality of opportunity appears to work neither in theory nor practice. We have linked this moral failure to the debate about educational inequality. Normatively, equality of opportunity seeks to provide every citizen with an equal chance to become unequal. This is illogical thinking since it does not address structural inequality. It embeds social inequality as normal in society. In practice in a stratified world where class, race and disability often coalesce on an intersectional basis, equality of opportunity can result in greater disadvantage and discrimination. Is this morally acceptable in a democracy? The answer must be an emphatic 'No', but is anyone listening? Few it would seem are listening because they think the system is fair!

There are other models to choose from. Equality of condition, for example, offers an alternative that treats all citizens broadly the same, so that no child is disadvantaged. But does that sound like communism to many people? Nobody wants communism any more. It is widely (and with good reason) viewed as a recipe for tyranny. In realty, equality of condition is potentially a strategy for the practice of humanism in a democratic society. Every citizen is entitled to similar respect and recognition in achieving their aspirations to live a fulfilled life. On the other hand, opportunity pluralism pragmatically offers a diversity of pathways between further education and higher education. That is a positive development. But, opportunity pluralism also reflects the historic dichotomy between education and skills that evokes traditional class divisions. The exposure of the myth of social mobility goes to the core of the problem. The class system does not change but creates well-honed and cleverly marketed political and sociological rhetoric to obscure this seminal truth of a system based on class and racial privilege that is dividing society and leaving its most vulnerable citizens behind – a denizen class populating the ghettos of our unequal world.

5

Snakes and ladders: aspirations and barriers

Life and destiny are largely determined by birth and social class position, as Salman Rushdie (1981: 141) contends in his Booker Prize-winning magical realist novel *Midnight's Children*: 'All games have morals, the game of Snakes and Ladders captures as no other activity can hope to do, the eternal truth that for every ladder you climb a snake is waiting just around the corner, and for every snake a ladder will compensate.' The novel is a loose allegory based on events coinciding with Indian independence in 1947 and demonstrates the impact on children born at that moment in history.

Those who experience disadvantaged childhoods find themselves locked into a world dominated by poverty, discrimination and exclusion from which it is very difficult to escape. Education purportedly provides the ladder of opportunity to an autonomous and prosperous life, but participation is already constrained for young working-class people and marginalised ethnic minorities by a lack of what Pierre Bourdieu has called cultural, social and economic capital. Bourdieu (1973: 60) argued that the main function of education is the cultural and social reproduction of power relationships and the maintenance of privilege and social hierarchy across the generations:

> By making social hierarchies and the reproduction of these hierarchies appear to be based on the hierarchy of 'gifts', merit or skills established and ratified by its sanctions, or, in a word, by converting social hierarchies into academic hierarchies, the education system fulfils a function of legitimation which is more and more necessary to the perpetuation of the 'social order'.

DEIS schools seek to compensate for often invisible inequalities hidden in divergent expectations, cultural codes and popular vernacular shared meanings. Disadvantage is also visible in the material poverty of children's lives, where every day is a struggle for existence, including adequate nourishment and food security. At the core of educational inequality is the class system based on a binary between privilege and disadvantage that has both objective and subjective dimensions.

Pierre Bourdieu, at a conference in Grenoble in December 1997, delivered a paper entitled *La Precarite est aujoud hui partout*, in which he identified alienated youth as 'the precariat', recognising the vulnerability and support needs of this marginalised group. In understanding the ontological experience of the education system in shaping the biographies and identities of young people, Bourdieu's concept of symbolic capital is also important. Symbolic capital is the power to establish, reproduce and construct social reality. Charles Masquelier (2018: 1) asserts that in order to achieve adjustment to this 'symbolic kind of domination' the individual must accept this 'kind of symbolic power' as the natural order of society (orthodoxy). In a comment on the impact of symbolic capital in defining the social reality of young people in Seoul, Mun Young Cho (2022: 473) notes: 'The affective discourses of fairness and security, which are often embodied and fetishized by precarious youth who are struggling to survive, have fostered a deeper marginalization and criminalization of the urban poor.' Young people universally experience the hegemonic influence of symbolic capital in shaping their educational journey and how they experience it.

In this chapter we explore the relationship between access and opportunity as a game of chance (with a lot more snakes than ladders) for most students from disadvantaged communities. Their fate, we argue, is arbitrarily determined by structural influences, notably, poverty, ethnicity and territorial stigmatisation, rather than individual attributes. Disadvantage, we contend, severely constrains the educational progression and achievements of working-class people. It is not all gloom, however. Some students from disadvantaged communities succeed against the odds. What were the factors that influenced their progression to higher education? We start the chapter with the positive experiences of 16 HEAR students studying at UCC. The chapter then focuses on an analysis of a survey of 303 senior-cycle DEIS school students on their educational aspirations and reasons for wanting to go on to third-level education. In terms of the critical relationship between aspiration and achievement, what emerges has been called the 'aspiration gap' (Blower, 2020). We explore the barriers and facilitators shaping students' progression. Finally, we consider the relationship between schooling and student failure in an alienating learning environment.

Access, motivation and support: students' views

The research team asked the HEAR student group at UCC why they chose to go to university. Nearly all of them spoke about their hopes of getting a 'good' job and enjoying a better standard of living than they had experienced growing up. In some cases, students referred to the low wages and job insecurity their parents had faced as a motivation to further their education, thereby improving their career prospects. A university degree was seen as a route to a better life, as the following examples illustrate:

'I think all my life I kind of wanted to go to university. Because I didn't really come from the richest of homes. As, you know, everyone knows education is key to success. Well, one of the key ways anyway. … My mum didn't go to college and she always told me, "Oh, if I had gone to college, I could have done this, and my life would have been better". So that kind of stayed in my head – to go to college, and make sure you have a good degree, get a good job. So that's kind of why I went to college.

I come from a family that would be quite poor; there wouldn't be much money there. None of my brothers and sisters went to college and I, kind of, it's not that I was judging anyone, but I kind of wanted to better myself. I wanted to be comfortable in life and I wanted to experience college. I've always wanted a job in healthcare.

If you want a good job, if you want to have a nice home, go on holidays, all that kind of stuff … if you want that kind of life, then I would definitely recommend going to university.'

HEAR students' motivations were often expressed in generic terms ("nice home", "good job"). Indeed, some spoke in greater detail about the kind of lifestyles or occupations they did *not* want in the future as a reason for going to university. For example, one student described her motivation in the following terms:

'I wanted to come to college because I am from a disadvantaged area. And it's not a nice place to be, you know! And the kind of people that I am surrounded by – I didn't want a life like them, you know. I didn't want to be on the dole or to be playing with children's allowances and having a corporation house. I wanted to have a proper career and – not that I am saying that there is anything wrong with it, but I didn't want that lifestyle, I wanted a better one. The only way I was going to do it was to go to college and to get a degree and follow on, get my career.'

Other students spoke of the type of low-paid jobs they did not want, including cleaners, care assistants, or (as in the following example) working in a supermarket:

'I knew to get a job; you know, to get a decent job you needed to get a degree. I worked in places like supermarkets and all that and I don't really want to do that … it would make you work a little bit more in your Leaving Cert to make sure you get more, I won't say better, but yeah, I guess, a better job, yeah. … Well, some people enjoy that kind of work, so it's fair enough if they want to work like that. It's no disrespect to them.'

The HEAR students were asked about what or who had helped them get to university. Most mentioned the importance of financial support through the SUSI (Student Universal Support Ireland) grants scheme as instrumental in getting to university. Students also spoke in detail about people who had supported them, including parents, other family members and teachers. Parental/family support was generally in the form of encouragement and, in some instances, limited financial support. Teachers were often credited with providing the type of information and advice on higher education that students were unlikely to receive at home. In the following extract, a student describes how her career-guidance teacher influenced her subject choice:

'My careers counsellor, she went through my CAO [application form] with me. And I originally wanted drawing and fine art and that kind of stuff. And she was like, "You can do that as a hobby". She said, "With these grades, you could do [science]". I was getting As in honours biology and she said, "You should do science". And she told me a story about her niece. Her niece actually did a genetics programme in Dublin. And she told me about the amazing career that she had, the car she was driving and, do you know, just the comfortable lifestyle kind of thing. And I was like [laughs], "I suppose I could keep drawing as a hobby".'

In some cases, teachers seemed to have had an even more profound influence – three of the 16 participants said that the initial impetus to go to university came from their teachers. They believed that without their teachers' interventions, it is unlikely that they would have entered higher education. In all three cases, students said they had been unaware of their own potential, as the following example illustrates:

'It was the careers counsellor that kind of – I never even thought about university until she said it to me. And then when I realised I had the potential, then I kind of was like, "Yeah, I want to go for it". … The school [teachers] were amazing. The careers counsellor – I'll never forget her. She helped with everything … I definitely had a lot of teachers who kind of made me feel confident in my education, you know, 'cause I never knew how smart [I was]. That sounds really arrogant maybe. But I didn't know that I had the potential that I had. And if it wasn't for the teachers at school, saying, "You can do this", I wouldn't have thought I could.'

Teachers' knowledge of the following student's background and difficult home circumstances made them particularly supportive:

'They kind of knew my backstory as well; do you know, where I had come from and, do you know, that I was kind of on my own kind of thing. So,

> I think that is why they gave me ... that little bit of extra support as well. Other people have their parents going through their CAO with them and stuff like that. Whereas, I didn't, so I think they did that.'

Although this student's parents were described as being "super proud" of her going to university, she felt they had played no role in helping her to get there ("I never had any motivation from them"). A second student also credited his teachers with helping him realise his potential:

> 'I suppose when I was in first year, second year and third year, I kind of thought I was a kind of cool lad – I never wanted to go into classes, [I'd] ditch classes and mess and just totally waste all my ability. But I remember there was a group of five or six of us and we were going for detention or something and the principal called me out into his office and said: "You have [ability] and you really should give this a go. Just stop being such a fool." So I actually did; I listened to him and left my five best friends and actually started studying, and I can honestly say if it wasn't for him I'd just, I would be, I'd be drawing the dole, 100 per cent I have to say.'

In our third example, one teacher appeared to play an even more substantive role – not only building up the student's self-confidence to enable her to apply for university, but also meeting with her parents, who were initially opposed to her plans because she had experienced discrimination in secondary school. As a member of the Traveller community, this student came from one of the most chronically under-represented groups in Irish higher education (1 per cent). Looking back, the student recalls that she had never thought of going to university because it 'seemed like something that someone from my background could never get'.

The aspiration-achievement gap: a poverty trap?

Alex Blower (2020) poses the question in a UK Higher Education Policy Institute blog: 'Is a simple "lack" of aspiration a sufficient explanatory model for a stark disparity in university access?' Neil Harrison and Richard Waller (2018a and b) have partly answered the question, concluding that the British evidence does not stack up in favour of aspiration-raising as a 'silver bullet for social mobility'. The UK evidence, according to Blower, demonstrates three things. First, disadvantaged young people do not have notably lower aspirations than their better-off peers (Baker et al, 2014). Second, in reality, some young peoples' aspirations may be unrealistically high (St Clair et al, 2013). Third, it is argued that there is no strong evidence that aspirations drive motivation and achievement (Gorard et al, 2012). Other UK researchers argue that there is good evidence of a link between expectations and disadvantage (Archer et al, 2013).

Irish evidence indicates a close correlation between social structure and individual achievement. The HEA published data at the end of 2020 that offers an insight into the spatial and socio-economic profile of the Irish student population. The data is based on Deprivation Index Scores (DIS), which measure the relative affluence or disadvantage of a particular geographical area based on data from the Irish census. The data (HEA, 2020: 1) revealed:

- In terms of ratios, there were 4.9 students from disadvantaged areas to every 10 students from affluent areas participating in higher education, but this does vary across institutions.
- 10 per cent of all students were classified 'disadvantaged', while 20 per cent were classified as 'affluent'.
- In terms of fields or areas of study, courses such as finance, banking and medicine have a high DIS (5.3 and 6) – they attract more-affluent students. Just 4 per cent of medical enrolments were from disadvantaged areas.
- The higher education student population did not reflect the diversity of the rest of the population in Ireland.

The Education Indicators for Ireland Report (2023: 30) estimates the progression rate from DEIS schools to higher education in 2021 at 43.4 per cent compared with 69.3 per cent from non-DEIS schools.

The contemporary Irish media frenzy with school league tables exposes a sharp educational divide between postcode areas in Dublin, where the affluent middle-class neighbourhoods of south Dublin – with postcodes 4, 6, 6w and 14 – all record progression rates of around 100 per cent. In contrast, working-class areas of Dublin, such as postcode districts 10, 11 and 22, all record much lower progression rates, falling below 20 per cent (*The Irish Times*, 5 December 2017). The explanation for this divide is clearly linked to class, geography and community, which constitutes 'a tale of two cities'. Postcodes matter because they spatially reflect social division in which the lottery of life is determined at the expense of the disadvantaged. Youth biographies are shaped by geography and the identities ascribed. Arguably, students from disadvantaged communities are caught in a poverty trap. Some struggle to set themselves free from a destiny of poverty and deprivation. Others are already trapped in lives of poverty.

Resilience, disadvantage and aspirational optimism

A DEIS school principal observed in an interview with the research team: "I think the key area is listening to the voice of the student and what they are telling us." When children grow up in a disadvantaged urban community, it is important to reach beyond ascribing a ghetto mentality and accord them the respect they deserve. That is the DEIS school principal's essential point, on which he elaborated in relation to student resilience:

> 'We did some research during the week on attendance and asked students how we can help you come to school more often and how you can help yourself and we found out really interesting stuff ranging from making the school interesting, methodologies, it can be boring, to health issues, kids feeling ill, feeling sick. I think a significant challenge of a school like ours is the whole area of resilience and students signing out early from school. We've data on that … there is a significant number of kids that don't finish the school day.
>
> Resilience, stickability, and once again some kids are born with this in terms of their temperament, their fortunate in their gene pool to have resilience. Maybe Mom says – and Mom is a very significant person – from a very early stage says, "You are going to school. Get up, get your two feet on the ground and get to school". That starts at four, five, six, seven, eight years of age. "Get yourself together, get your lunch and get into the car and get to school." Now, if you've got a lot of issues going on in your life, sometimes the easy option is to say, "Yeah, well, stay in bed".'

Clearly, the home environment and the role of the mother are fundamental influences in shaping resilience. However, poverty remains central to determining life chances through the mechanisms of segregation and exclusion that defines the world, self-confidence and opportunities available to the left-behind class. Zygmunt Bauman (2001: 119) asserts:

> To be poor in a rich society entails having the status of a social anomaly and being deprived of control over one's collective representation and identity; the analysis of public taint in the American ghetto and the French urban periphery [shows] the *symbolic dispossession* that turns their inhabitants into veritable social outcasts.

Diane Reay (2017) has adopted the game Snakes and Ladders as a powerful metaphor for working-class students' progression (or more accurately the lack of it) through the British education system, which she views as a pernicious game of life chances. Educational progression is, as Reay suggests, analogous to playing Snakes and Ladders in which the student's fate is largely determined by their class position. These are profound issues that inform and shape the definition and foundational meaning of youth, youth policy and childhood in a postmodern world, where the social is decentred and identities are destabilised. Reay (2017: 112) asserts: 'Social mobility comes with a neoliberal vocabulary of aspiration, ambition, choice and self-efficacy', which, in the case of a disadvantaged student's biography, 'there is no sense of confidence or entitlement but, rather, a frightening cocktail of fear, bewilderment and ignorance'. Reay's research findings suggest working-class students discover how the education system works too late because of their lack of economic, social and cultural capital. This is the dark side of working-class aspirational optimism, where students' hopes and dreams are shattered by the realities of social disadvantage.

Chris Barber (2008: 408) observes in contemporary society: 'Youth is not so much a biological category overlaid by social consequences as a complex set of shifting cultural classifications marked by difference and diversity', concluding 'however we define it youth remains an ambiguous concept'. The 'schoolification of society' concept (discussed later) suggests that free play at school and at home are being eroded in favour of structured academic, sporting and cultural pursuits (Weale, 2021). This is the meaning of class difference being played out in real time, shaping real lives for better or worse. It is a fundamental social injustice that undermines the changing aspirations of DEIS school students.

Changing aspirations: school students' views on higher education

In our UCC survey of senior-cycle students, we asked what they would like to do when they finished school (Table 5.1). A total of 66 per cent of respondents said that they wanted to progress to higher education, though a slightly smaller proportion (60 per cent) said that they were 'very likely' or 'fairly likely' to apply. These findings are significant because earlier Irish research indicated that young people from disadvantaged backgrounds saw higher education, particularly universities, as being remote and unattainable (Lynch and O'Riordan, 1998). Several teachers in our six case-study schools also spoke of a generational change in the educational aspirations of young people from disadvantaged communities.

The students who said that they wanted to go on to higher education, and who indicated that they were definitely or probably going to apply or who were still deciding (190 of them) were asked a series of questions about motives, choice of college and so on. The findings are presented in Table 5.2.

The survey found that the vast majority of those who wanted to go on to higher education were motivated by a desire to improve their job prospects and increase their chances of working in an area that interests them. Social and personal reasons also featured prominently, including a desire to become more independent; to meet new people and make new friends; and to experience life as a student.

Students' reasons for wanting to progress to higher education, and their impressions of college life, were explored in more detail through the focus

Table 5.1: DEIS school students' educational aspirations

Aspiration	Frequency	Percentage
Go to university	135	44.6
Study at an institute of technology (technological university)	54	17.8
Go to teacher training college	11	3.6
Study at a further education college	26	8.6
Start working	10	3.3
Start an apprenticeship / learn a trade	25	8.3
Don't know	17	5.6
Other	13	4.3
No response	12	4.0
Total	**303**	**100**

groups. Improved career prospects were by far the strongest motivational factor identified across all seven focus groups. Participants spoke about not wanting to "get stuck in a dead-end job", "work on the minimum wage" or "end up on the dole". In their view, higher education meant getting a well-paid job, having a career and better life opportunities. There were some differences of opinion, however, with regard to the value of education, as the following extract from a focus group in Dublin illustrates. While most young people in this group felt that higher education was a prerequisite for secure, well-paid employment, one participant questioned this assumption:

Student 1: With education you get more money.
Student 2: Some people didn't even go to school and ... they have jobs.
Student 3: Yeah and they're getting shit pay. ... The reason I'm staying at school, and what college is for ... is to make a future for myself. If I have kids, to provide for them.
Student 2: You don't have to go to college for that ...
Student 1: But you don't get as much money just doing a normal job.
Student 3: I know my mam had to go back to college to finish her [Manpower] levels for childcare before she got a proper job in Montessori.
Student 1: Everything – you just need to have certificates for everything nowadays, that's all.
Student 2: What?
Student 3: It's all down to one certificate and one degree on one piece of paper, and that's all.

Table 5.2: Reasons for wanting to go on to higher education

Reason	Very important %	Important %	Fairly important %	Slightly important %	Not important %	N*
To improve my job prospects	63	32	4	–	–	185
To study a subject that really interests me	68	27	3	1	0.5	184
To become more independent	41	38	15	4	2	184
To improve my chances of working in an area that interests me	74	23	2	–	–	183
To meet new people and make new friends	24	45	21	8	2	184
To train for a particular career	55	39	6	–	–	184
To experience life as a student	24	42	23	8	2	184
To put off getting a job until I'm older	9	12	15	18	46	183

*N is the number of participants who answered each question, out of a possible 190.

Focus-group participants also identified a range of positive experiential and social dimensions associated with college life, including meeting new people, a vibrant social life, access to sports and leisure facilities, and being able to study a subject of interest. In addition, young people spoke about going to university as a chance to mature and gain independence. In their discussions they often contrasted their experience of school with the anticipated independence of university life. As one student pointed out: "Your school life, until you go to university, from junior infants to sixth year, you are conforming your whole life. And when you get to university it's completely different, it broadens horizons, it's all new." Similarly, another student noted: "Your experiences are a lot different when you are in university – you are your own person, you can do what you want." Some young people also spoke about gaining autonomy as learners: "Secondary school kind of tells you what to think, but third level allows you to have your own opinions on things." This particular factor (the development of independence and autonomy) is also a well-established key feature of overall youth transition. Coles (1995), Walther et al (2006) and Furlong and Cartmel (2007) all refer to the natural motivator of growing up and wanting to reduce dependence on family as an integral part of moving from youth towards 'full' adulthood.

Finally, a small number of focus-group participants referred to a desire to make their family proud or to become the first member of the family to progress to higher education. For these young people and their families, progress to third level is seen as a visible indicator of success.

The fact that a majority of the senior-cycle second-level students surveyed in DEIS schools aspire to progress to higher education is a significant finding, because (as noted) earlier Irish research indicated that young people from disadvantaged backgrounds saw higher education, particularly universities, as being remote and unattainable. There are some signs that attitudes and aspirations among working-class students may be changing. A number of studies in the UK and Australia have challenged the idea that young people from working-class backgrounds are not interested in higher education (James, 2002; Bradley and Miller, 2010; Kettley and Whitehead, 2012). Our research lends further evidential weight to a more positive vision of the higher-education aspirations of working-class students. But is this hope likely to fall victim to what has been described as 'cruel optimism' (Berlant, 2011)? Major barriers stand in the way of disadvantaged students realising their dreams.

Barriers to accessing higher education

While the majority of young people (66 per cent) in our six case-study schools aspire to go on to higher education, the reality is that a significantly lower proportion are likely to enrol, based on progression rates from previous years and HEA statistics quoted earlier (13.5 per cent). The findings from our research suggest that a range of economic/financial and psychosocial factors influence access to higher education, including: the costs of higher education; poverty and social deprivation; lack of confidence; family history of higher education; and levels of attainment at school.

Costs of higher education

A HEA (2023) publication entitled *Eurostudent VIII: Report on Living Conditions of Higher Education Students in Ireland* calculated that one-third of students in colleges and universities were experiencing serious financial problems, with accommodation costs accounting for 35 per cent of all their expenditure.

The interviews and focus groups carried out by our UCC research team suggest that the cost of higher education continues to be a source of concern for potential entrants and their families. Teachers and community groups reported that, generally speaking, families in disadvantaged areas would not be able to afford the costs of higher education. Consequently, the student grants (SUSI) system was seen as the key to progression to higher education. Difficulties arose, however, when families were marginally outside the qualifying range, as might be the case in a household where both parents work, albeit in low-paid jobs. Parents worried that their children might not qualify for the full grant, that the grant would not be adequate, or that some costs (such as deposits on accommodation) might be payable before the grant was issued. Reliance on a grant presented challenges, particularly for those who were not familiar with the qualifying criteria or application process. The possibility of students taking out a loan was rarely mentioned as an option by any of the participants. Financial considerations were also a significant theme in the focus groups. Students, for example, spoke of their concerns about becoming a financial burden on their families if they entered higher education. Their comments recall Ball et al's (2002b) argument that, for young working-class people, decisions around whether to participate in higher education are never straightforward and have to be weighed up on a number of fronts, with costs featuring as an important consideration.

It was clear that financial considerations also placed restrictions on where young people went to college and, in some instances, what they studied. In the student survey, over three-quarters of respondents said that the 'cost of living and studying' was an 'important or very important' consideration when choosing where to apply. A recurring theme in the interviews and focus groups in the four city schools was that young people would apply to local universities or institutes of technology (now called technological universities) so that they could continue to live at home, thereby saving the costs of accommodation. Students from the two rural schools did not have the option of living at home, if they wanted to attend university. Therefore, the cost of accommodation was a significant factor in their choice of where to study. The high cost of living in Dublin was raised by students from both of the rural schools, one of whom asserted: "No one goes to Dublin 'cause there's no accommodation; it's just too expensive."

Poverty and social deprivation

Tina MacVeigh (2006: 68) notably observed: 'The extent to which pupils from disadvantaged areas are disadvantaged in education is reflected in differences in access to third-level education.' Clearly, students from disadvantaged areas are particularly vulnerable to financial poverty, but there is variation between areas. While all of the DEIS areas were categorised as 'underprivileged', head teachers and community workers noted that there were considerable variations between different housing estates and households, with some young people living in conditions of extreme poverty. We engaged with one catchment area in Dublin described as being among the most deprived in the country. The poorest areas were particularly hard hit by the recession that unfolded from 2008 onwards, which led to rising unemployment and welfare retrenchment. Food poverty continues to be a significant problem in socially deprived areas of Dublin and Cork, with young people coming to school hungry and being unable to concentrate on their studies. As one youth worker put it:

> 'Parents want their kids to do well, but it [education] just kind of falls down the priority list; poverty is still a big issue. Food poverty – it's a big issue that kids are going to school hungry. Now one school started a breakfast club, because kids were just coming [to school] with no food. ... Youth workers here would find a big issue with kids coming for drop-in sessions and stuff, that they're really coming for a sausage sandwich because they've had nothing to eat.'

In a report on the extension of the hot school meals programme to all DEIS schools from September 2023 and for all students by 2030, *The Irish Times* (30 March 2023) noted that a survey of 773 school principals, 407 parents and 109 providers had found the provision of hot school meals 'reduced levels of food poverty amongst children'. One DEIS school principal from the survey stated that the provision of hot school meals had very beneficial consequences: "We noticed a huge transformation with the kids in the afternoon. Some of the kids would normally be half asleep and not participating in the classes but now they are awake because they have been fed." Another observed: "We can talk about attendance and improving their academic path but feeding a hungry child is something we must do."

Homelessness, substandard housing and overcrowding were also seen as significant social challenges in urban areas. Moreover, the stresses associated with poverty, such as threats of eviction and household debt, had a knock-on effect on the mental and physical health of both parents and children, which in turn impacted on school attendance, academic performance and aspiration. Teachers and youth/community workers consistently reported that when families were struggling to make ends meet, education was inevitably pushed down the list of priorities. In some instances, young people had to take on additional responsibilities, particularly the care of younger siblings, which further impacted on school performance and attendance. As one school principal told us: "I have a girl here in third year. She's extraordinarily bright. We spoke this morning; she was late for school, she was telling me that she was helping her mother with the younger children. She is put in a parent role at a very young age." Having caring responsibilities for family members was also raised in several focus groups with young people, particularly in Dublin, and these tasks were seen as potentially barriers to accessing higher education, for example that they might have to take care of their parents. It is not possible to tell if these young people were referencing personal experience or it was something they had observed in other families, but it is nonetheless significant that care-giving was raised in relation to barriers to education and future plans. It is indicative of the kinds of responsibilities that young people from disadvantaged communities have to assume, in addition to school work. In recent decades, there has been an increasing recognition of the role that children and young people play in providing care for other members of the family, and the impact this potentially can have on school attendance, student performance and opportunities to progress to higher and further education (SCIE, 2005; O'Connell et al, 2008; Fives et al, 2010). Nonetheless, the scale of these informal caring practices is believed to be underestimated because of the relative invisibility of young care-givers (Fives et al, 2010).

Anxiety and lack of confidence about going to university

As noted earlier, the young people in our research were interested in progressing to higher education and had generally positive views of university life, thanks in part to the access initiatives in which their schools participate. Despite these positive impressions, however, some young people found it difficult to picture themselves going to college. When asked what might make it difficult to get to college, or what might deter them from applying, students in all seven focus groups mentioned feelings of anxiety and a lack of confidence. In some instances, young people reported doubts about their academic ability to achieve the necessary entry points or meet the standards of work in higher education. Another major area of concern related to the social and relational dimension of college life. Some participants worried about not knowing anyone in college, and having to make new friends in unfamiliar surroundings. As one student observed:

> 'There is social anxiety. Say you feel comfortable in the school 'cause you basically know most of the people in the school, and say you were to go to UCD [University College Dublin] or Maynooth [University]: there's going to be hundreds, thousands of students; the place is going to be huge; you'll be anxious and all; you wouldn't know what to do.'

For those who want to move to another part of the country to attend college, there was the additional worry of moving into accommodation with strangers and potentially losing contact with existing friends. While university was viewed as a sociable space, with many opportunities for making new friends, some young people appeared unsure of their own ability to fully participate in the social and relational dimension of college life. Their concerns about settling in were further compounded by the size and unfamiliarity of the campuses and numbers of students. A lack of familiarity with the higher-education system, and the consequent difficulties involved in decision-making, were also raised in the student survey: just over 50 per cent of students who wanted to go on to higher education agreed with the statement, 'I don't know what to expect', while nearly 60 per cent agreed that 'it's very difficult choosing where to go and what to study'. Although it was clear from the focus groups that participants had favourable impressions of higher education, the idea of going to university was still a leap into the unknown and fraught with potential risks.

The issue of confidence was also raised by other participants, both in relation to education and work opportunities. One community worker in Dublin, for example, told us that young people from this area feel: "If I put down [my address] and they discover it is a halting site, even if I had 20 degrees, whose going to want me?" Parents made similar points about their children's lack of self-belief and how this shaped their future plans. One mother described her unsuccessful attempts to build up her daughter's confidence to apply to go to university: "She feels like she's not good enough, that she's not brainy enough, and it's like talking to a wall telling her. 'You can do it, you can do it'."

Comparatively few young people explicitly raised concerns about 'not fitting in' because of their social class background, which has in the past been a significant theme in the literature on barriers to higher education (for example, Archer et al, 2007). This may in part be due to a reluctance on the part of young people to discuss their views in class terms, particularly in Ireland where 'there is a marked ambivalence about class' and where 'the organised working class has been quite weak' (Finnegan and Merrill, 2017). While issues relating explicitly to class differences was not a prominent theme in focus groups, however, there was one notable exception where students at a Dublin school asserted that higher education institutions (HEIs) were less likely to accept applicants from poorer areas. The following is an extract from that discussion:

Student 1: If there is someone, say, from ... Blackrock [middle-class area] and they see an application from [this disadvantaged area] they are going to pick the person from Blackrock.
Student 2: Yeah, more than likely. If it's between two of you and you have the higher points, then they might pick you, but if they are the same. ... If people have paid for their education, they look at them as smarter somehow, even though that's not the case.
Student 3: Because you come from a disadvantaged area, or what people think is a disadvantaged area. They know that there is crime in your area. They probably think you are going to come in and start knocking down their statues or something. [Laughter]

This extract reveals a good deal about how these young people think they will be perceived within higher education: as less able because they are not privately educated, and 'trouble-makers' because they come from a 'disadvantaged' area. In a tiebreak situation, college administrators are perceived to discriminate on the basis of area and, by extension, social class. HEIs are constructed as essentially middle-class institutions, in which working-class applicants are likely to be excluded or positioned as the 'other', to be monitored for lower academic standards and disruptive behaviour. Given the importance of a sense of belonging, both for higher-education access and retention (Lehmann, 2009), the concerns about territorial stigmatisation articulated by these young people are particularly significant to debates on widening participation.

Family history of higher education and home support for education

Parental attitudes and support for education in the home are often posited as key factors in educational outcomes and access to higher education (Kirk et al, 2011). In our study there was general agreement among different participants that working-class parents would be supportive of their children if they wished to progress to higher education. The majority of the respondents in the student survey reported, for example, that their parents would like them to progress to higher education. In the interviews, parents whose children planned to go to university described themselves as being "proud", "thrilled" and "delighted" (see Chapter 6). Moreover, teachers and community workers consistently reported that parents valued education as a route to a better future for their children. Most teachers qualified their responses, however, by suggesting that parents were not always in a position to provide the kinds of support, encouragement and advice that would improve their children's chances of educational success and progression to higher education.

Teachers raised three main issues which impacted on progression to higher education by young people from different socio-economic backgrounds. First, there is the expectation of middle-class households that young people will go on to higher education – this is nurtured by parents from an early age. While young people from disadvantaged backgrounds may *aspire* to progress to higher education, their middle-class counterparts tend to view going to university as the norm. As one school principal asserted: "If they [middle-class parents] say their child is going to university, they *are* going to university." Second, parents in disadvantaged areas want their children to do well in school, but this does not necessarily translate into support in the home, which in turn impacts on attainment. A recurring theme in teacher observations was that parents did not always 'push' their children to succeed academically:

'They [parents] are ambitious for them, but sometimes they don't put that together with the work that is required of the students to get to that. There's sometimes a bit of a gap there between ambition and how to encourage them to work at home afterwards. They don't sometimes realise how much is required to get to [university].'

Middle-class parents, by contrast, are perceived to be far more driven and controlling when it comes to their children's education and career decisions. For example, one career-guidance teacher asserted that these parents "are nearly consumed by the child that's doing their Junior or Leaving certificate: it's all about them for that period of time". Finally, teachers and community workers noted that most parents in disadvantaged communities would not be familiar with the higher-education system, and might not be in a position to advise and support their children on matters such as course or university choice. A frequent example given by career-guidance teachers is that they have to fill out the university entrance (CAO) forms with young people, whereas in middle-class households these forms would be completed at home with parental support and supervision. Several of the parents we interviewed acknowledged their lack of familiarity with the higher-education system and their reliance on schools and universities to provide information and advice (see Chapter 6).

Levels of attainment

International research suggests that social class is still 'a powerful predictor of educational attainment' and that 'a smaller proportion of young people from lower socio-economic groups achieve the entry qualifications for higher education' (Hutchings and Archer, 2001: 70). In our study, teachers (particularly those in urban schools) reported that significant numbers of young people were not achieving the entry points for higher education, which they attributed largely to the long-term processes of disadvantage and discrimination already discussed, including poverty and unequal access to educational resources and services. It was noted that middle-class students have a competitive advantage over their working-class peers who can afford private tuition (grinds), which is now a significant part of exam preparation in Ireland (Smyth, 2009). Furthermore, teachers in the two Dublin schools reported that many of their students work part-time (both in the evenings and at weekends), which resulted in less time for homework and exam preparation. Young people from poorer families were reluctant to give up this source of income, even in their final year.

It was beyond the scope of our study to explore the complex issue of attainment levels in any detail. Nonetheless it is important to raise this issue here as a reminder that the key processes impacting on higher education entry occur much earlier in the educational process (McCoy et al, 2010). As O'Connell et al (2006) argue, social selectivity in access to higher education is a cumulative process whereby 'retention in the second-level system and performance in the Leaving Certificate are important determinants of entry to higher education, and that retention and performance are in turn heavily influenced by socioeconomic background'.

Factors that facilitate access to higher education

Students and teachers at the six case-study schools were asked what would help or enable young people from DEIS schools to go on to higher education. As might be expected, the availability of student grants was seen as key to facilitating access. Focus-group participants noted that qualifying for a grant to cover registration and living expenses would be the single greatest determinant of whether they went on to higher education. Some students noted the importance of the HEAR scheme, which offers places on reduced points and extra college support to school leavers from socio-economically disadvantaged backgrounds. They were also aware of alternative routes to higher education, outside the standard school entry system based on exam performance, including accessing university through post-leaving certificate (PLC) courses, FETAC, or as mature students (of 23 years and over).

Teachers reported that higher-education access events and initiatives, such as open days, Easter/summer camps and homework clubs, have helped to break down some of the barriers to higher education. They identified several benefits of university access programmes. First, they fostered an interest in higher education among young people who had no family history of higher education. Second, they helped school students prepare for college and gave them a better sense of what to expect. Finally, some access programmes contributed to school work and exam preparation, for example through homework and revision clubs run by college students. In the following extract a school principal describes the benefits her pupils derive from homework clubs, which provide practical support while also sparking an interest in higher education:

> 'I think the strength is that you're getting people talking about university. That's a good thing. It's in the landscape; it's there, and I think it's wonderful that we have volunteers from [the university] who come up to our students. There's kind of a twin; there's a dual purpose to that. One is they're helping them with their homework practically, but in a very real sense they're having conversations as well about college and university. And these are people that our students can relate to, you know – they're not that much older than them. It isn't a case of just coming up, helping with their homework. It's much more than that, you know, it's much more than that.'

While the feedback from teachers on different access schemes was generally very positive, it was noted that schools outside the cities are less able to take advantage of certain initiatives, particularly those provided on an ongoing basis such as the homework clubs. College summer and Easter camps may also be difficult for pupils from rural schools to attend because of the need to arrange accommodation.

Both teachers and young people noted the importance of the role of parents in supporting their children to go on to higher education. One principal, for example, stated that it was a combination of factors, including the support of a significant person, usually a mother:

> '[I]f you look at the students who are achieving very, very well in their Leaving Certificate, they availed of all of the supports that are in the school, and there are significant supports in the school. And one thing they have in common is they have a significant person in their lives – really, really significant – who is supportive – doesn't need to know everything about the Leaving Certificate and [CAO] points and everything, but they're a strong person for them. Very often it's a mother.'

Receiving adequate support, encouragement and career guidance from teachers was identified in the focus groups as important in enabling young people to progress to higher education. Students reported that their teachers had organised open days, helped them to complete CAO forms and provided them with course information. However, not all young people felt they were receiving enough career guidance, or were reticent about approaching teachers for further information. As one student pointed out: "You can't ask them [career guidance teacher] every single question. You can't be annoying them."

While we found that the DEIS schools in our study were exceptionally committed to and supportive of their students, schooling is not without its critics. As noted earlier, Bourdieu points to the role of symbolic capital and the function of cultural and social reproduction in constructing the learning environment of schooling. The resulting stratification of the school learning environment may impose a further layer of disadvantage on working-class students. We have already discussed the significant barriers students from disadvantaged communities confront during their educational learning and progression. Critics over the years have also pointed to the control culture of schooling as a social institution (Holt, 1964; Illich, 1971; Giroux, 1994). In this stratified social space of schooling, some students will be included and others excluded, and some will exclude themselves (Lareau, 2011) as part of their personal adaptation strategies. DEIS schools seek to be inclusive through their supportive student environment. That makes them valuable to society because they seek to compensate for the underlying inequities of the education system that Bourdieu has identified. There is room, however, for curriculum development that connects with students' interests and futures. A UK report entitled *All Our Futures* (NACCE, 1999: 5) asserted in relation to the need to rethink the purpose of schooling:

> By creative education we mean forms of education that develop young people's capacities for original ideas and action: by cultural education we mean forms of education that enable them [students] to engage positively with the growing complexity and diversity of social values and ways of life. We argue that there are important relationships between creative and cultural education, and significant implications for methods of teaching and assessment, the balance of the school curriculum and for partnerships between schools and the wider world.

All Our Futures (1999: 23) concluded that the social challenge of the school is 'to provide forms of education that enable young people to engage positively and confidently with far reaching processes of social and cultural change'.

Conclusion

This chapter has sought to explore the factors that impact on levels of participation in higher education by young people from lower socio-economic backgrounds. In line with previous research (Forsyth and Furlong, 2003; McCoy and Byrne, 2011), we found that economic factors continue to have an important influence and arguably have become more significant over the last eight years in the wake of the economic recession. While some financial barriers occur at the point of entry (such as registration fees and accommodation costs), others reflect structural problems, notably poverty and unequal access to educational resources. Teachers and community workers, particularly in the city schools, noted that there were different levels of disadvantage within disadvantaged communities: some young people lived in conditions of extreme poverty and their families faced an uncertain future. In these circumstances, education is pushed down the list of priorities, with knock-on effects on school attendance and academic attainment and aspirations.

Some of the key themes to emerge from the research concerned young people's aspirations and orientations towards higher education. Most of the young people in our research said that they would like to go to college and had positive views of what college would entail. This is in line with a number of studies that suggest that attitudes to higher education in working-class communities are changing (James, 2002; Bradley and Miller, 2010; Kettley and Whitehead, 2012). While these young people liked the idea of university life, however, this was countered by a lack of confidence in their own ability to access and participate fully in higher education, both on an academic and social level. They displayed none of the assuredness about their future or sense of 'university entitlement' often associated with higher socio-economic groups (Crozier et al, 2008). Teachers, community workers and a few parents located this lack of confidence in a broader context, including traditionally low levels of family/community participation in higher education. Coming from areas that have been designated as 'disadvantaged' also appears to impact on young people's levels of confidence. Our findings suggest that there is a need for critical reflection to identify the processes through which young people from lower socio-economic groups come to feel they are 'not good enough' for university. Moreover, rather than individualising this issue, lack of confidence needs to be located within a wider social context as constructed through poverty, social inequalities and other forms of discrimination.

6

Social class and parental attitudes to education and career choices

Parental attitudes and support for education in the home are often posited as key factors in educational outcomes and access to higher education (Kirk et al, 2011). Moreover, since the late 1980s, there has been an increased outsourcing of educational learning to the home (Buckingham and Scanlon, 2003) and an expectation that working-class parents will take on responsibility for reversing educational inequality (Reay, 2017). International research has explored parents' orientations to further and higher education and how the nature of parental involvement can vary significantly depending on socio-economic background (Ball et al, 2002a; Irwin and Elley, 2011 and 2012). In their research on ethnicity, social class and participation in higher education, Ball et al (2002a) found that college-educated parents are able to mobilise various forms of support and information and are directly involved in choice-making, for instance in making visits to universities and commenting on university application forms. Similarly, Crozier et al (2008) argue that parental knowledge and social networks contribute to a sense of 'university entitlement' among middle-class young people, which is largely absent in the case of their working-class counterparts (see also Evans, 2009). A number of studies indicate that while working-class parents value higher education and often have high expectations for their children, their efforts to support them are hampered by unfamiliarity with college requirements, concerns about affordability and limited awareness of financial-aid opportunities (Ball et al, 2002a; Kirk et al, 2011). On the other hand, Irwin and Elley (2011), while acknowledging the links between social class and familial orientations to higher education, caution against overstating the internal homogeneity of middle-class and working-class experience. Studies in the US and the UK have highlighted the fact that parental orientations to education can vary within, as well as across, classes, and can change over time, in response to a number of factors (see Goldenberg, 2001; Mistry et al, 2009; Irwin and Elley, 2011 and 2012).

Bourdieu's model has been an influence on the analysis of differences in parenting styles between social classes. As sociologist and educationist, Annette Lareau (2011: 361), puts it:

> Pierre Bourdieu provides a context for examining the impact of social class position. His model draws attention to conflict, change and

systemic inequality, and it highlights the fluid nature of the relationship between structure and agency. Bourdieu argues that individuals of different locations are socialized differently. This socialization provides children, and later adults, with a sense of what is comfortable or what is natural (he terms this *habitus*). These background experiences also shape the amount and forms of resources (*capital*) individuals inherit and draw upon as they confront various institutional arrangements (*fields*) in the social world.

Lareau (2002 and 2011) coined the terms 'unequal childhoods' and 'invisible inequalities' in her pioneering research into the causes of educational stratification. Lareau draws on the theoretical ideas of Bourdieu in analysing the relationship between class and culture during the formative years of childhood, which she applies to families in the US in her book *Unequal Childhoods* (2011: 5):

> Middle-class parents who comply with current professional standards and engage in a pattern of concerted cultivation deliberately try to cultivate their children's development and foster their cognitive and social skills. The commitment amongst working-class and poor families to provide comfort, food, shelter, and other basic support requires on-going efforts, given the economic challenges and formidable demands of child-rearing. But it stops short of deliberate cultivation of children and their leisure activities that occurs in middle-class families. For working-class and poor families, sustaining natural growth is viewed as an accomplishment.

Lareau's work is of seminal importance in applying Bourdieu's analytic framework to unravelling the cultural codes that underpin parenting and child socialisation. She concludes (2011: 6): 'Thus, middle-class children were trained in "the rules of the game" that govern interaction with institutional representatives. … The working-class and poor children, by contrast showed an emerging *sense of constraint* in their interactions with institutional settings.'

While it is widely accepted that parental attitudes are of seminal importance in shaping children's education, very little research on this topic has been carried out in Ireland. As part of the 'Widening Access to Higher Education' project we interviewed 25 parents – 24 mothers and 1 father – drawn from six case-study schools in deprived rural and urban areas. Parents were asked about their children's plans for the future and their engagement in their children's education and career choices. The resulting data was revealing in terms of parental aspiration, the value they attached to education and their perceptions of what constituted a good future.

As we shall see in this chapter, parental reactions to their children's imagined futures varied widely from 'delight' to a few cases of scepticism, disappointment and opposition. There were also notable variations in terms of parents' level of engagement in their children's education and decision-making for the future. A few parents expressed scepticism about the social inequality that provided the context for the realisation of their children's hopes and ambitions – the aspiration-achievement gap – which closely correlates with social class position. Most parents, however, appeared to subscribe to the meritocratic ideal of working hard to gain a college degree, which would in turn help to ensure occupational success.

Most parents said their children were likely to undertake post-secondary education or vocational training. The option of going straight to work after school was mentioned in only a few cases. This was broadly in line with the findings of our research with school students and teachers who reported that the majority of young people who completed the Leaving Certificate exam, progress to FET, higher education or, in a small number of cases, join the police or army.

Parents' orientations towards higher education

Of the 25 parents interviewed, nine said they expected their children to go on to higher education: in some cases, they named specific careers and/or subject areas, including teaching, architecture, computer science and health. These parents – most of whom had left school by 16 years of age – expressed feelings of pride and strong approval ('delighted'; 'very happy') at their children's future plans. They valued higher education as a means of giving their children the opportunities that they themselves had missed.

While all parents were enthusiastic about the prospect of their children going on to higher education, it is clear that some were more proactive than others and had steered their children in a particular direction from an early age. In this respect they exhibited a type of 'strategic orientation' to their children's education, described by Irwin and Elley (2011 and 2012). These parents told us that they discussed career options with their children from primary school onwards, advised them on subject choices – with a view to future careers – and attended campus open days and information events run by the school so that they could become better equipped to support their children. In a few cases, parents were able to enlist the help of other family members who had progressed to higher education to provide guidance and act as role models for their children. Some parents advocated 'pushing' their children to achieve and had a strong sense of their own role in shaping their children's futures. At the same time, these parents did not see themselves as putting undue pressure on their children or forcing them into careers that they would not be suited to. Rather, they described situations in which they weighed up their children's strengths and interests and how these might be channelled into graduate-level careers.

Monica was one of the most strategically oriented parents in the group and exemplifies several of the themes just noted. A strong believer in education as a means of social mobility, she repeatedly mentioned the importance of 'pushing' children to achieve. She had no experience of third-level education herself, having left school at 15 to start work. Monica had three sons, the oldest of whom (Brian) wanted to be an architect. It was clear from Monica's account that she not only supported her son in this ambition, but saw herself as having played a key role in helping him to *reach* this decision, for example by advising him on subject choices and career options. In addition, she drew on a family connection to encourage her son to consider architecture. In this respect, Monica displayed an awareness of the value of accessing first-hand knowledge of the higher education system and professional careers pathways, to which families from lower socio-economic groups would not usually have access (Ball et al, 2002a; Reay et al, 2002). She felt that her son was now 'on the right track' and heading for a career in architecture, though there was little sense of complacency: "I still will push him. I think parents should push their children. It's not saying it's easy. We know it's hard."

Other strategically oriented parents provided similar accounts of steering their children towards higher education and graduate careers. Fara, a mother of two originally from Nigeria, saw education as a means to a better life for her daughters, a view which she believed was shared by other members of the Nigerian community in Ireland:

'And some of the ones from my background will want their children to progress [to higher education] because to us this is an opportunity to give our children a better life, better opportunities, so we kind of push our children to grasp the opportunity, to be able to have their third level [education]. It really sets them up for life so they are always surrounded by people that think that way.'

Fara appeared to be deeply committed to her children's educational advancement and development of cultural capital. Pathways through education and career opportunities were discussed from an early age:

'I think from primary school it's good to have a good grounding in certain things. So, from primary school I allow them to do [afterschool activities]. As soon as they get to sixth class, we start having a discussion about what secondary school is about. What expectations are for third level and all that.'

Fara went on to say that she had discussed a range of career possibilities with her daughters. When selecting subjects for the Junior and Leaving Certificate exams they had considered what careers these subjects might lead to. In terms of aspiration and strategic thinking, Fara appeared to be no different from any highly motivated middle-class parent in her approach to planning for her children's future. However, there is a crucial difference in the availability of financial resources, which she acknowledged frankly in the course of the interview.

In other households the impetus to go to university appeared to have come largely from the *child*, with little or no apparent 'pushing' from their parents. While these parents supported their children's plans to apply for higher education, they spoke about their children's aspirations with a degree of detachment, which was quite different from the strategically orientated parents just described, as the following comments from two of the mothers illustrate:

> 'Oh, I don't mind [what college course she does] – it's her choice. She's the one doing it. She's the one who does the work. She's good at work. She is very determined. If she decides something she is going there, she is doing it.
>
> I just kind of listen to what he [her son] says because I don't know. It's him that is looking into all this.'

It was clear from the interviews that this apparent detachment did not indicate a lack of interest on the parents' part, but rather a lack of familiarity with the educational system and how best to help their children navigate their way through it. The following was a typical comment:

> 'And you know, when they're questioning you about college, I didn't go to college, neither did my husband. … She [her daughter] would come home from school and she'd be saying, 'If I want to go to college to do this, what would I have to do?' and I mean, I don't know. I didn't go to college. I'm trying to find bits of information.'

Similarly, another mother explained that she relied on the higher-education system itself to provide her daughter with information: "I would be more depending on the college to give her information. I left school when I was just started third year. My mother had a [serious illness] so basically I just had to leave and stay at home to clean and cook."

While acknowledging their lack of familiarity with the higher-education system, parents did not necessarily see this as problematic. They felt the young people themselves – with support from the school and universities – were able to source information on the internet and make their decisions about third-level education. As one parent asserted: "They're smarter: this generation are way smarter than we were." Our findings here are reminiscent of Ball et al (2002b), who note that, in households where parents did not attend college themselves, 'the process of information gathering and choice are mostly left to the student'. By contrast, middle-class parents are often directly involved in choice-making in relation to higher education. Similarly Irwin and Elley (2012) found that some parents in intermediate or working-class circumstances 'felt they had a relatively limited influence over their children's futures, and often conceded greater autonomy to their children than did any of the middle-class parents'. The issue of parental engagement with the educational system was a recurring theme in our interviews with teachers, many of whom reported that, while parents wanted their children to do well academically and progress to college, they were not always in a position to provide effective advice and support because of their own limited experience of the education system, or they saw this as being more the domain of the school.

Parental perspectives on the value of higher education and their concerns for the future

All of the parents described here valued education and strongly supported their children's aspirations to go on to higher education. In explaining *why* they thought higher education was important, parents frequently drew on their own life experiences. Most of this group had left school at 16 years of age, usually to start work, and now look back with some regret on what they felt they had missed. These parents saw education, particularly higher education, as a means of providing their children with the opportunities they never had, as the following comments illustrate:

> '[I told my son] "I want you to be staring your life with a good job; you're stable, and then move on with your life" 'cause I never got an education. I left school at a very young age. I was from a family of six, the eldest girl, we had no money at the time. I left school. I got a job, and, I remember, I was 15 years old working in a restaurant.
>
> I am a hundred per cent interested in my child's education because I left school early myself and it is obvious now [my daughter] won't be going down the route that I did. I had a child very young. I was pregnant at 17 and I had him when I was 18. So, I am interested very much in her education. … She wants to go to university and get a degree.'

It was also clear from the interviews that parents believe education has become more important over time. They noted that even low-skilled jobs now required a Leaving Certificate, whereas in the past, few or no formal qualifications would have been expected. To achieve any kind of upward social mobility, third-level education was seen as essential. Indeed, one parent commented that we are reaching the stage where young people will need a degree to work in a shop – a point that was also made by community workers we spoke to. While these remarks were made humorously, they nonetheless point to concerns about 'credential inflation', whereby young people are having to remain in education for longer in order to compete for jobs.

When asked if they had any concerns, or could foresee any barriers to their children progressing to higher education, the main issues – unsurprisingly – related to financial cost and lack of familiarity with student grant application procedures. Parents voiced a number of concerns about eligibility and whether the student grant would be sufficient to cover all costs. Some parents also worried that the prohibitive costs of going to university might negatively impact on their children's aspirations.

Ball et al (2002a) note that going on to higher education is seen as a natural progression in middle-class households and in this sense it is a 'non-decision'. While the parents in our research were hopeful for their children's futures, there was no evidence of this type of assuredness and entitlement. Indeed, one parent said that her daughter had not told anyone else that she was hoping to go to university because she feared they would "bombard" her with questions and if she did not subsequently go to college she would have "wasted their time". Even among the strategically oriented parents, there was little sense of complacency: children needed to be 'pushed' and careful plans had to be put in place, particularly around the affordability of college. One mother described how location and public transport routes, for example, were key factors when she and her daughters discussed possible universities. Certain colleges were shortlisted while others were more or less ruled out on the basis of bus routes. In nearly all cases, with the exception of students in rural locations, parents said that their children would attend a college that was within a commutable distance in order to continue living at home and save on accommodation costs.

Parental attitudes to further education and training

We will now discuss another group of parents, whose accounts of their children's futures did not include higher education. In most cases these parents reported that their children were planning to enrol in a FET programme, such as courses in childcare, hairdressing, animal husbandry, an apprenticeship, or (in one case) join the police. A few said their children wanted to start work straight from school or were still undecided about their futures. Like the parents described earlier, these parents valued education and wanted their children to progress further in the education system than they had done. At the very least they wanted their children to complete the Leaving Certificate at the end of their schooling and then go on to further education and training. Again, parents' hopes for their children were linked to their own experiences (of leaving school early) and a perception that education had become more important over time. There are parallels here with Irwin and Elley's (2011: 484) research with working-class parents in the UK, the majority of whom reported that education is now more important than in the past. The authors attribute this to changes over recent decades: 'Whereby qualifications have overtaken work-based routes to successful working-class employment.'

When asked for their views on their children's plans for the future, the responses were largely positive. For example, one father – whose son was applying to join the police force – said he was "delighted with it – it's a great profession, its brilliant, it would be a great job". Similarly, another parent told us that she was delighted that her son had chosen to do a carpentry apprenticeship because "it's a good job ... my cousin is a carpenter and he does well". Her older son had already started an apprenticeship, which combined study with on-the-job training.

Like Erwin and Elley's (2012: 119) UK research, we found some parents regarded a trade as a good career option. At the same time this positivity was tempered by an awareness of the precarity of the construction industry, on which these trades heavily depend for employment. Parents in one rural school, for example, reflected on the local impact of the downturn in the construction industry after the 2008 financial crash, but were cautiously optimistic that the economy was improving and new jobs were opening up for young people. In the following extract, an aunt speaks positively about her nephew's decision to forego third-level education and instead take up an apprenticeship:

> 'My nephew was very good at school, he did his Leaving Certificate, but before the Leaving Certificate, people came to speak to them [about apprenticeships for electricians]. My nephew took the apprenticeship and he is in his second year now ... and loves it. And all along leading up to it he was going to Cork, to college, but it just happened that way and he took it, him and another boy. And he just went and is happy. ... His friends from school, the group he was with, they went to college.'

A recurring theme with this group of parents was that their children had made the most appropriate choice given their particular abilities and interests. For example, several parents said their daughters did not want to work in offices and would be happier with 'hands-on' occupations, such as childcare. While it is clear from the interviews that parents discussed possible futures with their children, they emphasised that it was ultimately up to the child themselves – within certain limits – to make decisions on their future. Several parents explicitly rejected the idea of 'pushing' their children in a particular direction as this was seen as ineffective ("I don't go on or anything as it gets boring and you are wasting your time"), puts young people under undue pressure and could lead to careers in which they are not happy. Michael, whose son wanted to join the police, was particularly emphatic on this point:

> 'We haven't forced it upon him, he came up with the idea himself. We are aware as parents that "pushing" kids to do certain jobs because they are financially … they would be financially better off, but my son came up with the idea himself. … We wouldn't push him in for financial reasons.'

Similarly, another participant suggested that parents ultimately have limited influence over their children and the best they can do is support them:

> 'I leave him make the decision and all I can do as a parent is support his decision. Because it doesn't matter if I say, "No you are not to do that", and he says he is going to do it. Just the same as when we were young and people were telling us what to do, we would do it anyway. So, it's best if we just leave him off and support him along the way, any way that I can.'

While affording their children a good deal of agency, there were some options that parents ruled out in the strongest terms, including 'hanging around the house', 'signing on' or going to work in 'dead-end' jobs. Where tensions arose, it was usually when parents felt children were not putting enough effort in at school or had no particular plans for the future and consequently were at risk of drifting into low-paid or precarious employment. As noted, parents were very aware of how the jobs market had changed since they were at school. Therefore, leaving school early was not an option, as one mother explained:

> 'You need your Leaving Certificate in this day and age. You didn't 20 years ago, it didn't matter what you did … you always got a job. But you need to be the right age and you need your Leaving Certificate, definitely. … They wouldn't take you on anywhere without your results, no, not now anyway. Young people still drop out anyway, but there is nothing there for a 16-year-old drop-out. There is nothing there for them: they don't get the dole, they get nothing.'

In a few cases, parents felt that their children could have progressed to higher education had they worked harder or had more self-confidence.

Participants in one paired interview also spoke of how the universities are still seen as remote by young people in their community, which deterred potential applicants. While these mothers may have felt some element of disappointment that their children were not progressing to higher education, they were generally satisfied with their plans for the future, particularly where these plans included further education or training. However, there were two notable exceptions, where parents and children reached an impasse on the issue of third-level education. Two mothers from a Dublin school wanted their daughters (who were in their final year at school) to progress to higher education, but they had steadfastly resisted. Both parents believed that their daughters were academically capable but lacked confidence in their abilities, which in turn impacted on motivation and work ethic. Like the strategically orientated parents described earlier, these mothers advocated 'pushing' children, though they appeared to have had limited success. We will look at their stories in further detail in the following section, as they illustrate the tensions that can arise when parental expectations are significantly at odds with those of their children.

Conflicting aspirations: parents' and children's attitudes to higher education

Gill, a mother of two who had left school at the age of 14, wanted her daughters to complete their Leaving Certificate and then go on to higher education. While she had the same aspirations for both daughters, her level of involvement in their education appears to have varied significantly. Gill's eldest daughter (Maire) was highly motivated to progress to higher education. She carried out extensive research on the different courses and institutions and eventually applied for a degree course with little or no apparent consultation with her parents. In this instance, Gill's role was similar to that of the parents described earlier in this chapter who encouraged their children's aspirations without necessarily offering 'tangible support or facilitation' (Ball et al, 2002b). However, with her younger daughter (Sinead), Gill had taken on an active role in trying to steer her towards college. She was frustrated by Sinead's apparent lack of motivation and concerned that she might 'end up with nothing' once she finished school. Sinead wanted to start work straight from school as a shop assistant, an option that her mother vehemently opposed on the grounds that it was a dead-end job.

To appreciate Gill's perspective on the importance of education, it is informative to look at her own biography. She had left school early, started work in a factory and was now determined that her children would take a different path in life:

'I push them, do you know what I mean. … Because I only did first year and second year in secondary school. And at the time me mam let me leave on the condition I got a job. … And I got a job in a factory. And I *hated* it. Absolutely *hated* it. … And I always swore if I've any kids they're going all through school. They're doing something with themselves.'

Our second parent, Patricia, also valued education as a means of social mobility. While also expressing frustration with her daughter's decision not to go on to higher education, she acknowledged the significant social and economic barriers faced by young people from lower-socio-economic backgrounds. Patricia recognised the importance of geographical inequality in determining children's opportunities and the impact of territorial stigmatisation on student's life chances and careers. She comments insightfully on how territorial stigmatisation is internalised by students from disadvantaged areas creating psychosocial barriers, which inhibits the realisation of their academic aspirations:

'It's 'cause they're from [this area] that they don't think they'll get in [to university]. They don't think they're good enough. Or they don't see themselves as part of that. When [I] look at the kids in Michelle's class and it's university and the likes of Trinity [College] and UCD [University College Dublin], they have them up here and have themselves down so low. They think the universities are above them. And I'm forever going, "No, they're not. Just because you're from here doesn't mean to say that you're not going to get in anywhere". … It's like college – it's not part of their world, do you know what I mean? It's kind of normal for them not to go … it's just not part of the culture in [this area].'

Patricia's comments suggest that young people's minds are significantly influenced by their local community. However, she also suggests that DEIS schools are making a difference for at least some young people in disadvantaged areas, and that it is important to get young people to think about university from an early age: "Putting it into their heads from a really young age that university is the best option … you'll always find something. … I don't think it really matters what you have your degree in, as long as you have your degree. … It kind of gives you a leg-up."

In some respects, Gill's and Patricia's experiences and outlook are reminiscent of the middle-class parents described in previous research (such as Lareau, 2011) who had a strong sense of the value of education and 'push' their children to succeed. However, while these mothers clearly saw higher education as a route to social mobility, this was discussed in generic terms. Patricia's comment that "it doesn't really matter what you have a degree in, as long as you have your degree" is particularly telling in this regard. There are echoes here of Ball et al's (2002a) and Reay et al's, (2002) research with working-class families which found that neither family nor student have much sense of the different kinds and statuses of higher education on offer or what higher education study will be like. While their own experience of leaving school early made them want their children to progress to higher education, it also meant that they were sometimes ill equipped to support them in terms of information and guidance.

Conclusion

Parental attitudes and support for education are often seen as key factors shaping educational outcomes and progression to higher education. In the data we have presented there was general agreement among participants that parents valued education, even when they had been denied it themselves, and were supportive of their children if they wanted to progress to higher education. Parents whose children were planning on going to university described themselves as "proud", "thrilled" and "delighted". There was no lack of support, even when parental involvement was constrained by a lack of first-hand knowledge. Only in cases where children did not want to engage with a career choice did parents withhold their support and approval. Even when parents were critical of the opportunity structure, positive attitudes towards higher education and its impacts and possibilities for the lives of their children were maintained.

The interviews provided an insight into the experiences of parents who grew up in working-class communities at a time when the prospects of going on to higher education were remote. Indeed, most did not complete secondary school, but left at 15 or 16 to start work. Despite their own limited experiences of formal education, these parents valued education and wanted their children to progress further than they had done themselves. One of the teachers in our research made the point that there had been a generational change in young people's educational aspirations and expectations. Much the same could be said of their parents. Furthermore, there was a considerable level of agreement among the other participants in the study – teachers, community workers and young people – that parents in disadvantaged communities valued education and would be supportive of their children if they wanted to go on to college. There was a notable difference with Lynch and O'Riordan's (1998) study, in which teachers reported that working-class people 'did not value education' and that some parents and children, particularly in the Dublin schools, were 'hostile or indifferent to education'. In line with Kettley and Whitehead's (2012) research, we found little evidence of parental attitudes to higher education that could be characterised as ambivalent or negative.

A number of issues were raised in the interviews that shed light on parental orientations to education and why these have changed over time. First, there was a perception that the jobs market in Ireland had altered significantly over the last 20 years and that the level of educational qualifications required for all jobs had increased. In order for their children not to be 'left behind' in a competitive jobs market, parents believed that they had to remain in the educational system for longer. Further education and vocational training were valued, while higher education was seen as a route to more significant social mobility. Second, parents noted that there are now more educational opportunities for young people, which has contributed to raising expectations. Parents praised the schools for their efforts to encourage children to stay in school and then go on to further or higher education. They also commented favourably on the various access initiatives run by higher-education institutions that had helped to raise awareness and aspirations among young people. There was a sense that higher education is being considered as an option by families in disadvantaged communities in a way that it was not in the past. Finally, parents' own biographical experiences of leaving school early shaped their orientation to their children's education and future careers. Several parents felt that they had 'missed out' and wanted their own children to have the opportunities that they had not. Like Irwin and Elley (2011 and 2012), our research found that, while all parents were concerned about their children's education and future career prospects, this was expressed in different ways and with varying levels of confidence. At one end of the spectrum were parents, like Monica, who took a highly strategic role in planning their children's education and future career. More typical were those parents who, while providing support and encouragement, seemed to play a less-active role, largely because of their lack of familiarity with the educational system. Parents tended to rely on teachers and young people themselves to source information on higher education and make course choices. In these cases, the aspirations and strong academic performances of their children appear to have raised parental expectations; a finding that resonates with previous studies (Goldenberg, 2001; Mistry et al, 2009).

Our research points to the need to make information on post-secondary options more accessible to parents, so that they feel confident in providing guidance to young people as they progress through the education system. The findings also highlight an area where parents in disadvantaged areas provide a particularly important support to their children, without which they would be less likely to progress to higher education, and this is in the provision of accommodation during their years in college. Young people from these communities generally select institutions that are within a commutable distance of home in order to save on accommodation and living expenses. The practical role that parents – many of whom are on very limited means – play in enabling young people from disadvantaged communities to progress to higher education is often overlooked.

7

Structural racism and Traveller education

Ireland's 30,987 Traveller population was officially recognised as an ethnic minority on 1 March 2017. It was the culmination of a long campaign by Travellers to have their identity, culture and unique social position recognised by the Irish state as constituting a separate ethnic group. Public recognition was a mark of respect towards an ethnic minority that has long experienced discrimination and racism in Irish society. While it was symbolically a historic moment, it did not resolve the problems of poverty and social inequality that are at the core of the marginalised status of Travellers in Ireland. Nor did recognition as a minority ethnic group represent a qualitative change in the Traveller community's social status. Travellers and Roma continue to experience discrimination and racism in their everyday lives, as the comment by Maria Quinlan (following) clearly illustrates. There are no official statistics regarding the number of Roma in Ireland but the population is estimated to be between 3,000 and 5,000 people.

The president of Ireland, Michael D. Higgins, in a message for Traveller and Roma Day, 8 April 2021, declared:

> The statistics are appalling in terms of what has persisted as exclusion. Today only 14 per cent of Traveller women have completed secondary education, compared to 83 per cent of the general population. Some 60 per cent of Traveller men have not progressed beyond primary education. This is compared to 13 per cent of the general population. Yes, it is true that the number of Travellers with third-level education has doubled in the last number of years, and that is to be welcomed – what a great achievement – it is ground-breaking and exemplary – but it represents just half of one per cent of the Traveller population. The figure for the general population with third-level qualifications is 47 per cent.

Maria Quinlan (2021: 60), in a report entitled *Out of the Shadows*, quotes ironically:

> [W]e talk all the time [about] the assimilation policy, we see education and I'm sure the government sees education as another way of making us settled people. They provide for us what they provide for settled

people. And we tag along with that or else we don't get anything. …
You know, we're not looked at as an ethnic group … we should be
grateful like. That's structural racism … and schools become resentful
when we [aren't grateful]. 'We gave you everything.' … We were saying
yes you're spending millions, but you're not spending it the right way.
You need to listen to us.

In this chapter we look at the issues of poverty and discrimination among
the Irish Traveller community. Drawing on the findings from the UCC
Widening Participation in Higher Education Project, we explore Traveller
experiences of the educational system and the barriers to progression to
third-level education. We commence with an exploration of the language of
inclusion involving a term called 'interculturalism', which can be described
as a diluted form of multiculturalism. Through an analysis of the evolution
of social policy, the chapter tracks positive policy changes in official reports
over time. The chapter focuses in particular on educational inequality and the
exclusion of 99 per cent of Travellers from higher education. It constitutes
a public scandal, but is rarely acknowledged as such in political discourse
with the important exception of the widely respected President Higgins,
who has spoken out strongly on Traveller and Roma rights.

Multiculturalism and interculturalism

Henry Giroux (1994: 325) observes: 'Multiculturalism has become a
central discourse in the struggle over issues regarding national identity,
the construction of historical memory, the purpose of schooling, and the
meaning of democracy.' Multiculturalism moves the concept of equality
beyond a materialist definition, based on class and redistributive justice,
to embrace a cultural definition based on the recognition of identity and
difference. This has led to a reconfiguration and transformation of the
meaning and scope of equality in public discourse into a more complex
social phenomena and the emergence of identity politics.

In Ireland, 'interculturalism' has emerged in policy discourse as the
preferred term in relation to Travellers, the country's oldest minority ethnic
group. The term interculturalism means the promotion of interaction,
understanding and respect between people from different cultural and
ethnic backgrounds. Bryan Fanning (2002: 186) describes interculturalism
as 'weak multiculturalism', adding 'the terms "interculturalism" and to a
lesser extent, "integration" have become the predominant terms to depict
the ethos of initiatives by the state and other sectors in Ireland to address the
needs of Travellers, asylum-seekers and refugees'. Its ambitions are modest.
It lacks a transformative agenda and is more about toleration than liberation.
Yet, some view interculturalism as a step forward from the status quo. In

1998 the Irish National Teachers Organisation argued that interculturalism education policies were necessary to address xenophobia and racism (cited in Fanning, 2002: 186):

> The monocultural education system in Ireland has to change in order to counteract racism and discrimination in schools. This is best achieved through the integration of intercultural education in the school curriculum. The INTO (Irish National Teachers Organisation) supports the view that intercultural education is the foremost strategy of schools against xenophobia and racism.

Clearly, the adoption of interculturalism in relation to the Travelling community in Ireland was a tentative step in opening up dialogue between Traveller and settled communities. It was also an important recognition of the existence of xenophobia and racism in Irish society.

Social policy towards the Travelling community

Social policies for Travellers in Ireland have evolved slowly and painfully from a hostile environment with little evidence of understanding or toleration. For many years, the policy logic was driven by the desire to find a solution to the 'Traveller problem' (McVeigh, 2008: 91). Bryan Fanning (2002), in his book *Racism and Social Change in the Republic of Ireland*, has analysed shifting policy trends since modernisation commenced at the beginning of the 1960s, when Ireland was transformed from a predominantly rural and traditional society into a modern developed economy, which displaced many people living in the countryside to become urban dwellers. The traditional nomadic lifestyle of Travellers was eroded by modernisation and the normative demands to conform to the new expectations of social life in an urban environment.

Fanning (2002: 153) has commented on the social consequences of modernisation for the Travelling community:

> Travellers were constructed as a problem for Irish society. Their cultural distinctiveness became constructed, within a highly racialised discourse of Traveller deviance and inferiority, as a justification for spatial exclusion and discrimination. Within the dominant discourses of the time Travellers were not to have equal rights to welfare unless they first ceased to be Travellers. The price of social citizenship within the assimilationist logic of social policies which emerged to address the 'problem of itinerancy' included surrendering identity and difference.

A series of official reports were delivered over the ensuing decades of modernisation including by: the Commission on Itinerancy, 1963;

the Travelling People Review Body, 1983, and the Task Force on the Travelling Community, 1995. Fanning (2002) identifies two key shifts in official discourse contained in these reports. First, there has been a shift from constructing Travellers as a problem experienced by 'normal' people (the settled community) to constructing the problem in terms of the relationship between Traveller and settled communities with, by 1995, some emphasis on discrimination against Travellers. Second, there was a growing public acceptance that Travellers have a distinct culture and, by 1995, acknowledgement that this culture is not inferior to that of the dominant community.

The *National Traveller and Roma Inclusion Strategy 2017–2021* (Department of Justice and Equality, 2017: 17) provides us with a 21st-century insight into the evolution of social policy in relation to the Traveller community, asserting: 'Discussions with Traveller and Roma representatives and other relevant stakeholders has resulted in a change of emphasis from *integration* to *inclusion* which is seen as better capturing what we want to achieve for these communities in society.' It also decided (p 18) that 'the question of recognition of Traveller ethnicity would be considered in the context of this inclusion strategy'. In relation to cultural identity, the Strategy set out a number of principles (p 25):

- Traveller culture, identity and heritage is supported and valued within Irish society.
- Travellers and Roma should be supported to develop, preserve and promote their cultural heritage.
- Intergenerational learning, cultural continuity and positive self-identity for Travellers should be facilitated.

With regard to education, the Strategy committed to a number of fundamental policy changes with regard to education (pp 25–26):

- Access, participation and outcomes for Travellers and Roma in education should be improved to achieve outcomes that are equal to those of the majority population.
- There should be a positive culture of respect and protection of cultural identity of Travellers and Roma across the education system.
- There should be improved opportunities for Traveller and Roma men to engage in culturally appropriate apprenticeships, training and lifelong learning.

There have been numerous reports, policies and strategies over the years that have aimed to improve Travellers' quality of life. The Programme for Government contains eight commitments that include the Traveller community by name, across mental health, drug use, health, housing and education. The *National Traveller and Roma Strategy 2017–2021* includes 149 actions across a range of areas. The Expert Review Group on Traveller Accommodation published its report in July 2019, and the Ombudsman for Children published a report in 2021 on the conditions faced by children on one halting site. Despite these and other initiatives, Travellers do not report improvements to conditions on the ground. It is evident that improving the quality of life for Travellers is not solely an issue of policy making; it is also an issue of implementation, oversight and a socially inclusive environment.

Challenges facing the Traveller community in Ireland

According to the 2016 census, the 30,987 Travellers in the Irish state constituted just 0.7 per cent of the total population. Just over 58 per cent of Travellers are under the age of 25 years, compared with 33.4 per cent of the general population. Although a relatively small group in Ireland, Travellers have been identified as experiencing 'extreme disadvantage' and exceptionally strong levels of prejudice (Watson et al, 2017: 1).

A number of reports have highlighted the challenges facing the Traveller community, from poverty and high rates of unemployment to health inequalities and poor living conditions (Department of Health, 2010; Watson et al, 2017; Department of Justice and Equality, 2017; Houses of the Oireachtas, 2021). The 2016 census revealed that Travellers were more than three times as likely to live in multiple-family households compared with the general population. According to the *Report of the Joint Committee on Key Issues Affecting the Traveller Community* (Houses of the Oireachtas, 2021), many Travellers are living in overcrowded and substandard accommodation. They are significantly more likely to be affected by the homelessness crisis in Ireland and are 22 per cent more likely to become homeless. Moreover, the high level of 'hidden homelessness', including overcrowding, couch surfing and precarious tenancies mean the homelessness crisis is worse than recorded in official statistics.

Problems with overcrowding are also raised in an report by the Economic and Social Research Institute (Watson et al, 2017), which notes that 56 per cent of Travellers lived in overcrowded accommodation, compared with 6 per cent of the non-Traveller population. Nearly one-third of Travellers lived in accommodation with three rooms or fewer, compared with 6 per cent of non-Travellers. Overcrowding was more common among children under 15 years of age, which has implications for school performance. These statistics are significant social indicators of extreme deprivation among the Irish Traveller population.

Available figures suggest that Irish Travellers experience considerable health inequities and higher morbidity and mortality rates than the general population. Their life expectancy is 15.1 years less for men and 11.5 times less for women (HSE, 2020; Houses of the Oireachtas, 2021). Travellers also experience significant mental health issues, with suicide rates at 11 per cent – seven times higher for males than the national average (Tanner and Tanner, 1990). There are several contributing factors to Travellers' poor physical and mental health and health outcomes, including poverty, high unemployment levels, poor living conditions and poor diet. In addition, concerns about discrimination can lead to lower rates of engagement with the health services (Houses of the Oireachtas, 2021).

Travellers and education

The picture in relation to Travellers' engagement with the formal education system and educational outcomes is equally stark. The Joint Committee Report (Houses of the Oireachtas, 2021: 17) notes:

> 28 per cent of Travellers leave school before the age of 13, compared to one per cent of the general population. Only eight per cent of Travellers have completed education to Leaving Certificate level, compared to 73 per cent of non-Travellers, while only one per cent of Travellers aged between 25–64 have a degree, compared to 30 per cent of non-Travellers. Half of Travellers have poor functional literacy.

Poor educational outcomes are located in a complex web of interconnected issues (p 18):

> The Committee was struck by the interconnected nature of the issues facing the Traveller community which they examined. Deficient and substandard living conditions precarious accommodation and homelessness have severely detrimental effects on both mental and physical health, and brutally impact Traveller children's ability to thrive in education. Lower educational outcomes have a damaging impact on employment opportunities. Chronic unemployment causes stress and has negative consequences for mental health. It is clear that these issues will not be solved in isolation and must be tackled through a whole of Government and a whole of society approach.

In assessing the statistical data on Traveller education and outcomes, Watson et al, 2017: 34) conclude: 'These patterns seem to suggest that improvements in education level across the general population have not been shared by Travellers. As a result, Travellers have been left further behind in terms of their capacity to take advantage of employment opportunities and other advantages associated with improved levels of education.' Travellers are one of the most under-represented groups in higher education, as the president of Ireland noted in his salutary commentary, which is supported by a number of reports (O'Connell et al, 2006; HEA, 2015).

Previous research documents the negative experiences of Travellers in formal education, including bullying, social exclusion and low expectations on the part of teachers (see, for example, Knipe et al, 2005; Padfield and Cameron, 2009; Department of Health, 2010; Biggart et al, 2013). The report *Out of the Shadows* (Quinlan, 2021), commissioned by the National Traveller and Roma Inclusion Strategy, found that Traveller children experience 'daily discrimination and racism' in the Irish education system, describing name-calling by peers, exclusion and a sense of being ignored by some teachers. The Traveller Community National Survey (O'Mahony, 2017) reported that four out of ten Travellers said that they or their children had been bullied in school because of their identity as a Traveller. A culture of low expectations for Traveller students is often reported.

Existing evidence also suggests that Travellers do not associate education with social mobility because of the high level of discrimination they face when seeking employment (Knipe et al, 2005). As a result, some Travellers may 'deny their identity' in order to 'fit in' at school or find work (Department of Health, 2010, 120).

The Joint Committee Report (Houses of the Oireachtas, 2021) notes that cuts were made to Traveller-specific educational supports after the financial crash of 2008, including the Visiting Teacher Service for Travellers and Resource Teachers for Travellers. Segregation of Traveller education was phased out in a process of 'mainstreaming', but there are concerns that, without focused supports within mainstream education, Traveller students are struggling. Traveller organisations have reported regression in the progress rates of Traveller students since these cuts were made.

Reflecting on the changes in educational policy and practice, and editorial in *The Irish Times* (1 October 2021) concluded: 'Though we have progressed from the days of blatant discrimination against Traveller children, which saw them separated from their peers into different classes or even different schools, it is clear the education system is still often not meeting the needs of the community's children.'

Research findings on Traveller education

As part of the Widening Access project, exploratory research was carried out in relation to access to higher education for young people from the Traveller community. Interviews were carried out with representatives from a Traveller health and community project, a third-level Traveller access programme and a youth organisation that works with Travellers who return to education. An in-depth interview was also held with a Traveller student as part of research with students from lower socio-economic backgrounds who had entered higher education through the DARE programme. The findings suggest that poverty and limited expectations on the part of schools impact on educational outcomes and progression rates for Traveller children. At the same time, there were indicators that young Travellers are staying on in school longer and that some are returning to education as adults. The main points raised in the interviews are outlined in the following sections.

Past and present experiences of education in the Travelling community

The UCC research study revealed many Traveller parents and grandparents had a negative experience of schooling, which continues to impact on engagement with the education system. A representative of a Traveller health and community project explained the legacy issues:

> 'Their [parents'] experience will taint children's experience because they are afraid their child is going to undergo the same bullying and segregation and ill-treatment. I personally had a good experience of education but I was put into segregated education at the start until my mother stopped it. But other Travellers have had horrific experiences at school, where even in the 1980s they were showered and washed down in front of other children because they were Traveller children. Because the assumption was that every Traveller child needed to be washed before they came to school. And [children were] separated in the playground – Travellers on one side and the rest on the other. Separated by teachers not by students. That's not long ago – the 1980s isn't that long ago, to have that happen. So, you have a whole host of background as to why Travellers aren't thriving in school. That's not to say that every Traveller isn't thriving in school, but the feeling in the county is that parents are very nervous of the education system.'

One of the outcomes is that parents from the Traveller community may not have the confidence to engage with schools, or raise issues with teachers, such as their child's need for additional support. This is one of the reasons why the role of Visiting Teacher for Travellers was viewed as important for Traveller children and families – because it brought an advocacy dimension to bear on the education system.

The challenges that young Travellers face in primary and secondary education were also raised in interviews with representatives from a third-level Traveller access programme, which supports Traveller students at school and in higher education. It was noted that some schools appeared to have lower expectations for Traveller children in terms of academic outcomes and attendance, and a different set of rules and standards seemed to apply.

Keeping Travellers in school appeared to be an end in itself ('the box is ticked'), with little reference to how the students are achieving. One of the interviewees (Moira) – who regularly met with young Travellers in secondary schools – recalled meeting a student who had reached fifth year without being able to read or write. Figures that suggest Travellers are staying on longer in education, according to this source, disguise the fact that they are leaving with few, if any, qualifications. Moira noted that, in order to increase Traveller access to higher education, policy makers and educators first need to address failures within the primary and secondary school system. Where there was an issue with low attendance, schools needed to think about *why* it was that Traveller children did not want to go to school. Rather than simply pointing to 'Traveller culture', Moira suggested that there needs to be a greater reflection on the nature of the education system. At the moment, young Travellers are 'going through the system', without concerns being raised about levels of attainment: "I think there's low expectations there for Travellers and it's happening in primary school, so if you are given a bad report from primary, what makes the teacher in secondary have any faith in you?"

Representatives from the youth service, who work with Travellers in the Youth Reach programme (which provides opportunities for young people who leave school without qualifications) also reported that, while young Traveller people were staying on in education longer, they were leaving school with poor exam results. They pointed out that it was important to look not only at how long Traveller young people remain in education, but also educational outcomes. As one youth worker put it: "I think we need to ask as well the deeper question – why are they coming out with such low results?"

Poverty and educational outcomes

Poverty – including overcrowded accommodation and lack of financial resources – was identified as one of the main barriers to educational progression among young people from the Travelling Community:

> 'If you are living in cramped quarters with ten different family members and you don't have a desk, it's hard to mind your stuff and do your homework. Also, if you look at what you need to go to school, it's expensive to go to school. The back-to-school grant covers people who have a medical card. But what about the working poor? What about people who are barely over the breadline? Poverty sets an awful lot of people in Ireland back – not just Traveller children – from participating, especially if you have other issues. So, you can overcome one issue at a time. So, if it's poverty, you can overcome that. If it's racism, maybe

you can overcome that. If you are a child who has to overcome poverty, lack of space, discrimination – if you are a child that has to overcome all that, that's when it becomes difficult. And this is my analysis of what is happening to Traveller children. They are dealing with more than one issue. And it is too much for one person's shoulders.' (Travellers' health and community project representative)

This interviewee went on to point out that children of more-affluent parents were able to afford a range of extra curriculum activities (such as music lessons), which gave their children an added advantage over deprived children. However, "a lot of Traveller children and children from disadvantaged backgrounds don't have that – not because parents don't want it, but because parents can't afford it". The emphasis on extra-curriculum activities and educational supports (such as grinds) was seen as a significant change from the past ("It was enough to go to school before") and one that further disadvantages poorer families. The loss of services due to austerity policies over the past decade, including a Visiting Teacher for Travellers, has also had a negative impact, particularly on the poorest families:

'The loss of the Visiting Teacher and other resources has had a massive negative impact on Traveller education locally. The Visiting Teacher for Travellers was like an ambassador and an advocate in the school and with the parents as well. Ensuring the children were in school, that the children had school books, that the children had uniforms. We were dealing with a case recently where a woman wasn't sending her children to school on a regular basis, and when it came down to it, it turned out her children didn't have shoes, her children didn't have school books, she didn't have money to prepare lunches. The school made a lot of assumptions about the woman's situation. That woman was living in dire poverty, even though on the outside everything seemed fine.'

The interviewee noted that there were variations in income and wealth levels within the Traveller community. Some young people have the option of becoming self-employed, with the help of their family. However, young people from poorer Traveller backgrounds would not have the same kinds of opportunities. For them, education offers the only route out of poverty:

'They [parents] want the best outcomes for their children. We have the same aspirations as everybody else. We want them to be happy, healthy successful and have a purpose in life. The difference we would say is that education is important, but the other things in life are important too, like having a family, like having a purpose in life, whether it's being in self-employment. So, for us, whether the young person expresses an interest in enterprise and self-employment and they come from a family that can support that … we would encourage them to go that route. But the worrying case would be where a child comes from a place in which they have little opportunity to support themselves down the road. Then we see education as being pivotal for lifting those children and our community out of poverty.'

"It's an old system": the need for a new education approach

So, what is to be done? Some of the participants in the UCC study suggested that we need a new education philosophy that entirely alters our way of thinking. This is a challenge to current incremental initiatives. For example, programmes that target senior-cycle students come too late for some young Traveller people because they have already left school or fallen behind their classmates. To be effective, initiatives need to begin at primary school.

Looking to the future, participants in the UCC study reported that Traveller education needs dedicated supports, which should be developed in conjunction with the Traveller community and young people themselves. According to representatives from a local Traveller project:

'We need role-modelling, investment. We need investment in Traveller education. We need supports, and those supports need to be developed in conjunction with Traveller academics, Traveller parents, the Traveller community and Traveller organisations. This is pivotal to their success, and in conjunction with young people. The young people's voice needs to be heard.'

Furthermore, it was contended that a complete re-evaluation of Traveller education was necessary:

'I find with education, [Traveller] parents and young people are blamed. And sometimes the schools are blamed. So, there's a lot of finger pointing, but the time for finger pointing is over. We need to get down to action. … Nearly all the resources invested in Traveller education were taken away and we need those reinstated, and used properly, not how they were used before. We need a complete SWOT analysis, if you like, of Traveller education. And we need all the supports analysed to see what exactly has been the benefit of the outcomes for Traveller young people in education.'

Similarly, the youth workers argued that for some vulnerable young people – not just those in the Traveller community – the current schooling system was 'not working' and that a complete re-examination of how society educates children is necessary to bring about real change:

> 'I do think it is as basic as changing the education system. It's as deep-rooted and fundamental and simple, in a way, as that. It's not working. It doesn't work. It doesn't even work for young people who manage to navigate it and come out the other end. … It just needs a massive, massive overhaul, and the resources and commitment from educators, to travel that path. And teach in new ways. And to teach new things that are more relevant to life, to their skills. … It's an old system. It hasn't changed or modified itself to any real degree for centuries. It's time for change. If you look at countries which have vibrant education systems, they are very different from ours.'

She went on to argue that we also need to think of new ways of assessing children's ability, as the current exam system is not fit for purpose:

> '[We need to look at] how they learn and what they learn. And being able to learn independently, on their own. Being given the task to complete, you know. I often even think that the exams – that's not the real way [of testing ability]. Who is given a task within any work situation that they have to sit there, at a desk, for two hours without any tools whatsoever and complete it? We don't work like that. We're given a task, we go off and we are resourceful enough to go to the library, to go to a computer, to do interviews, to talk to people. And that's how we will get the job done. Sitting in a room for a period of time, at a desk, isn't about getting the job done, you know. Why, that's no way to do anything! [Laughs]'

Several interviewees emphasised the importance of role models and 'success stories' as a way of encouraging young Travellers to stay on in school and progress to higher education. As one participant put it:

> 'Also being able to see the future, the benefits of education. It's important for our children to have supports and role models from an early age, like pathways from an early age. Even from primary school, to start visualising their futures because, by the time they get to secondary school, a lot of the literacy and numeracy support they need, while it's never too late to intervene, it's a bit late then. … But we need success stories coming out of the education system to encourage young people to stay in there, you know. We want to see them becoming doctors, we want to see them becoming nurses. We want to see them becoming, I don't know – teachers, classroom assistants,

shopkeepers, you know, if that's what they want for themselves. But we need to see them being successful and coming through. To have a currency for them.'

Interviewees also noted, however, that young people who progress to higher education and graduate careers may not disclose their Traveller identity because of fears of discrimination. So, it is more difficult for role models to emerge. As part of our research with UCC students, we spoke to a young Traveller (Mary) who had not told her fellow students that she was from the Traveller community because she had experienced discrimination in the past. Her family objected to her participation in higher education on the grounds that she was likely to experience discrimination – both at university and in the workplace – and lose her Traveller identity. Their reactions and Mary's reluctance to disclose her identity to fellow students need to be understood in the context of Travellers' experience of social exclusion. It would appear that Mary's decision to withhold her Traveller identity is not unique and her family's misgivings reflect a wider mistrust in the processes and outcomes of the formal educational system experienced by Travellers.

While our interviews highlighted the challenges that young people from the Traveller community face within the education system, several participants also noted that attitudes to education among the Travelling community are gradually changing. Youth workers reported that young people from the Traveller community are staying longer in the school system, relative to their parents and grandparents:

'If I look at the young people that I worked with, in the early 1990s, their parents would have absolutely, never really gone to school at all. And they may have gone a certain way, not even to Junior Certificate; they would have left maybe after primary. Very poor literacy and numeracy. They are now parents themselves and they want their children to complete education. Now, they might limp through the Leaving Certificate. But you can be sure when those young people have children, they will be pushing them through [the education system]. So, generationally it is changing, bit by bit.'

There were a number of reasons for changing attitudes towards, and engagement with, education. Youth workers noted that some mothers who left school early had returned to education as adults. This experience meant that Traveller parents were better able to support their children's home work:

'And I think it gives them a greater understanding as parents. In their support role, do you know? And what it takes to learn; you know, there's a fuller understanding of the learning process. So, if I am learning myself and I know how challenging and difficult that is for me, I have greater understanding of how challenging this is for my child, and so will support them more, with their homework or whatever.'

Youth workers reported that returning to education also made Traveller parents more aware of the importance of education. These parents were now encouraging their children to complete school and go on to further education and training:

'Even just this week, I would have three girls, on three different occasions, whose mothers were past Community Training Centre trainees. And they [mothers] would have made them [children] stay in school, up to the Leaving Certificate. Now they struggled in their Leaving Certificates, you know – not enough [points] to go further. But now their parents are making them look at Youth Reach, to get a better Leaving Certificate, to get to PLC, to get a job, to get wherever. So, yeah, it's definitely changing, and you will see it then, like you said, have kids and make them stay on, and encourage them. So, it's definitely changing.'

Other interviewees also reported that Travellers, particularly women, were returning to education, in part to support their children: "Women are more confident; women are more eager to learn now for their children". One participant went on to say that education was not only important for employment, but in addressing mental health issues within the Traveller community:

'I fully believe Travellers' mental health is all to do with lack of education. I know, accommodation, all of them things, but it might be a lack of accommodation, no hopes for the future and never getting employment, and I think that if Travellers could get that small bit of confidence to get in, get educated, find a job, their own mental health, their self – the difference it would make to their life.'

Conclusion

In this chapter we have examined the experience of Travellers within the Irish education system. There is a long history of problematising the Traveller community. Assimilationist policies were advocated as the solution, with Travellers being invited to live a settled life. Modernisation forced changes to Traveller lifestyles. Social policy gradually moved in the direction of cultural pluralism. Interculturalism became the guiding philosophy. It has been described as a form of 'weak multiculturalism'.

While the Traveller experience of education has been marred by poverty and discrimination, there are positive signs of change. Pressure is mounting for rethinking the philosophy of education that might make it more inclusive and multidimensional. Parental involvement in Traveller children's education has increased, leading parents back into the system. Clearly, there are fundamental resource issues at stake with a need for far greater investment in Traveller education. The will to forge Traveller equality with the settled community looms as the major challenge of the 21st century. Education will be a decisive influence on the future of the Traveller community.

8

Conclusion: Global lessons

This book is based on a sociological analysis and policy discussion of educational stratification, meritocracy and widening participation. The theory of Pierre Bourdieu has been particularly helpful in illuminating our analysis, notably his concept of cultural capital. His intellectual legacy has transformed understanding of educational inequality and its complexities.

Our study is also informed by empirical research based on the experience and aspirations of students, parents, teachers and youth and community workers living and working in disadvantaged areas and communities in the European Union (Ireland). The participants' voices contextualise the profound issues at stake, which are global in scope.

The analysis takes place at a time when major changes are occurring globally in post-industrial society, which have produced new forms of labour based on educational attainment, new identities – the appearance of a 'left-behind' class – and changed political allegiances – the emergence working-class conservatism. The precariousness of life for working-class and ethnic young people in the gig economy is the devastating social reality of our times. It is potentially returning social relations to the inequalities of Victorian society, as the safety net of the welfare state is gradually dismantled. In this closing chapter we address the future of education through the prism of transformative change and what it would look like in a world liberated from Aristotle's hierarchical prescription for society.

The symbolic and material treatment of young people in post-industrial society reflects broad social and cultural shifts placing education at the centre of youth policy. While these changes have transformed the lives of many young people for the better, others have been left behind. This has created a potentially dangerous aspirational-achievement gap in global society. For disadvantaged working-class young people, biographical choices, lifestyles and consumption are limited and identities destabilised by precarious lives. Poverty and marginalisation constrain their lives and generate a sense of powerlessness, social discredit and hopelessness, leaving them viewing themselves as 'minor citizens' (Powell et al, 2012). Higher education has emerged in this new social order as a pivotal societal influence in terms of the pursuit of social equality and human flourishing. It offers new grounds for hope for many young people, but does it pass the social justice test?

This book challenges the historically received wisdom that the working class are not interested in participating in higher education in a meritocratic society. Our research revealed that 66 per cent of senior-cycle students in DEIS schools aspired to participate in higher education. This is a more positive result than most research to date, and questions traditional assumptions that working-class students and their parents are not interested in higher education. They are! Young working-class people and their parents are responding to a changing labour market and the realisation that they need to possess higher-level qualifications to obtain a decent job and enjoy a good life.

The problem is that working-class people historically have been globally excluded from higher education through the existence of a system of economic barriers and cultural codes – in both visible and invisible inequalities – that are deeply embedded in the social structure. Poverty is at the core of this educational disadvantage. These influences prevent people from working-class communities and minority ethnic groups from fully participating in higher education. But educational equality is not and should not be only about a narrative of individual escape from deprivation. It is about promoting the common good through equality of condition by transforming the social structure to achieve a better and more democratic society. The net of participation in higher education needs to be cast widely and inclusively if popular aspirations to access higher education are to be achieved. Michael Sandel (2020: 224) offers a humanist vision of equality of condition:

> It is often assumed that the only alternative to equality of opportunity is a sterile, oppressive equality of results. But there is another alternative: a broad equality of condition that enables those who do not achieve great wealth or prestigious positions to live lives of decency and dignity- developing and exercising their ability to work that wins social esteem, shared widely by a diffused culture of learning, and deliberating with their fellow citizens about public affairs.

He raises some fundamental questions. What can be done to bring about equality of condition in terms of equalising citizens' life chances in a free society? Are universities capable of democratisation through widening participation (Benson and Harkavy, 2000)? The answer is both simple and complex. A simple answer is to give every citizen the right to go to university. It is possible. In South Korea the higher-education participation rate is 85 per cent (Grove, 2018). In reality, widening participation should involve the creation of a 'knowledge society', scaffolded on the humanistic principles of equality of condition, social inclusion and ethnic diversity. A knowledge society, in our view, would be:

- built on the foundation of community schools that: (a) embrace the democratic, secular and universalist ethos of public education; (b) include

curriculum reform based on creative and cultural education rather than competition and rote learning; and (c) addresses the social needs of students from disadvantaged communities, including free (hot) school meals, childcare and youth and community work supports, counselling and sporting and cultural facilities;
- the presence locally of well-stocked public libraries with books, digital facilities, study spaces and artistic and musical instruments, designed as neighbourhood cultural hubs;
- funding for every third-level student's tuition fees – the right to free higher education;
- free accommodation and maintenance through the provision of grants from a national learning bank for a minimum of five years in third-level education and training – this is arguably a fundamental issue of intergenerational justice;
- adequate student support services including counselling and health and an independent student ombudsman service to protect students' rights;
- the total elimination of child poverty as the highest social priority.

It is our basic conclusion that child poverty and social inequality have been the nub of the problem of under-representation of the working class, poor people and minority ethnic groups in higher education in the past and remains so today. It demands a fundamental rethink of what we mean by social justice and the contribution of universities. The report by the UK Commission on Social Justice (1994: 147) concluded: 'Educational improvement is a social and economic mission central to our vision of a more inclusive, productive and cohesive society.' Its realisation as a policy objective depends on a social consensus around rethinking the role and purpose of universities as socially inclusive civic institutions and shared cultural spaces. The problem with the current model of widening participation is that it may continue to exclude working-class and poor students from the elite universities, for example Oxford and Cambridge, and prestigious courses, such as medicine, finance and law). As Diane Reay (2017: 125) puts it: 'Widening participation to a very unequal, hierarchical field is a very crude response to an intractable problem that requires a much more sophisticated, morally informed solution.'

The paradox of widening participation in Britain, according to Reay (2017: 118), is that 'exclusion from the system has been replaced by exclusion within it'. Jack Grove (2018: 3) similarly noted that the removal of the cap on student numbers in Australia 'helped spark a 50% rise in the number of students from disadvantaged backgrounds between 2008–2015, reaching 146,000 entrants out of a total of 1.4 million. However, in the country's oldest universities, the Group of Eight, the share of places has barely shifted since 2009'. We have discussed in this book similar hierarchical patterns of participation in Irish higher education that reflect educational and social stratification. So, what can be done to equalise the system in a direction that moves social inclusion beyond the crude policy goal of numerically widening participation?

The answer is clearly complex, but points to embracing *equality of condition* as the only authentic means to equalise the system of higher education by treating all students broadly the same in terms of their entitlement to life chances. There are two dimensions to achieving equality of condition. First, there are 'reformist reforms', such as the Irish HEAR and DARE programmes, that are broadly affirmative-action initiatives opening up access to all universities. The policy is having a tangible impact on the system, as we have seen in the book, especially in relation to students with disabilities, where there has been a dramatic spike in participation rates. But, even these modest forms of affirmative action are being judicially outlawed, notably in the US. Furthermore, the cost of participation for many potential students may be prohibitive in terms of travel, subsistence and accommodation. There is a need for much greater investment in student maintenance and supports to scale up access numbers across the higher-education system. That requires a fundamental rethink about the role of the welfare state in developing a knowledge society in which a university education becomes a tangible social benefit free to all citizens and migrants as a right from the point of admission to completion of studies.

DEIS schools are significant initiatives designed to equalise the education system and, clearly, make a difference against the odds. They are part of an international evolution of publicly funded schools into community schools. However, massive investment in DEIS schools is required, similar to pandemic-level crisis spending, in order to turn these schools into what has been described as fully functioning community facilities not just focused on teaching students to read and write but also providing childcare for working families, food for hungry children and a sense of cohesion for neighbourhoods. Equality of condition is currently somewhat derisively called 'levelling up' in the UK. What it means in theory is greater redistributive justice targeted at the poor and disenfranchised working class, living in marginalised communities in a post-industrial society. In practice, levelling up is vaguer, suggesting a rhetorical device rather than a coherent policy strategy based on human rights and the redistribution of wealth and opportunities. The bottom line is that, while additional targeted public spending in disadvantaged areas undoubtedly makes a difference to improving the lived experience of poor students and their families, it won't change their world. It will, however, help to improve the lives of many children living in deprived communities in quite fundamental ways, such as providing food security through the provision of free school meals.

That brings us to the second dimension of achieving equality of condition through transformative change. It involves fundamentally changing the social system and its underlying cultural and political assumptions and addressing what we mean by the 'common good'. Aristotle put social hierarchy at the centre of the education system. Little has changed in public thinking about education in the succeeding millennia, except that the elite are today produced by meritocracy rather than aristocracy. It begs the question: 'How do we align education with human flourishing, which Aristotle equated with a happy and virtuous life?'

In *The Meritocracy Trap*, Daniel Markovits (2019: 275) identifies the complexity of the challenges involved for rethinking educational inequality:

> Unwinding meritocratic inequality is 'the work of a civilisation'. It requires a comprehensive adjustment – to government, private associations, cultural habits, and individual consciousness – on a scale equivalent to the changes that built up meritocratic inequality to begin with. The meritocratic trap was constructed over generations and will take generations to dismantle.

Markovits' analysis captures the scale and complexity of the transformative change involved in achieving educational equality. It would require moving away from Aristotelian hierarchical thinking about who should be educated to a project of social inclusion in which education would be reinvented in a new democratic world order. Markovits (2019: 275–276) offers 'two paths to reform' based on incremental change rather than total system renewal:

> First, education now concentrated in the extravagantly trained children of rich parents must become open and inclusive. Admissions must become less competitive, and training less consuming, even at the best schools and universities. Second, work – now divided into gloomy and glossy jobs – must return mid-skilled labour to the centre of economic production. Industry that is now concentrated in a superordinate working class must be dispersed widely across a broad middle class.

Markovits (2019: 276) acknowledges the limitations of his vision for change, arguing that transformative change is a generational project that will take time:

> Of course, these precepts do not yield instructions for curing meritocratic inequality entirely. Like every generational project, the campaign to build democratic equality cannot be planned out in advance. Instead, it will require committed but flexible and opportunistic action, on many fronts at once, in a movement – that develops and adapts as it grows. It is a fool's errand to spell out a complete reform all in one place – a policy wonk's checklist or even

a politician's programme – in advance of the first practical efforts to adopt any element of it.

While Markovits' argument in favour of cautious incremental delivery of new principles is well made, it is essential to acknowledge that transformative change is urgent and will require both political ambition and crisis level economic investment – sustained into the long term – if the goal of genuine educational equality of condition through equalising the life chances of all classes and ethnic groups in society is to be achieved. Moreover, this fundamental change will require massive public spending and a renewal of the welfare state, redesigned to meet the needs of the 21st century –when education has become essential for human flourishing and intergenerational justice.

It will also require society to rethink its cultural assumptions about the nature and meaning of equality of opportunity, particularly in terms of fairness. That will involve real philosophical challenges in relation to addressing Pierre Bourdieu's 'utopian possibilities' and transformative policy initiatives on the scale that Paulo Freire envisaged in *Pedagogy of the Oppressed* (1970). Freire urged the empowerment of the poor, who were being turned into an underclass in the megacities of the world. Freire's contribution was to revolutionise thinking about the education of the poor and working class into a democratic act of liberation. It imagined a world of genuine equality where Aristotle's cultural and social elitism would be finally banished. This is what transformative change means in terms of bringing social justice to education and bringing about *real* social change.

Change needs to start from the premise that a competitive education system is incompatible with democratic values – because it polarises society. We have suggested that creative and cultural education need to be at the centre of the school curriculum. There are broad parallels between the imperatives of achieving educational equality and tackling climate change in terms of human sustainability, the scale of investment required and the cultural and philosophical tasks of reimaging the world. The scale of the change required is also potentially very challenging in terms of how citizens think about freedom, and the financial costs are substantial. But the results of achieving equality of condition will build a better and more sustainable world, where democracy can endure and no citizen will be left behind. Everybody will have the potential to experience what Aristotle called human flourishing as a democratic goal and human right. That is probably as close to utopia as we are likely to get!

References

Adams, R. (2021) Gap widens between private and state schools, *The Guardian*, 11 August.
Adamy, J. (2023) Most Americans doubt their children will be better off, *The Wall Street Journal*, 24 March.
Alberti, G., Bessa, I. and Hardy, K. (2018) In, against and beyond precarity, *Employment and Society*, 32 (3): 447–457.
Appiah, A. and Gates, H. (2004) *Civil Rights,* Philadelphia, Running Press.
Appiah, A. and Gates, H. (2005) *Africana, Volume 4,* Oxford, Oxford University Press.
Archer, L., Hollinsworth, S. and Halsall. A. (2007) University's not for me – I am a Nike person, *Sociology*, 41 (2): 219–237.
Archer, L., De Witt J. and Wong, B. (2013) Spheres of influence: what shapes young people's aspirations at age 12/13 and what are the implications for education policy?, *Journal of Education Policy*, 29 (1): 58–85.
Aries, P. (1973) *Centuries of Childhood,* London, Penguin.
Aristotle (1944) *Collected Works,* Cambridge, Ma, Harvard University Press.
Baker, J., Lynch, K., Cantillon, S. and Walsh, J. (2004) *Equality from Theory to Action,* London, Palgrave Macmillan.
Baker, W., Sammons, P., Siraj-Blatchford, I. et al (2014) Aspirations, education and inequality in England, *Oxford Education Review*, 40 (5): 525–542.
Baldwin, J. (2017) *I Am Not Your Negro,* documentary, Velvet Film Productions.
Ball, S., Reay, D., David, M. (2002a) 'Ethnic choosing': minority ethnic students, social class and higher education choice, *Race, Ethnicity and Education*, 5 (4): 333–357.
Ball, S., Davies, J., David, M. and Reay, D. (2002b) 'Classification' and 'judgement': social class and the 'cognitive structures' of choice in higher education, *British Journal of Sociology of Education*, 23 (1): 51–72.
Barber, C. (2008) *Cultural Studies,* London, Sage.
Barry, B. (2005) *Why Social Justice Matters,* Cambridge, Polity Press.
Bauman, Z. (2001) *Community,* Cambridge, Polity Press.
Beattie, C. (1982) Rawls and the distribution of education, *Canadian Journal of Education*, 7 (3): 39–50.
Benson, L. and Harkavy, I. (2000) Higher education's third revolution, *Cityscape*, 5 (1): 47–56.
Berlant, L. (2011) *Cruel Optimism,* Durham, NC, Duke University Press.
Berlin, I. (1958) *Two Concepts of Liberty,* Oxford, Clarendon Press.
Bhopal, K. (2018) *White Privilege: The Myth of a Post-Racial Society,* Bristol, Policy Press.
Biggart, A., O'Hare, L. and Connolly, P. (2013) A need to belong?, *Irish Educational Studies*, 32 (2): 179–195.

References

Blower, A. (2020) Navigating the aspiration trap, blog, London, Higher Education Policy Institute, https://www.hepi.ac.uk/2020/04/21/navigating-the-aspiration-trap-white-working-class-students-and-widening-access-to-higher-education/

Bok, D (2006) *Our Underachieving Colleges,* Princeton, Princeton University Press.

Bolton, P. (2022) *Higher Education Numbers,* London, House of Commons Library.

Bourdieu, P. (1973) *Knowledge, Education and Social Reproduction,* London, Routledge.

Bourdieu, P. (1986) The forms of capital, in J. Richardson (ed) *Handbook of Theory and Research for Sociology of Education*, Westport, CT, Greenwood, pp 241–258.

Bourdieu, P. (1997) *La Precarite est audjourd hui partout,* paper, Grenoble Conference, 12–13 December.

Bourdieu, P. (1998) *Acts of Resistance,* Cambridge, Polity Press.

Bourdieu, P. (2005) Habitus in E. Roosky and J. Hillier (eds) *Habitus: A Sense of Place,* Aldershot, Ashgate.

Bourdieu, P. (2020) *Habitus and Field*, Cambridge, Polity Press.

Bourdieu, P. (2021) *Forms of Capital*, Cambridge, Polity Press.

Bourdieu, P. and Eagleton, T. (1992) Doxa and common life, *New Left Review*, 191 (1): 111–121.

Bourdieu, P. and Wacquant, L. (1992) *An Invitation to Reflexive Sociology,* Cambridge, Polity Press.

Bourdieu, P. and Grass, G. (2002) The 'progressive' restoration, *New Left Review*, 14, March/April: 63–77.

Bradley, J. and Miller, A. (2010) Widening participation in higher education *Educational Psychology in Practice*, 26 (4): 401–413.

Bray, A., Banks, J., Devitt, A. and Ni Chorcora, C. (2021) Connection before content, *Irish Educational Studies*, 40 (2): 431–441.

Brock report (1934) *Report of the Committee on Sterilisation*, London, HMSO.

Buckingham, D. (2011) *The Material Child,* Cambridge, Polity Press.

Buckingham, D. and Scanlon, M. (2003) *Education, Entertainment and Learning in the Home,* Milton Keynes, Open University Press.

Burleigh, M. (2000) *The Third Reich: A New History*, London, Palgrave Macmillan.

Case, A. and Deaton, A. (2020) *Deaths of Despair and the Future of Capitalism,* Princeton, Princeton University Press.

Central Statistics Office (2021) *Educational Attainment Thematic Report,* Cork, CSO.

Cho, M.Y. (2022) The precariat that can speak, *Current Anthropology*, 63 (5): 473–614.

Cohen, A. and Rutter, J. (2007) *Constructions of Childhood in Ancient Greece and Rome,* Athens, American Schools of Classical Studies.

Coles, B. (1995) *Youth and Social Policy,* London, University College London.

Commission on Social Justice (1994) *Social Justice: Strategies for National Renewal,* London, Vintage.

Conman, J. (2020) Michael Sandel: 'The populist backlash has been a revolt against the tyranny of merit', *The Guardian,* 6 September.

Coulson, S., Garforth, L., Payne, G. and Westell, E. (2017) Admissions, adaptations and anxieties, in R. Waller, N. Ingram and M. Ward (eds) *Degrees of Injustice,* Abingdon, Routledge.

Courtois, A. (2017) 'Thousands are waiting at our gates': moral character, legitimacy and social justice in Irish elite schools, *British Journal of Sociology of Education,* 36 (1): 53–70.

Crossley, S. (2017) *In their Place,* London, Pluto.

Crozier, G., Reay, D., Clayton, J. and Grunstead, J. (2008) Different strokes for different folks, *Research Papers in Education,* 23 (2): 167–177.

Cullinane, C. (2020) How the republic can avoid the calculated grades disaster, *The* Irish Times, 19 August.

Dahl, R (1956) *A Preface to Democratic Theory,* Chicago, Chicago University Press.

Dáil Éireann debate (2022a) Priority questions: Education Schemes, 1 February, www.oireachtas.ie/en/debates/debate/dail/2022-02-01/18/#s23

Dáil Éireann debate (2022b) Educational Disadvantage, 29 June, www.oireachtas.ie/en/debates/question/2022-06-29/95/

Department of Health (2010) *All Ireland Traveller Health Study,* Dublin, Government of Ireland.

Department of Justice and Equality (2017) *National Traveller and Roma Inclusion Strategy 2017–2021,* Dublin, Government of Ireland.

de Sousa Santos, B. (ed) (2007) *Another Knowledge is Possible,* London, Verso.

Dewey, J. (1916) *Democracy and Education,* London, Macmillan.

Donegan, M. (2022) This year I'm thankful for the US public libraries: beautiful icons of a better civic era, *The Guardian,* 29 December.

Doyle, L. (2021) It's about service rather than power, *The University Times,* 9 February.

Drudy, S. and Lynch, K. (1993) *Schools and Society in Ireland,* Dublin, Gill & Macmillan.

Dukelow, F. and Considine, M. (2017) *Irish Social Policy: A Critical Introduction,* Bristol, Policy Press.

Durkheim, E. (1953) *Suicide,* London, Routledge and Kegan Paul.

Dworkin, R. (1998) *Taking Rights Seriously,* London, Duckworth.

Epstein, H. (2020) Left Behind, *New York Review of Books,* 25 March: 28–30.

Esping-Andersen, G. (1990) *The Three Worlds of Welfare Capitalism*, Cambridge, Polity.

European Union (2017) *European Pillar of Social Rights*, Brussels, European Union.

Evans, S. (2009) In a different place, *Sociology*, 43 (2): 340–355.

Fanning, B. (2002) *Racism and Social Change in the Republic of Ireland*, Manchester, Manchester University Press.

Fanon, F. (1961) *The Wretched of the Earth*, London, Penguin.

Ferguson, D. (2017) Working-class children get less of everything in education – including respect, *The Guardian*, 21 November.

Finnegan, F. and Merrill, B. (2017) 'We're as good as anybody else': a comparative study of working-class students' university experiences in England and Ireland, *British Journal of Sociology of Education*, 38 (3): 307–324.

Fishkin, J. (2014a) *Bottlenecks: A New Theory of Equal Opportunity*, Oxford, Oxford University Press.

Fishkin, J (2014b) *Bottlenecks: The Real Opportunity Challenge*, Washington, DC, Brookings Institute.

Fives, A., Keenan, D., Brady, B., and Cairns, D. (2010) *Study of Young Carers in the Irish Population*, Dublin, Office of the Minister for Children and Youth Affairs.

Forsyth, A. and Furlong, A. (2003) Access to education and disadvantaged young people, *British Educational Research Journal*, 29 (2): 205–225.

Foti, A. (2017) *General Theory of the Precariat: Great Recession, Revolution, Reaction*, Amsterdam, Institute of Network Cultures.

Foucault, M. (1967) *Madness and Civilization*, London, Tavistock.

Foucault, M. (1977) *Discipline and Punish*, London, Penguin.

Foucault, M. (1980) *Power/Knowledge*, Brighton, Harvester Press.

Fraser, N. (1997) *Justice Interruptus*, London, Routledge.

Freire, P. (1970) *The Pedagogy of the Oppressed*, London, Penguin.

Freire, P. (1972) *Cultural Action for Freedom*, London, Penguin.

Friedman, S. (2018) What is habitus clive?, *Sociological Review*, 3 December.

Friedman, S. and Laurison, D. (2019) *The Class Ceiling: Why it Pays to be Privileged*, Bristol, Policy Press.

Furlong, A. and Cartmel, F. (2007) *Young People and Social Change*, Milton Keynes, Open University Press.

Gawande, A. (2020) Why Americans are dying of despair, *The New Yorker*, 16 March.

Geismer, L. (2023) Third way to nowhere, *The Nation*, January: 16–21.

Geoghegan, M. and Powell, F. (2009) Community development, the Irish state and the contested meaning of civil society, in D. Ó Broin and P. Kirby (eds) *Power, Dissent and Democracy: Civil Society and the State in Ireland*, Dublin, A.A. Farmar.

Gerrans, P. (2005) Tacit knowledge, rule following and Pierre Bourdieu's philosophy of social science, *Anthropology Theory*, 5 (1): 53–74.

Giddens, A. (1998) *The Third Way,* Cambridge, Polity Press.

Giroux, H. (1994) Insurgent multiculturalism and the promise of pedagogy, in D. Goldberg (ed) *Multiculturalism: A Critical Reader*, Cambridge, MA, Blackwell.

Giroux, H. (2013) The disimagination machine and the pathologising of power, *Sympoke*, 21 (2): 257–269.

Goffman, E. (1968) *Stigma: Notes on the Management of Spoiled Identity*, London, Penguin.

Goldberg, D. (1994) *Multiculturalism: A Critical Reader*, Oxford, Blackwell.

Goldenberg, C. (2001) Cause or effect? A longitudinal study of Latino parents' aspirations and expectations, *American Educational Research Journal*, 38 (3): 547–582.

Goldthorpe, J., Lockwood, D., Bechofer, F. and Platt, J. (1967) The affluent worker and the thesis of embourgeoisement, *Sociology*, 1 (1): 11–31.

Gorard, S., See, B. and Davies, P. (2012) *The Impact of Attitudes and Aspirations on Educational Attainment and Participation*, York, Joseph Rowntree Foundation.

Gorz, A. (1982) *Farewell to the Working-class,* London, Pluto.

Gough, I. (1979) *The Political Economy of the Welfare State,* London, Macmillan.

Government of Ireland (2022) *Our Public Libraries: Inspiring Connection and Empowering Communities*, Dublin, Government of Ireland.

Government of Ireland (2023) *Education Indicators for Ireland Report*, Dublin, Department of Education.

Gramsci, A. (1971) *Prison Notebooks,* London, Lawrence and Wishart.

Grove, J. (2018) Which countries are best at widening participation in universities? *Times Higher Education Supplement*, 5 December, pp 7–8.

Habermas, J. (1987) *Theory of Communicative Action,* Boston, Beacon Press.

Hall, R. (2021) UK students pay 60% more for halls of residence than decade ago, *The Guardian*, 10 December.

Harrison, N. and Waller, R. (2018a) Aspirations, expectations and rethinking outreach, blog, London, British Education Research Association.

Harrison, N. and Waller, R. (2018b) Challenging discourses of aspiration, *British Education Research Journal*, 44 (5): 914–938.

HEA (Higher Education Authority) (2015) *National Plan for Equity of Access to Higher Education 2015–2019*, Dublin, Department of Further and Higher Education, Research, Innovation and Science (FHERIS).

HEA (2018) *Progress Review of National Access Plan,* Dublin, Department of FHERIS.

HEA (2020) *New HEA Data Provides In-Depth Insight into Socio-Economic Profiles of Our Universities and Institutes of Technology*, Dublin, Department of FHERIS.

HEA (2021) *National Access Plan 2022–2026*, Dublin, Department of FHERIS.

HEA (2023) *Eurostudent VIII: Report on the Living Conditions of Higher Education Students in Ireland*, Dublin, Department of FHERIS.

Heller, N. (2023) The end of the English major, *The New Yorker*, 6 March.

Herrnstein, R. and Murray, C. (1994) *The Bell Curve,* New York, Free Press.

Higgins, M.D. (2021) President marks International Traveller & Roma Day 2021, president.ie/en/diary/details/president-marks-international-traveller-roma-day-2021/video

Hoffman, S. (1986) Monsieur Taste, *New York Review of Books,* 10 April.

Holt, J. (1964) *How Children Fail,* London, Penguin.

hooks, bell (2014) *Talking Back,* London, Taylor Francis.

Houses of the Oireachtas (2021) *Final Report of the Joint Committee on Key Issues Affecting the Traveller Community*, Dublin.

House of Commons Education Committee (2021) *The Forgotten: How White Working-Class Pupils Have Been Let Down and How to Change It*, London, House of Commons.

House of Commons Education Committee (2022) *Is the Catch-up Programme Fit for Purpose?*, London, House of Commons.

Howell, J. (1972) *Hard Living on Clay Street,* New York, Knopf Doubleday.

Hughes, G. and Moondey, G. (1998) *Community in Imagining Welfare Futures*, London, Routledge.

Hunt, J. (2023) Shelf life: libraries thrive in modern age, *Irish Times Magazine*, 29 April.

Hunt Report (Department of Education and Skills) (2014) *National Strategy for Higher Education to 2030,* Dublin, Government of Ireland.

Hutchings, M. and Archer, L. (2001) 'Higher than Einstein': constructions of going to university among working-class non-participants, *Research Papers in Education*, 16 (1): 69–91.

Ife, J. (2002) *Community Development in an Uncertain World: Vision, Analysis and Practice*, Frenchs Forest (NSW), Pearson Education Australia.

Illich, I. (1971) *Deschooling Society,* London, Marion Boyars.

Irwin, S. and Elley, S. (2011) Concerted cultivation?, *Sociology*, 45 (3): 480–495.

Irwin, S. and Elley, S. (2012) Parents' hopes and expectations for their children's occupations, *Sociological Review*, 61: 111–130.

Jack, A.A. (2019) *The Privileged Poor: How Elite Colleges are Failing Disadvantaged Students*, Cambridge, MA, Harvard University Press.

James, A., Jenks, C. and Prout, A. (1998) *Theorising Childhood*, Cambridge, Polity Press.

James, R. (2002) *Socio-Economic Background and Higher Education Participation*, London, Department of Science and Training.

Jesse, R. (2022) *They Look Down on Us,* London, CLASS Report.

Joint Committee on Education and Skills (2019) *Report on Education, Inequality and Barriers and Barriers to Education,* Dublin, Dáil Eireann.

Jones, O. (2012) *Chavs: The Demonization of the Working Class*, London, Verso.

Kamenetz, A./*New York Times* (2022) What is school for?, *The* New York Times, 4 September.

Keane, E. (2009) Fictional relationships … tension in the camp: focussing on the relational in understanding student's experiences in Higher Education, *Irish Educational Studies*, 28: 85–102.

Keane, E. (2011) Dependence-deconstruction, *Teaching in Higher Education*, 16 (6): 707–718.

Kettley, N. and Whitehead, J. (2012) Remapping the landscape of choice, *Educational Review*, 64 (4): 493–510.

Kirk, C., Lewis-Moss, R., Nilsen, C. and Colvin, D. (2011) The role of parent expectations on adolescent educational aspirations, *Educational Studies,* 37 (1): 89–99.

Knipe, D., Montgomery, A. and Reynolds, M. (2005) *Traveller Children's Experiences in Mainstream Post-Primary Schools in Northern Ireland*, Belfast, Department of Education.

Kolkman, D. (2020) 'Fxxk the algorithm?' What the world can learn from the UK's A-level grading fiasco, LSE, blog, 26 August, https://blogs.lse.ac.uk/impactofsocialsciences/2020/08/26/fk-the-algorithm-what-the-world-can-learn-from-the-uks-a-level-grading-fiasco/

Koshy, Y. (2021) The last humanist: how Paul Gilroy became the most vital guide to our age of crisis, *The Guardian*, 5 August.

Lamont, M. (2000) *The Dignity of Working Men,* Cambridge, MA, Harvard University Press.

Lareau, A (2002) Invisible inequality, *American Sociological Review*, 67 (5): 747–776.

Lareau, A. (2011) *Unequal Childhoods: Class, Race and Family Life,* Berkeley, University of California Press.

Ledwith, M. (2005) *Community Development: A Critical Approach,* Bristol, Policy Press.

Lehmann, W. (2009) University as vocational education, *British Journal of Sociology of Education*, 30 (2): 137–149.

Le Monde (2023) Death of Nahel M.: Responses to the anger and fear are needed, 1 July, editorial.

Levitas, R. (1998) *The Inclusive Society,* London, Macmillan.

Lewis, O. (1961) *Children of Sanchez,* New York, Vintage.

Lewis, O. (1966) *La Vida,* New York, Vintage.

Littler, J. (2018) *Against Meritocracy: Culture, Power and the Myths of Social Mobility,* London, Routledge.

Lovett, T. (1989) Adult education and the working class, in D. O'Sullivan (ed) *Social Commitment and Adult Education*, Cork, Cork University Press.

Lynch, K. (2020) Class and wealth, not merit, are rewarded in Ireland's education system, *The Journal*, 30 September.
Lynch, K. (2022) *Care and Capitalism: Why Affective Equality Matters for Social Justice,* Cambridge, Polity Press.
Lynch, K. and Baker, J. (2005) Equality in education: an equality of condition perspective, *Theory and Research in Education*, 3 (2): 131–164.
Lynch, K. and O'Riordan, C. (1998) Inequality in higher education, *British Journal of Sociology of Education*, 19 (4): 445–478.
Mac Sweeny, N. (2023) *The West: A New History of an Old Idea,* London, WH Allen.
MacVeigh, T. (2006) Education, life chances and disadvantage, in B. Fanning and M. Rush (eds) *Care and Social Change in Irish Welfare Economy*, Dublin, University College Dublin Press.
Major, L.E. and Machin, S. (2018) *Social Mobility and Its Enemies*, London, Pelican.
Mandela, N. (1995) *Long Walk to Freedom,* London, Little Brown.
Mangabeira Unger, R. (2022) *The Knowledge Economy,* London, Verso.
Markovits, D. (2019) The Meritocracy Trap, London, Penguin.
Marshall, T.H. (1973) *Class, Citizenship and Social Development*, Westport, CT: Scientific Research Publishing.
Masquelier, C. (2018) Bourdieu, Foucault and the politics of precarity, *Distinction Journal of Social Theory,* December: 1–10.
McAuley, J. (2022) A failure of imagination, *New York Review of Books*, 21 April: 59–62.
McCoy, S. and Byrne, D. (2011) 'The sooner the better I could get out of there': Barriers to higher education access in Ireland, *Irish Educational Studies*, 30 (2): 141–157.
McCoy, S., Byrne, D., O'Connell, P. et al (2010) *Hidden Disadvantage?*, Dublin, HEA / Dept of FHERIS.
McKnight, A. (2015) *Downward Mobility, Opportunity Hoarding and the 'Glass Floor'*, London, Social Mobility and Child Poverty Commission.
McLaren, P. (1994) White terror and opposition agency: towards a critical. multiculturalism, in D.A. Goldberg (ed) *Multiculturalism: A Critical Reader*, Oxford, Blackwell.
McLaren, P. (2021) The perilous road to justice: an interview with Peter McLaren, *Journal of Higher Education and Leadership Studies*, 2 (1): 145–156.
McMillan Cottom, T. (2018) *Lower Ed: The Troubling Rise of For-Profit Colleges in the New Economy*, New York, The New Press.
McVeigh, R. (2008) The 'Final Solution': reformism, ethnicity, denial and the politics of anti-Travellerism in Ireland, *Social Policy and Society*, 7 (1): 91–112.
Mervosh, S. (2022) The pandemic erased two decades of progress in math and reading, *The New York Times*, 1 September.

Mishra, P. (2017) *Age of Anger,* London, Allen Lane.

Mistry, R., White, E., Benner, A. and Huynh, V. (2009) A longitudinal study of simultaneous influence of mothers and teachers, *Journal of Youth Adolescence*, 38: 826–838.

NACCCE (1999) *All Our Futures: Creativity, Culture and Education*, London, DfEE.

Neary, M. and Winn, J. (2017) Beyond public and private: a framework for cooperative higher education, Open Library of Humanities, 3 (2): 2. Doi: https://doi.org/10.16995/olh.195.

New York Times (2022) What is school for?, 4 September.

Novak, T. (1998) *Poverty and the State,* Milton Keynes, Open University Press.

O'Brien, C. (2021a) Leaving certificate calculated grades, *The Irish Times*, 22 February.

O'Brien, C. (2021b) Private schools say exclusion from state grants discriminatory, *The Irish Times*, 27 December.

O'Brien, C. (2022) Education remains underfunded compared to EU, *The Irish Times*, 28 September.

O'Connell, C., Finnerty, J. and Egan, O. (2008) *Hidden Voices: An Exploratory Study of Young Carers in Cork*, Dublin, Combat Poverty.

O'Connell, P., Clancy, P. and McCoy, S. (2006) *Who Went to College in 2004?*, Dublin, HEA/Dept of FHERIS.

O'Connor, J. (1973) *The Fiscal Crisis in the Welfare State*, London, Routledge.

OECD (Organisation for Economic Co-operation and Development) (2018) *A Broken Elevator? How to Promote Social Mobility*, Paris, OECD.

OECD (2021) *Education at a Glance 2021*, Paris, OECD.

Offe, C. (1984) *Contradictions of the Welfare State*, London, Hutchinson.

O'Mahony, J. (Behaviours & Attitudes) (2017) *Traveller Community National Survey*, Dublin, National Traveller Data Steering Group/Community Foundation for Ireland.

Orwell, G. (2000) *1984,* London, Penguin.

O'Sullivan, D. (1993) *Commitment, Educative Action and Adults*, Aldershot, Avebury.

O'Toole, F. (2012) *Up the Republic,* London, Faber.

O'Toole, F. (2021) Fianna Fáil has had two long lives – there will not be a third act, *The Irish Times*, 13 July.

Packer, R. (2021) The four Americas, Atlantic, July/August: 64–78.

Padfield, P. and Cameron, G. (2009) *Inclusive Education for Children and Young People*, London, Routledge.

Parsell, C. (1981) Genetics and cultural deficit theories, *Black Studies*, 12 (1): 19–37.

Piketty, T (2014) *Capitalism in the Twenty-First Century,* Cambridge, MA, Belknap Press.

Polanyi, K. (2001) *The Great Transformation*, Boston, Beacon.

References

Powell, F. (2001) *The Politics of Social Work*, London and New York, Sage.
Powell, F. (2009) Think globally, act locally, *Geojournal*, 77: 141–152.
Powell, F. (2013) *The Politics of Civil Society*, Bristol, Policy Press.
Powell, F. (2017) *The Political Economy of the Irish Welfare State: Church, State and Capital*, Bristol, Policy Press.
Powell, F. and Guerin, D. (1997) *Social Policy and Civil Society: Voluntarism in Ireland*, Dublin, A&A Farmar.
Powell, F. and Scanlon, M. (2015) *Dark Secrets of Childhood*, Bristol, Policy Press.
Powell, F., Geoghegan, M., Scanlon, M. and Swirak, M. (2012) *Youth Policy, Civil Society and Modern Irish State*, Manchester, Manchester University Press.
Powell, F., Scanlon, M. and Galvin, M. (2018) *Making a Difference: A Research Report on Student Volunteering in UCC*, Cork, Institute of Social Science in the 21st Century.
Putnam, R. (2000) *Bowling Alone*, New York, Simon and Schuster.
Putnam, R. and Feldstein, L. (2004) *Better Together: Restoring American Community*, New York, Simon and Shuster.
Quinlan, M. (2021) *Out of the Shadows – Traveller & Roma Education*, Dublin, Government of Ireland.
Rainwater, L. (1970) *Behind Ghetto Walls*, London, Penguin.
Read, B., Archer, L. and Leathwood, C. (2003) Challenging cultures, *Studies in Higher Education*, 28 (3): 261–277.
Reay, D. (2005) Doing the dirty work of social class? Mothers work in support of their children's schooling, *Sociological Review*, 53 (2): 104–116.
Reay, D. (2017) *Miseducation: Inequality, Education and the Working Classes*, Bristol, Policy Press.
Reay, D. (2020) The perils and penalties of meritocracy, *Political Quarterly*, 91 (2): 405–412.
Reay, D., Crozier, G. and Clayton, J. (2009) Strangers in paradise: working-class students in elite universities, *Sociological*, 43 (6): 103–112.
Reich, C. (1971) *The Greening of America*, New York, Random House.
Reich, R. (2021) The true meaning of 6 January, *The Guardian*, 28 December.
Rogalsky, J. (2009) 'Mythbusters': dispelling the culture of poverty myth in the urban child classroom, *Journal of Geography*, 108 (405): 198–209.
Rooney, S. (2019) *Normal People*, London, Faber & Faber.
RTÉ (2023) Is it fair that public money helps to fund private schools?, 6 March, rte.ie/news/upfront/2023/0218/1357271-is-it-fair-that-public-money-helps-to-fund-private-schools
Rushdie, S. (1981) *Midnight's Children*, London, Jonathan Cape.
Saltmarsh, J. and Hartley, M.(eds) (2011) *'To Serve a Larger Purpose': Engagement for Democracy and the Transformation of Higher Education*, Philadelphia, Temple University Press.

Saltmarsh, J. and Hartley, M. (2016) The inheritance of the next generation engagement scholars, in M. Post, E. Ward, N. Longo and J. Saltmarsh (eds) *Publicly Engaged Scholars*, Stirling, VA, Stylus.
Sandel, M. (2010) *Justice: What is the Right Thing To Do?*, London, Penguin.
Sandel, M. (2020) *The Tyranny of Merit*, London, Penguin.
Sandel, M. (2021a) Toppling the myth of meritocracy, *Harvard Gazette*, 5 June.
Sandel, M. (2021b) The future of democracy, *Noéma*, 7 December.
Schoenbaum, N. (2023) The Supreme Court inadvertently instituted affirmative action for white men, *Politico*, 19 July.
SCIE (Social Care Institute for Excellence) (2005) *The Health and Wellbeing of Young Carers*, London, SCIE.
Sellgren, K. (2020) Elitist curriculum not serving white working classes, *BBC News*, 13 October.
Sibieta, L., Tahir, I. and Waltmann, B. (2022) *Adult Education: Past, Present and Future*, London, Institute of Fiscal Studies.
Silver, H. (1994) Social exclusion and social solidarity: three paradigms, *International Labour Review*, 133 (5–6): 531–578.
Shields, L., Newman, A. and Satz, D. (2017) Equality of educational opportunity, *Stanford Encyclopaedia of Philosophy*, Stanford, Stanford University Press.
Smyth, E. (2009) Buying your way into college: private tuition and the transition to higher education in Ireland, *Oxford Review of Education*, 35 (1): 1–22.
Snoussi, D. and Mompelat, L. (2019) *'We are Ghosts': Race, Class and Institutional Prejudice*, London, Runnymede Trust and CLASS.
Solas, *Adult Literacy for Life*, Dublin, Government of Ireland.
Spicker, P. (1993) *Poverty and Social Security*, London, Routledge.
Standing, G. (2014) *The Precariat*, London, Bloomsbury.
Standing, G. (2018) *The Precariat are Not the Left Behind*, Davos, World Economic Forum.
St Clair, R., Kintrea, K. and Houston, M. (2013) Silver bullet or red herring? New evidence on place of aspirations in education, *Oxford Review of Education*, 39 (6): 719–738.
Stern, F. (1961) *The Politics of Cultural Despair*, Berkeley, University of California Press.
Stewart, M. (2018) The 9.9% is the new American aristocracy, *The Atlantic*, June: 50–54.
Stone, I.F. (1988) *The Trial of Socrates*, New York, Anchor.
Tanner, D. and Tanner, L. (1990) *History of the School Curriculum*, New York, Macmillan.
Tawney, R.H. (1922) *Secondary Education for All*, London, Allen and Unwin.
The Telegraph (2009) Professor Brian Barry, obituary, 5 April.

Thompson, I. and Ivinson, G. (2020) *Poverty and Education Across the UK,* Bristol, Policy Press.
Tilly, C. (1998) *Durable Inequality,* Berkeley, University of California Press.
Titmuss, R. (1962) *Income Distribution and Social Change*, London, Allen and Unwin.
Tormey, R. (2010) The silent politics of education disadvantage, *Irish Educational Studies*, 29 (2): 189–199.
Towles, A. (2021) Trumpism is absolutely tied to the failure of the American dream, *Irish Times*, 28 October.
Turchin, P. (2023) *End Times, Counter Elites and the Path to Political Disintegration,* London, Allen Lane.
UCAS (2020) *What Happened to the Covid Cohort? Lessons in Levelling Up in 2021 and Beyond*, London, UCAS.
United Nations (1948) Universal Declaration of Human Rights, New York/Geneva.
Wacquaint, L. (2022) *The Invention of the 'Underclass'*, Cambridge, Polity.
Walther, A., du Bois-Reymond, M. and Biggart, A. (eds) (2006) *Participation in Transition: Motivation of Young Adults in Europe for Working and Learning,* Frankfurt, Peter Lang.
Watson, D., Kenny, O. and McGinnity, F. (2017) *A Social Portrait of Travellers in Ireland*, Dublin, Economic and Social Research Institute.
Weale, S. (2021) Call for more play time amid 'schoolification' of UK childhood, *The Guardian*, 23 April.
Wilkinson, R. and Pickett, K. (2009) *The Spirit Level,* London, Allen Lane.
Willet, C. (1998) *Theorizing Multiculturalism: A Guide to Current Debate,* Oxford, Blackwell.
Williams, J.C. (2018) Angry young men, *Times Literary Supplement*, 6 July.
Wood Report (1929) *Report of the Joint Committee on Mental Deficiency*, London, HMSO.
Wuthnow, R. (2018) *The Left Behind: Decline and Rage in Rural America*, Princeton, Princeton University Press.
Young, M. (1958) *The Rise of Meritocracy*, Piscataway, NJ, Transaction.
Zimmerman, J. (2020) What is college worth?, *New York Review of Books*, 2 July.

Index

A

Abbot, Greg 74
academic transition 100–103
access to higher education vii–ix, 1, 13, 128–148
  alternative routes 145
  aspirations 132–133
  barriers to 15–18, 28–29, 63, 93–94, 107, 138–145, 155, 159, 171–172, 178–181
  changing aspirations 135–138
  entrance requirements 91, 93, 114–115, 120–123, 145–146
  facilitators 130–132, 145–147, 159, 161
  as game of Snakes and Ladders 134–135
  lack of confidence 141–143
  motivations 129–130, 135–138
  reforms 182–183
  resilience 133–134
  social structure and achievement 133
  transition to 96–103, 141–143
  Traveller community 168–177
  widening participation 92–104, 180
  see also parents
accommodation
  cost of 93, 139–140, 155, 162
  Traveller community 167, 168, 171
Adams, R. 111
Adamy, J. 35
adult education ix, 16, 87–92, 175–176
adult literacy 66–67
affective justice 23–24, 118
affirmative action 74, 95–96, 181
Afghanistan 105
Alberti, G. 37, 38
alienation 28, 37–38, 40–41, 56–57, 63
anomie 40–43
Antigonish Community, Canada 92
Appiah, A. 95–96
apprenticeships 116, 136, 156, 166
Archer, L. 53, 56–57
Arendt, H. 22
Aries, P. 46
Aristotle 1, 18, 23, 44, 45, 46, 182, 183
Arizona State University 76
attainment gap 50, 54, 66–68
austerity 6, 24, 43, 70, 80, 89–90, 172
Australia 57, 180

B

Baker, J. 117, 118
Baker, W. 57
Baldwin, J. 39, 40
Ball, S. 139, 149, 154, 155, 158, 160
banning books 73–74, 75
Barber, C. 135
Barry, B. 47, 115, 118–119
Bauman, Z. 134
BBC news report 50–51
Berlant, L. 138
Berlin, I. 4
Bhopal. K. 49
Biden, Joe 65, 94
Black Lives Matter 49, 62
Blair, Tony 92
blame, and poverty 62–65
Blower, A. 132
Booth, C. 41
Bourdieu, P. v, 6–7
  culture and class 3–4, 46, 47, 52–56, 71, 72, 128–129, 147
  globalisation vi
  meritocracy 106, 113
  neoliberalism vii, 73, 77–80
  and parenting styles 149–150
  precariat 37–38, 128–129
  and social mobility 125
  utopian possibility vii, 183
  welfare state 47, 78
Brazil 27
Britain *see* United Kingdom/Britain
Brock report (1934) 41
Buckingham, D. 111
Bush, George W. 3

C

Campus Engage Charter for Civic and Community Engagement 82, 83, 85
Canada 92
care 23–24, 44–45, 141
Cartmel, F. 138
Case, A. 7–8, 62, 63, 65
Catholicism 42, 44
Central Statistics Office in Ireland 37
children/childhood 43–46
  and capital 54
  child poverty 70, 115, 180
  COVID-19 pandemic 121–124
  rights 21, 59, 113, 126–127
  socialisation 44–45, 54–56, 66, 150
  Traveller community 169–176
  unequal childhoods 150
  see also parents; schools
Cho, M.Y. 129
citizen journalism 83
citizen science research model 83
citizenship 21, 22, 24, 69

civic and community engagement 82–86
civic virtue 6, 18, 69, 78, 109
civil society 73–82
Clarke, K. 45
CLASS 7, 27, 28
class (general)
   class divide 57–59
   concept of 27
   COVID-19 pandemic 122
   cultural capital 54–55, 106, 121, 135, 150, 152–153
   cultural politics 48–52
   dynamics of 7, 58
   educational attainment 133, 145
   educational disadvantage 65–71
   educational ladder 46–48
   equality of opportunity 113–115
   eugenics 47–48
   Gatsby Curve 57–58
   habitus 55–56
   and intelligence 47
   and meritocracy 106–114
   rethinking social inequality 26
   and social mobility 124–126
   see also middle classes; working class
cognitive justice 12, 15, 26, 40
Cohen, A. 44
Coles, B. 138
commodification 74, 77, 80, 93–94
common good 11, 107–108, 179, 182
community vi–vii
   community engagement 82–86
   as site of intervention 41–42
community schools *see* DEIS schools
conscientisation 11–12, 16, 87–88
Considine, M. 46
Coulson, S. 98
Courtois, A. 21, 22
COVID-19 95, 108, 121–124
creative education 147, 180, 183
credential inflation 155
critical literacy 12, 71, 105
critical pedagogy 10, 16, 39, 83, 87
critical race theory 49–50, 64, 71
critical theory/poststructuralist perspective of social justice 70–71
Crossley, S. 61
Crozier, G. 149
Cullinane, C. 122
cultural capital
   and class 54–55, 106, 121, 135, 150, 152–153
   equality of condition 118
   equality of opportunity 115
   and meritocracy 106, 110
   opportunity hoarding 121
   theory of 3–4, 6, 46, 52–56
cultural deficit theory 63–64, 66
cultural empowerment 11–12, 16, 86–92

culture of poverty thesis 63–64
culture wars 73–74, 75, 79, 82

D

Dahl, R. 77
Darwin, Charles 46, 48
deaths of despair 7–8, 62
Deaton, A. 7–8, 62, 63, 65
degrees, value of 35–36, 155
DEIS schools 14, 17
   access to higher education 15, 28–29, 138–148, 159, 179
   COVID-19 pandemic 123, 124
   cultural capital 54–55
   educational aspirations 135–138
   funding of 21, 80, 181
   and invisible inequalities 128
   opportunity pluralism 116
   and parental attitudes 151–160
   and poverty 140–141
   and private sector 120–121
   progression to higher education 133
   purpose and roles of 29–30, 81, 181
   and resilience 133–134
   success of 181
democracy
   civic and community engagement 83–85
   critical pedagogy 10
   and education v, 11–12, 19, 20
   and a fair society 21–26
   and humanism 77
deservingness 7, 107, 108
Dewey, J. v
difference principle 69
disadvantaged 59
   educational disadvantage 65–71
   see also access to higher education; DEIS schools; poverty; race; Traveller community; working class
dispositions 55
Donegan, M. 88–89
Doyle, L. 2
Drudy, S. 87–88
Du Bois, W.E.B. 95
Dublin 67, 133, 136, 140–143, 145, 158, 160
Dukelow, F. 46
Durkheim, E. 40–41, 42
Dworkin, R. 11

E

Eagleton, T. 56
economic barriers 17–18, 28–29, 63, 74, 93, 94, 107, 139–140, 145, 155, 159, 179–181
economic capital *see* financial capital
economic crisis (2008–2013) 37, 43, 80, 112, 169
Education Indicators for Ireland 133
Education Research Centre, Dublin 30

educational aspirations 10, 27–29, 132–133, 135–138, 158–160
educational attainment/outcomes
  access to higher education 145
  cultural deficit theory 63–64
  educational disadvantage 65–68
  employment and income 37, 48
  and mortality 62
  Traveller community 163, 168–169, 171, 175–176
  see also exams/qualifications
educational disadvantage 65–71
educational equality models 112–119, 127
educational ladder 46–48
educational stratification vii, 6, 18–21, 35–72
  alienation 3, 5, 56–57
  benefits of higher education 36–39
  blame 62–65
  Bourdieu, culture and class 52–56
  childhood 43–46
  class divide 48–52, 57–59
  educational disadvantage 65–71
  educational ladder 46–48
  Gatsby Curve 57–58
  as global problem 2–3
  great challenge of 9
  historically 18–19
  and meritocracy 8–10
  mirror image of society 39–40
  problem of anomie 40–43
  territorial stigmatisation 60–62
elite over-production 35, 36, 37
Elley, S. 149, 151, 154, 156, 161
embodied cultural capital 52, 56, 125
employment
  culture of poverty thesis 64
  gig economy 6, 38, 51, 64
  and knowledge economy 94
  as motivation 129–130, 135–137
  precariat 7, 37–38, 51, 109
  qualifications 154–155, 161, 179
  rates of 37
  reforms 182
  student 145
  Traveller community 167, 168, 169, 172–173
  unemployment 37, 167, 168
  wages 64, 94
  working class 7, 51
empowerment 20, 68, 183
  cultural empowerment 11–12, 16, 86–92
entitlement 54–55, 99, 135, 148, 149
equality, concept of viii–ix
equality of condition 3, 11, 46, 117–119, 127, 179, 181–183
equality of opportunity v–vi, 11, 48, 69, 113–115, 117, 127, 183
equality of respect and recognition 26, 118
eugenics 41, 47–48

European Union, inclusion strategy 43
exams/qualifications
  and class 67, 122–123, 145, 153, 156
  COVID-19 pandemic 122–123
  DEIS schools 54, 123, 145–146
  and economic capital 52–53
  and employment 37, 64, 94, 126, 155, 156, 161, 179
  private and state schools 111
  private tuition 120–121, 145
  Traveller community 163, 168, 171, 174, 175–176
  at university 102
  and university admission 91, 93, 114–115, 120–123, 145–146
  value of degrees 35–36, 155
extra-curriculum activities 55, 172
Eysenck, Hans 47

F

fair society, challenges of 21–26
Fanning, B. 164–166
Fanon, F. 41
Feldstein, L. 89
Ferguson, D. 23
field 54, 56
financial barriers *see* economic barriers
financial capital 47, 54, 55, 107, 110, 115, 118, 120–121, 130–131, 135
financialisation of higher education 35
Finland 47, 89
Finnegan, F. 142–143
Fishkin, J. 20, 114, 115–116
Florida 73–74, 75
food poverty 140
Foti, A. 38
Foucault, M. 60, 71
France 5, 38, 42, 52–53, 79
Fraser, N. 86–87
free tuition 16, 24, 35, 73, 116, 124, 180
freedom 4, 6, 10, 48, 105–106, 111
Freire, P. ix, 1–2, 10, 11–12, 16, 21, 83, 87, 105, 183
Friedman, S. 25, 43, 54, 55, 110–111, 125
funding
  adult education 90, 91
  schools 21, 30, 80, 181
  Traveller community 169, 172, 173
  universities 11, 16, 17, 76
  widening participation 93–94, 95
Furlong, A. 138
further education and training (FET) 116, 155–158, 176
Further Education and Training Awards Council (FETAC) 16

G

Gates, H. 95–96
Gatsby Curve 57–58

Gawande, A. 63
Geismer, L. 6
gender *see* men; women
genetics 46–47
Gerrans, P. 52
Giddens, A. 6, 11
gig economy 6, 38, 51, 64
Gilroy, P. 26
Giroux, H. 5, 10, 39, 164
globalisation v–vi, 42, 51, 108, 109
  and knowledge economy 2–5
Goffman, E. 60, 61
Goodwin, M. 51
Gorz, A. 51
Gramsci, A. 88
grants 28–29, 131, 139, 145, 155, 180
Grass, G. v, vii, 6–7, 73
grind schools 120–121, 145
Grove, J. 180
Guardian, The 5, 108–109, 111

H

Habermas, J. 16
habitus 54, 55–57, 98, 150
habitus clive 55–56
Harrison, N. 132
Hartley, M. 77, 84
Harvard Gazette 107–108
health inequalities 167–168
HEAR students 13, 97–98, 129–132, 181
Heller, N. 76, 77
hermeneutics of suspicion 22, 106–111
Herrnstein, R. 47
Higgins, M.D. 73, 163
higher education/universities (overview)
  affirmative action viii, 74, 95–96, 181
  alienation 56–57
  benefits of 8, 35–39
  civic and community engagement 76, 82–86
  entrance requirements 91, 93, 114–115, 120–123, 145–146
  eradicating educational stratification 19–20
  financialisation of 35
  funding of 11, 16, 17, 76
  in knowledge economy 73–78
  knowledge society 11–12, 76, 179–181
  participation rates in Ireland 13–14
  see also access to higher education; parents; public education; Traveller community; widening participation
Higher Education Authority (HEA) Ireland 13–14, 37, 139
Highlander Folk School, Tennessee 92
homework clubs 146
hooks, bell 11, 26

House of Commons Education Committee 50, 64, 121–122
housing 141, 167, 168, 171
Howell, J. 49
Hughes, G. 41–42
Hugo, Victor 4
human capital 110–111
humanism v, 11, 19, 35, 74, 76–78, 93, 127, 179–180
Humboldt, Wilhelm von 35
Hunt Report 85
Huxley, T.H. 46

I

identity politics 26, 86, 164
Ife, J. 68
independent learning 101, 102–103
information-age capitalism 6
Institute of Fiscal Studies (IFS) 89
institutionalised cultural capital 53
institutionalist concept of social justice 69–70
intelligence 46–48, 106
interculturalism 164–165
intersectionality viii, 26, 28, 43, 44, 47, 59, 65–68, 94, 95, 98–99
IQ tests 46–47, 106
Ireland (general) vi–vii, 2–3
  alienation 57, 135, 138
  child abuse 44
  cost of higher education 14, 74, 139
  COVID-19 pandemic 123
  economic crisis 37, 80, 112
  education policy 2, 13–14, 29–30
  educational disadvantage 21, 65–68
  employment 37, 161
  equality of opportunity 117–118
  funding of education 2, 17, 21
  meritocracy 1, 110
  private sector 21–22, 120
  public education 73, 82–83, 85, 89–91
  quality of life ranking 16–17
  school league tables 133
  social class 58–59, 142–143
  social exclusion 42
  social structure 133
  student grants 29, 130–131, 139
  see also access to higher education; DEIS schools; Traveller community
Irish Independent 123
Irish Joint Committee on Education and Skills 117–118
Irish National Teachers Organisation 165
Irish Research Council 14
Irish Times, The 1, 2, 13, 14, 17, 21, 30, 73, 117, 169
Irish Universities Association 82, 85
Irwin, S. 149, 151, 154, 156, 161

Italy 88
Ivinson, G. 19

J

Jack, A.A. 49, 96–97
Jensen, Arthur 47
Jesse, R. 27, 28
Johnson, Lyndon B. 63
Joint Committee on Education and Skills, Ireland 67–68
Joint Committee Report, Houses of the Oireachtas 168, 169
Joint Irish Parliamentary Committee on Education and Skills 65
Jones, O. 48, 51–52
Journal, The 58, 110

K

Kamenetz, A. 1, 81
Kennedy, John F. 124
Kerr, C. 75
Kettley, N. 161
Kirby, P. v–vi
knowledge
  Bourdieu's theory 52
  civic and community engagement 83–84
knowledge economy 2–5, 36, 94
  and universities 73–75, 76–77
knowledge society 11–12, 76, 179–180, 181
Kolkman, D. 123

L

Lamont, M. 49
Lareau, A. 3, 106, 149–150
Laurison, D. 25, 43, 54, 110–111, 125
Le Monde 38
Ledwith, M. 68
left-behind class (overview) v
  concept of 4–5
  problem of anomie 40–43
  social construction 5–11
  see also working class
levelling up 43, 93, 125, 181
Levitas, R. 42
Lewis, O. 63–64
liberal concept of social justice 69
lifelong learning 16, 82, 90, 116
literacy 66–67, 121, 171
Littler, J. 106
Lovett, T. 88, 90
Lynch, K. 23–24, 57, 58–59, 87–88, 110, 117–118, 160

M

Mac Sweeny, N. 82
Machin, S. 58, 94–95, 119, 120, 124, 125–126
Macron, Emmanuel 5, 79
MacVeigh, T. 140
Major, L.E. 51, 58, 94–95, 119, 120, 124, 125–126
Mandela, N. 35
Mangabeira Unger, R. 3
Markovits, D. 25, 63, 110, 182–183
Marshall, T.H. 24, 69
Marx, K. 41
Masquelier, C. 129
mature students 13–14, 16, 91
McKnight, A. 119
McLaren, P. 10, 21
McMillan Cottom, T. 94
McVeigh, R. 165
men, White working class 48–49, 50–52, 62, 63, 64
mental health 168, 176
meritocracy vii–viii, 1, 16, 20, 24, 105–127
  and adult education 91
  aspirations of working class 27–28
  critique vii, 22, 25, 27–28, 91, 106–111
  dismantling 182–183
  and educational stratification 8–10
  equality of opportunity viii, 113–115, 117
  and 'fairness' 8, 9, 23, 25, 39
  models of educational equality 112–119
  origins 22
  and private sector 119–121
  and social mobility 25, 124–126
Merrill, B. 142–143
middle classes
  attainment gap 54
  class divide 57–59
  and cultural capital 54–55, 106, 150
  embodied capital 125
  navigating the system 106–107, 111
  opportunity hoarding 25, 119–121, 125, 145
  parents 55, 58, 59, 95, 106–107, 119–121, 144, 145, 149, 150, 154
  and social mobility 125–126
  socialisation 54, 55, 56, 150
  university entitlement 56, 99, 143, 144, 149, 155
Mishra, P. 40
Mompelat, L. 7, 9
Mooney, G. 41–42
mortality rates 62, 167–168
motivations of students 129–130, 135–138
multiculturalism 164–165
Murray, C. 47
Muslim students 79

N

National Access Plan, Ireland 13
National Council of Labour Colleges 90

National Traveller and Roma Inclusion Strategy 166, 167, 169
nature versus nurture 46–47
Neary, M. 74
neoliberalism vii–viii, 6, 23–24, 25, 59
  hegemonic impact of 15
  inspiration for 80
  knowledge economy 73–75
  and precariat 38
  re-stratification of society 7
  resistance to 77–78
  social democracy 6
  and universities 76–78
  and welfare state vii–viii, 24, 80
New York Times, The 75, 81, 121
New Yorker 76
No Child Left Behind Bill, US 3
noble lie concept 110

O

Obama, Barack 3
objectified cultural capital 52–53
Occupy movement 23, 38
O'Connell, P. 145
OECD 17, 20, 111, 124, 125
opportunity hoarding 25, 119–121, 125, 145
opportunity pluralism ix, 11, 16, 20, 115–117, 127
O'Riordan, C. 57, 160
Orwell, G. 9, 15
O'Sullivan, D. 65–66, 87
othering 60–62
O'Toole, F. 18, 44
Out of the Shadows 169

P

Packer, G. 71, 109
parents 149–162
  conflicting aspirations 158–160
  further education and training 155–158
  middle class 55, 58, 59, 95, 106–107, 119–121, 144, 145, 149, 150, 154
  no familiarity with higher education 153–154, 155, 161
  opportunity hoarding 25, 119–121, 125, 145
  providing accommodation 139–140, 155, 162
  rights of 21, 126
  shaping resilience 134
  socialisation 44–45, 54–56, 66, 150
  strategic orientation 151–153, 155
  Traveller community 170, 172–173, 175–177
  working class 149–161
Parsell, C. 63
Pickett, K. 117
Piketty, T. 23, 117

Plato 82, 110
pluralistic societies 114
Polanyi, K. 80
postgraduate studies 107
postmodernity 51, 71
poverty 5–6, 179, 180, 181, 183
  and blame 8–9, 62–65
  culture of poverty thesis 63–64
  educational disadvantage 66–67, 68
  food poverty 140
  levels of 17–18
  social exclusion 42–43
  and social justice 70
  structural 62, 63, 64, 65
  territorial stigmatisation 60–61
  Traveller community 167, 170, 171–173
  see also economic barriers
power 7, 53, 70–71, 118
precariat 7, 37–38, 51, 109, 114, 128–129
private sector 21–22, 75–76, 106–107, 111, 114, 119–122
  private tuition 120–121, 145
psychometrics 47, 48
public education 73–104, 180
  adult education 87–92
  civil society and humanism 75–82
  concept of 73
  cultural empowerment 86–92
  public libraries 88–90
  purpose and role 74–75
  schools 81–82
  and universities 73–75, 76, 82–86
  widening participation 92–103
public libraries 88–90, 180
Putnam, R. v, 89

Q

qualifications *see* exams/qualifications
Quinlan, M. 163–164

R

race
  affirmative action 74, 95–96, 181
  and class 26, 28
  critical race theory 49–50, 64, 71
  cultural deficit theory 63–64
  developmental goals 50
  educational disadvantage 65–71
  eugenics 47–48
  interculturalism 164–165
  and meritocracy 111
  and mortality 62
  multiculturalism 164–165
  structural racism 163–164
  student debt 94
  territorial stigmatisation 61–62
  'white is a metaphor for power' 39–40
  White privilege 26, 49–51

White working class 27, 48–52, 62, 63, 64
widening participation 95–97
Rainwater, L. 61–62
Rawls, J. 69
Read, B. 101
Reay, D. 23, 26, 51, 58, 76, 160
  educational progression 134–135
  equality of opportunity 113
  fitting-in to higher education 57, 98–99, 101–102, 103
  meritocracy 109–110
  opportunity hoarding 121
  widening participation 93, 180
redistributive justice 47, 69, 80, 181
Reich, C. vi
Reich, R. 5
relative social mobility 124–125
Report of the Joint Committee on Key Issues Affecting the Traveller Community 167
resilience 133–134
responsibilisation 25, 52
Ricoeur, P. 22, 71
rights 25, 73–4, 105, 114
  children's 21, 59, 113, 126–127
  civil rights 49, 91, 92, 95–96
  equality of condition 117–119
  equality of opportunity 48, 113–114
  opportunity pluralism 115–116
  parental 21, 126
  right to education 113
  right to have rights 22
  social justice 68–71
  see also race
Rogalsky, F. 64
role models 174–175
Roma *see* Traveller community
Rooney, S. 111–112
Runnymede Trust 7
Rushdie, S. 79, 128
Ruskin College, Oxford 90–91
Rutter, J. 44

S

Saltmarsh, J. 77, 84
Sandel, M. 17, 18, 25, 27–28, 39, 48, 107–109, 179
Schoenbaum, N. 74
Scholastic Aptitude Test, US 48
schoolification of society 135
schools (general)
  compared to universities 101–103
  COVID-19 pandemic 121–124
  creative education 147, 180, 183
  and critical race theory 49–50
  cultural deficit theory 63–64
  and culture wars 73–74, 75, 79
  educational disadvantage 50, 59, 64, 65–68
  equality of condition 3
  funding of 21, 80
  historically 45–46
  intercultural education 165
  knowledge society 179–180
  league tables 133
  and meritocracy 110
  poverty 17–18
  private 21–22, 75–76, 106–107, 111, 114, 119–122
  purpose and roles of 81–82
  segregation 95–96
  Traveller community 132, 165, 168–176
  see also DEIS schools; exams/qualifications
Scott Fitzgerald, F. 57–58
secularism 73, 79
segregation 95–96
self-belief 141–143
self-employment 172–173
Shaheen, F. 7
Shields, L. 113
Sibieta, L. 90
Snoussi, D. 7, 9
social capital 47, 54, 55, 106–107, 118, 120, 121, 135
social contract 24, 38, 78, 80
social Darwinism 46, 48
social democracy 6
social discredit 60–62
social division of labour 40–41, 42
social exclusion 42–43, 60, 66, 86–87
social inclusion 11, 13, 14, 17
social inequality, rethinking 26–27
social justice viii–ix, 23–24, 26, 47, 183
  adult education 91
  and educational disadvantage 68–71
  and equality of condition 118–119
  meaning of 68–69
  rethinking of 180
  and social mobility 124–126
  and welfare state 79–80
social mobility 9, 25, 109, 134–135
  habitus clivé 55–56
  myth of 124–126
Social Mobility and Child Poverty Commission 119
social reproduction 52, 53
social solidarity 107, 108
socialisation 44–45, 54–56, 66, 150
Socrates 19, 35, 39
Solas 66–67
South Korea 179
sovereign citizen movements 108
Spicker, P. 41
Standing, G. 4–5, 38
Stern, F. 3
Stewart, M. 110
stigmatisation 51–52, 58, 114
  territorial 60–62, 143, 159
structural concept of social justice 70

Index

structural poverty 62, 63, 64, 65
structural racism 163–164
student debt 11, 20, 24, 35, 63, 74, 77, 93–94, 139
SUSI grants 29, 130–131, 139
Sutton Trust 122
symbolic capital 54, 107, 129, 147

T

talking back 11, 16
Tawney, R.H. 19, 46
teacher support 80, 102–103, 131–132, 147
territorial stigmatisation 60–62, 143, 159
third mission of the university 82–86
Third Way 6, 79
Thompson, I. 19
Tilly, C. 119
Times Educational Supplement 19
Titmuss, R. 41
Tormey, R. 21, 66
Towles, A. 23
transformative change 16, 21, 181–183
Traveller community 163–177
  challenges facing 167–168
  and education policy 166
  and education system 168–173
  fitting-in to higher education 99–100
  multiculturalism and interculturalism 164–165
  new education approach 173–176
  poverty 171–173
  social policy 165–167
Traveller Community Survey 169
Trump, Donald 27, 63, 108, 109
Turchin, P. 35

U

UK Commission on Social Justice 68, 180
UK Social Mobility and Child Poverty Commission 119
unitary societies 114
United Kingdom/Britain
  alienation 56–57
  aspirations 132, 138
  class 7, 27
  COVID-19 pandemic 121–123
  creative education 147
  educational progression 134–135
  levelling-up 181
  meritocracy 91, 111
  parental support 119, 149, 156
  public education 89, 90, 103
  quality of life index 16
  social justice 68, 180
  social mobility 124
  tuition fees 93

White privilege 50
widening participation 92–93, 94–95
United Nations
  Human Development Index 16–17
  Universal Declaration of Human Rights 113
United States
  commodification 93–94
  COVID-19 pandemic 121
  critical race theory 49–50
  culture wars 73–74, 75
  despair 7–8
  funding of education 76, 94
  meritocracy 109, 110
  No Child Left Behind Bill 3
  poverty 61–62, 62–63, 65
  public education 81–82, 84, 89–90, 92, 94
  race 39, 49–50, 74, 94, 95–96, 181
  role of higher education 11
  Scholastic Aptitude Test (SAT) 48
  social inequality 27
  Supreme Court viii, 74, 95, 96
  territorial stigmatisation 61–62
  value of a college degree 35
universities *see* higher education/universities (overview)
Universities and Colleges Admissions Service (UCAS), UK 92–93
untested feasibility 21
utilitarianism 74
utopian possibility vii, 183

V

Varadkar, Leo 2
Visiting Teacher for Travellers 169, 170, 172
volunteering 85–86
Von Hayek, Friedrich 80

W

Wacquant, L. 5, 52
Wall Street Journal 35
Waller, R. 132
Walther, A. 138
Watson, D. 167, 168
welfare state 7, 12, 22, 23
  and capitalism 69–70
  conceptualisation of 24–25
  and knowledge society 181
  and neoliberalism vii–viii, 24, 80
  purpose and ethos 78
  reforms 79, 183
  and social justice 69–70, 79–80
  and social mobility 124–125
  undermining of 6, 78
White privilege 26, 49–51
White working class 27, 48–49, 50–52, 62, 63, 64

Whitehead, J. 161
widening participation vii–ix, 9, 10, 17, 20, 92–103
  academic transition 100–103
  desegregation and affirmative action 95–96
  and elite universities 180
  fitting-in 98–100
  hierarchical patterns of participation 180–181
  and knowledge society 179–180
  opportunity pluralism ix, 11, 16, 20, 115–117, 127
  paradox of 180
  policy context 92–95
  as policy solution vii, 10, 13, 16
  in practice 96–103
  size of challenge 1–2
Widening Participation in Higher Education project 14
Wilkinson, R. 117
Williams, J.C. 48–49
Willis, P. 49
Winn, J. 74
women
  access to education 20, 111
  ancient Greece 19, 45
  employment rates 37
  and freedom 105
  motherhood 44–45
  progressive individualism 25
  reproductive rights 25, 48
  Traveller community 176
Wood Report (1929) 41
Workers' Educational Association 89
working class
  adult education 88, 90, 91
  alienation 28, 37–38, 40–41, 56–57, 63
  aspirations 10, 27–29
  and blame 62–65
  and capital 53–54
  class divide 57–59
  cultural politics 48–52
  educational disadvantage 65–71
  employment 7, 51
  empowerment 183
  equality of condition 117–119
  equality of opportunity 113–115
  fitting-in to higher education 98–103
  further education and training (FET) 155–158
  habitus clive 55–56
  intersectionality 26, 28
  male identity crisis 49
  and meritocracy 9, 24–25, 27–28, 106–111
  negative impacts on 7–8
  opportunity hoarding 119–121
  opportunity pluralism 115–117
  othering 58
  precariat 37–38
  social construction of 5–8, 10, 42, 51
  social Darwinism 46–48
  social hierarchy 43–44
  social justice 68–71, 180
  social mobility 55–56, 124–126
  stigmatisation 51–52, 58, 114, 143
  territorial stigmatisation 60–62, 143, 159
  underclass 5, 41, 51, 61, 183
  White privilege 49–51
  White working class 27, 48–49, 50–52, 62, 63, 64
  see also access to higher education; DEIS schools; parents; poverty
World Economic Forum 4–5
Wuthnow, R. 27

Y

Young, M. 8, 9, 46, 106

Z

Zimmerman, J. 93–94

www.ingramcontent.com/pod-product-compliance
Lightning Source LLC
Chambersburg PA
CBHW051543020426
42333CB00016B/2077